TOP HAT & TAILS

To
Caroline for the patience
and understanding that only other author's
wives know and . . .

To
Suzzie without whom
this book could not have been written –
nor would it have its
happy ending.

TOP HAT & TAILS

The story
of
Jack Buchanan

Michael
Marshall

ELM TREE BOOKS · London

First published in Great Britain 1978
by Elm Tree Books/Hamish Hamilton Ltd
90 Great Russell Street, London WC1B 3PT

Copyright © 1978 by Michael Marshall

The extracts from the journal by Mrs Susan Sage
which features in Act 2 are copyright © 1978 by
Susan Sage and Michael Marshall

British Library Cataloguing in Publication Data

Marshall, Michael
    Top Hat and Tails.
    1. Buchanan, Jack 2. Entertainers – Great
    Britain – Biography
    I. Title
    791'.092'4   PN1583.B/

ISBN 0–241–89602–9

Typeset by Filmtype Services Ltd, Scarborough
Printed in Great Britain by
Ebenezer Baylis & Son Ltd,
The Trinity Press, Worcester, and London

Contents

Jack Buchanan and Fred Astaire performing 'I Guess I'll Have to Change my Plan' from The Band Wagon *in 1952.*

Foreword

by
Fred Astaire

JACK WAS ALWAYS AN idol of mine ever since the first time I saw him. When my sister Adele and I made our initial visit to England in 1923, Jack was in the show *Battling Butler*. He was the first English star we saw in London. He had a style and method all his own and at the end of the performance, there was tremendous enthusiasm. It was then that I heard for the first time the cries of 'core, 'core which, happily, I was later to learn at the end of my own show, meant that the audience was well satisfied.

I was captivated by his personal charm and comedy methods. I enjoyed watching him walk as well as his songs and dances. He always had a marvellous walk. Little did I think then that, some thirty years later, we would be working together when he came over to California to star with Cyd Charisse and me in *The Band Wagon* for M.G.M.

We had some amusing moments together in that very successful movie. One number in particular, 'I Guess I'll Have to Change my Plan', offered us a lot of enjoyment in rehearsals. It was complete with top hat, white tie and tails and canes – oh naturally, they had to be there. There were several tricks with these canes and when we were rehearsing, we got to laughing so much that we began to drop the canes quite frequently. Then the same thing happened with one of the hat tricks. So we decided to end the number that way by throwing the hats and canes on to the floor and becoming completely the opposite from the meticulously natty song and dance performers we started out to be. The idea paid off and it scored with the audiences. What was also very important – we enjoyed it.

I'm glad we got together in this way because, over so many

years, our careers ran in parallel. When I first appeared in shows on the London stage, Jack was making a huge success with Gertrude Lawrence and Beatrice Lillie in the Charlot Revues on Broadway. Then when I went to Hollywood, I just missed Jack who worked there in some of the early hit muscials. So it went on and it took the War to get us together for the opening of the Stage Door Canteen in London.

The Band Wagon confirmed what I had always suspected: that Jack – behind that seemingly casual style – worked as hard as I did to perfect his routines. I hope readers of this book may think, as I do, that 'I Guess I'll Have to Change my Plan' is one of the fitting memorials to this great artist in which I was proud to share.

Fred Astaire

Acknowledgements

IT IS SIGNIFICANT THAT the largest group of those who have made major contributions to this book are Jack Buchanan's fellow artists. Their willingness to do so is a reflection of their admiration of his work and, in many cases, their affection for him as a man.

I am particularly grateful to Fred Astaire for providing the Foreword which so appropriately links the two greatest top hat and tail men of this century. I am also especially conscious of the trouble which Vivian Ellis, Harold Hobson and Alan Melville have taken in their special written contributions for this book.

Others from the entertainment world who have given freely of their time in conversations and correspondence with the author include:

Nuala Barrie Allason, Liz Allen and Bill O'Bryen, Maidie Andrews, Tom Arnold, Adele Astaire, Roma Beaumont, Pandro S. Berman, Guy Bolton, Coral Browne, Douglas Byng, Irving Caesar, Cyd Charisse, Betty Comden, Robert Coote, Roland Culver, Constance Cummings, Bing Crosby, George and Eileen Cross, Lili Damita, Dorothy Dickson, Howard Dietz, Adele Dixon, Vivian Ellis, Fred Emney, Nanette Fabray, Douglas Fairbanks Jr, Harold French, Roy Fox, Margot Grahame, Peter Graves and Vanessa Lee, Olive Gilbert, Adolph Green, John Green, Hubert Gregg and Pat Kirkwood, Sir John Gielgud, Binnie Hale, Dorothy Hammerstein, Alfred Hitchcock, June (Mrs June Hillman), Harold Hobson, Stanley Holloway, Bob Hope, David Jacobs, Glynis Johns, Jack Hulbert, Gene Kelly, Bill Kendall, Evelyn Laye, Charles Lefeaux, Moira Lister, Bessie Love, Ben Lyon, Babbie MacManus, Alan Melville, Joseph

Meyer, Billy Milton, Vincente Minelli, Stephen Mitchell, Clifford Mollison, The late Phyllis Monkman, Robert Morley, Richard Murdoch, Anna Neagle and the late Herbert Wilcox, Robert Nesbitt, David Niven, Lord Olivier, Graham Payn, Jack Prendagast, Walter Pidgeon, Roy Plomley, Elsie Randolph, Gene Raymond, Leo Robin, Cyril Ritchard, Arthur Schwartz, Tony Smythe, Tommy Steele, Heather Thatcher, Austin Trevor, Jill Williams, Wyn Clare Williams, Yvonne Bose Williams, Googie Withers, and Wilfrid Hyde White.

There are many others who have given me professional help and encouragement particularly in the vast task of replacing and reassembling research material which was lost in wartime damage and post-war museum mishaps to Jack Buchanan's records. Among the individuals and institutions I would particularly thank are:

John Billingham, Kenneth Corden, Richard Hewlett, Chris Morgan, Tom Morgan, P. J. Saynor, Tony Trebble, Brian Willey and many of their colleagues at the B.B.C.; Jeremy Boulton at the British Film Institute; Bernard Crisp and Captain Law at Cunard; William Martin and Margaret Bannister at the Public Libraries in Dunbarton and Helensburgh; Chris Ellis at E.M.I.; Roger Morgan, Chairman of the Library Committee, and many of my fellow Members of the Garrick Club for their interest and helpful suggestions; Michael Griffith-Jones and his colleagues in the House of Commons' Library; Paul Myers and his associates at the Lincoln Center Library for the Performing Arts in New York; Mildred Simpson and the Library Staff at the Academy of Motion Picture Arts and Sciences in Hollywood; Raymond Mander and Joe Mitchenson and their Theatre Collection; Michael Pistor, lately Counselor for Public Affairs, United States Information Service in the American Embassy in London; Alexander Schouvaloss and Catherine Haill of the Theatre Collection at the Victoria and Albert Museum; AND Rufina Ampenoff, Edward Anderson, The late Lord Avon (Anthony Eden), Professor Malcolm Baird, Eric Braun, George Benning, Ian Bevan, Thomas Cassidy, Joan Childs, E. C. Court, Bryan Cowgill, Reginald Eagle, John East, Elaine Evans, Sam Gardiner, Melville Gillum, John Hallett, Minnie Harris, Mary Hutcheson, Bill Ireson, Rita Jackson, Richard and Carol King, Miles Kreuger, Betty Larkin, Cole Lesley, Kenneth MacDonald, Ian Main, Pauline Marks, Maxine Maxwell, John Montgomery, Lena Morigi, Lord Mountbatten, Roy Pearce, Eva Reveley, Neil Rimington, Robin Russell, Brian Rust, Margaret Scott, Frank Sleap, Lord Selsdon, Dennis Robert-Tissot, James Urquhart, Dr Peter Waddell, Allen Warren, Peter Warren, and Arnold Weissburger.

Apart from such professional help, my work has been made easier and more enjoyable by the contributions I have received from the many Jack Buchanan fans. I shall always be interested in hearing from other 'J.B.' admirers and hope that they may find pleasure in the book's shared memories.

Coming close to home, my special thanks to my secretary, Anne Buckingham, for her marathon typing efforts, to my old friend Reggie Vaughan for proof reading the manuscript and to my editor, Colin Webb, for unfailing help and encouragement.

In the dedication to this book I have paid tribute to my wife Caroline's patience but her help has been all embracing in research and constructive suggestions. The dedication also reflects my debt to Mrs Susan Sage in making the project possible but, beyond that, I am immensely grateful to her, to her husband De Witt Sage and to her daughter, Theo, for their encouragement, generous hospitality and sympathetic understanding.

The author and publishers would also like to thank the following for their kind permission to reproduce copyright material in this volume. For extracts from books and songs: Chappell & Co. Ltd: 'A Cup of Coffee, a Sandwich and You' (Joseph Meyer, Al Dubin and Billy Rose), copyright 1925 by Harms Inc., 'And Her Mother Came Too' (Ivor Novello and Dion Titheradge), copyright 1921 by Ascherberg Hopwood & Crew Ltd (Chappell & Co. Ltd), 'Dancing Honeymoon' (Philip Braham and Douglas Furber), copyright 1922 by Ascherberg Hopwood & Crew Ltd (Chappell & Co. Ltd), 'Fancy Our Meeting' (Joseph Meyer, Philip Charig and Douglas Furber), copyright 1928 by Harms Inc., 'I Think I Can' (Ray Noble and Douglas Furber), copyright 1935 by Sterling Music Publishers Ltd (transferred into Chappell & Co. Ltd), 'She's Such a Comfort to Me' (Arthur Schwartz, Douglas Furber and Donovan Parsons), copyright 1929 by Harms Inc., 'That's Entertainment' (Arthur Schwartz and Howard Dietz), copyright 1953 by Chappell & Co. Inc., 'The Big Tune' (M. Darewski and Douglas Furber), copyright 1925 by Ascherberg Hopwood & Crew Ltd (Chappell & Co. Ltd), 'The One I'm Looking For' (Joseph Meyer, Philip Charig, Douglas Furber and Ira Gershwin), copyright 1928 by Harms Inc., 'Weep No More My Baby' (John W. Green and Edward Heyman), copyright 1933 by Harms Inc., 'When Will They Liberate London' (Vivian Ellis), copyright 1945 by Chappell & Co. Ltd, 'Who Do You Think You Are' (John W. Green and Edward Heyman), copyright 1935 by Famous Music Corp.; Cinephonic Music Co. Ltd: 'I'm in a Dancing Mood'; Crawford Music Corp.: 'I'm in a Dancing Mood'; Elek Books Ltd: *British Music Hall* by Roy Busby; Francis Day & Hunter Ltd: 'They Didn't Believe Me'

Introduction

TOP HAT AND TAILS was one of the many revues in which Jack Buchanan starred. The title might equally well have applied to most of the forty-five shows and thirty-five films in which he appeared in a career which lasted from 1911 to 1956.

The image of Jack Buchanan will always be that of the most immaculate man of his day. One critic said that the word debonair might have been invented for him. Others said that he always looked as though he had been poured or born into top hat and tails.

But, in a professional sense, his success in revue (as in musical comedy and, later, in straight acting) was not simply a matter of his elegant appearance. It was in revue that he first made his name and it was in revue that British and American audiences came to appreciate his remarkable skill and versatility. For revue requires not only an ability to sing and dance but also a gift for instant and varied characterisation. All these Jack Buchanan had and it is upon this *range* of skills as well as his many other activities that this book is based.

In writing it, the author has found the revue connection irresistable. If *Top Hat and Tails* symbolises Jack's image and place in social history, it is *A to Z* which summarises his work and achievements. *A to Z* in 1921 was the best of the productions in which Jack worked for André Charlot and led to the British introduction of intimate revue on Broadway. In this show, each item followed alphabetically. Similarly in this book, the chapters follow the letters of the alphabet to suggest both words and music that seem appropriate in the many facets of the Jack Buchanan story.

As Jack himself sang:

> Everything that happens in life
> Happens in a show
> You can make them laugh,
> You can make them cry,
> Anything, anything can go . . .

> The clown with his pants falling down,
> Or the dance that's a dream of romance,
> Or the scene where the villain is mean –
> That's entertainment . . .

This was his opening to the song 'That's Entertainment' in the film *The Band Wagon* in 1952. The song – with its wide ranging list of what constitutes entertainment – was an apt summation of Jack Buchanan's own work. Indeed, his role in *The Band Wagon*, although exaggerated to the point of ego-mania, portrayed him as a dramatic actor, producer and former musical comedy star in a way which was clearly designed to draw on his talents in all these fields.

Yet even this list barely touches on many of the interests that made Jack Buchanan a star for over forty years. Recognised as an accomplished musical comedy and revue artist in the First World War, he became a truly international figure in the mid-twenties with his success on Broadway with Gertrude Lawrence and Beatrice Lillie in the Charlot Revues. A silent movie performer at the same time, he went on to star in several of Hollywood's first successful musicals in the thirties. As a producer of almost all his own West End musical comedies, he simultaneously directed and starred in film versions of many of these same shows. In the forties, he turned to straight acting, producing and directing with outstanding success and yet retained the musical-comedy zest which led to his Hollywood return and to a new television career in the fifties.

Even after his death, his durability as a star remains. In Britain, during the seventies when Christopher Gable made the transition from ballet to musical comedy in *The Good Companions*, the critics hailed him as 'a new Jack Buchanan'. In the same decade, Jack's recordings continue to sell well and, in recent years, he has been the subject of two major long playing records. In 1976, the photographer, dancer and impresario Allen Warren recorded his version of Jack's 1936 hit 'This'll Make You Whistle'. At the same time the director of the Merton Festival, the singer and guitarist Leonard Pearcey was recording Jack's best known solo number 'And Her Mother Came Too'.

In the United States, the most recent tributes to Jack's work came with M.G.M.'s two musical film compilations in 1974 and

1976 under the title of *That's Entertainment*. They reminded audiences around the world not only of the title song which Jack had introduced in *The Band Wagon* in 1952 but also of his comedy work with Fred Astaire and Nanette Fabray in the 'Triplets' number from the same film and, of the high style and magic when the two greatest top hat and tails men of their day combined to perform 'I guess I'll have to change my plan'.

In the Foreword to this book, Fred Astaire recalls his enjoyment in working with Jack. So, too, do many of Jack's other partners. His list of leading ladies is almost the women's 'Who's Who in the Theatre'. It includes : Irene Bordoni, Coral Browne, Martine Carol, Fay Compton, Constance Cummings, Lili Damita, Dorothy Dickson, Adele Dixon, Diana Dors, Binnie Hale, Glynis Johns, June, Gertrude Lawrence, Evelyn Laye, Vanessa Lee, Sylvia Leslie, Beatrice Lillie, Moira Lister, Jeannette Macdonald, Jessie Mathews, Phyllis Monkman, Anna Neagle, Heather Thatcher, Fay Wray, and his longest partner of all, Elsie Randolph. Many of them have a major part to play in this story.

So, too, do many of the men with whom J.B. worked. In Britain, they included Fred Emney, David Hutcheson and Bill Kendall who became Jack's 'Three Musketeers' both on and off stage. Internationally, his work included one memorable theatrical partnership with Bing Crosby and Bob Hope as well as co-starring in films with Maurice Chevalier and Fred Astaire.

These are some of the aspects of Jack Buchanan's career which made him the complete entertainer and which this book seeks to describe. In Act I (Chapters A to L) his work as a performer is described in detail. This is also the principal theme of the Entracte Chapter which describes the wartime years. It is in Act II (Chapters L to Z) that we learn most about Jack as a man – principally through the account of his wife, Suzzie, who shared the last nine years of his life.

If this format suggests a tribute, the author makes no apology. We live in an age when 'frank biographies' with their emphasis on the failings of the great are all the rage, when we seem only too willing to cast down our idols and when – especially in the case of great artists – it is fashionable to imply that public and private success are incompatible. Yet one of the most satisfying aspects in writing about Jack Buchanan has been the enthusiasm, generous co-operation, love and admiration expressed by so many whose work brought them into contact with him. Among the acknowledgements listed on page ix, are more than 100 of the greatest names in the entertainment world who have given generously of their time in meetings and correspondence with the author. They include some whose relationship with Jack was that of the professional rival, the disappointed in love and the press critic. Yet almost without exception their memories are happy and appreciative.

Jack Buchanan was no saint. He had his favourites, his fits of temperament, his maddening idiosyncrasies and, in his romantic life, caused havoc as an absent-minded heartbreaker. But these criticisms are relative and, in the opinion of almost all who knew him, he was a matinée idol both on and off stage. In a bitchy profession, there are few who have anything but admiration for him. As one of the contributors to this book, Wilfrid Hyde White, says: 'You never heard stories against Jack because there simply weren't stories to tell. He wasn't a subject for muck raking because there wasn't any muck'.

Not that his life was lacking in drama. His early struggles and near starvation; his major stage flops as well as his triumphs; the fortunes made and lost as an impresario and the effect of his secret and unhappy first marriage – all these events might have crushed a lesser man. But the key to Jack's character is that he regarded them as part of his *private* life. He came from a generation who believed that his public was entitled to retain the glamorous, happy and humorous image of the man in top hat and tails without concern for the man with private worries. He dressed up to go on stage and he dressed up when he left the stage door – conscious of his public in both places. But once away from the theatre, he guarded his private life jealously so that the press dubbed him 'The male Garbo'.

For despite all the household names among his friends and professional colleagues, J.B. remained an intensely private person. A friend of royalty, he never advertised the fact. Noted all his life for Saville Row elegance and the man about town image of top hat, white tie and tails, he much preferred the private relaxation of casual dress when with his close friends. The perpetual bachelor, pursued and adored by a massive female following, he found the greatest happiness in the last years of his life as a husband and step-father.

To the few who shared this intimate side of his life, he was 'Johnnie B' – a loyal friend and family man. To those who worked for him, he was 'J.B.' or 'The Guv' – a man who enjoyed boundless respect and affection. To theatre and film lovers on both sides of the Atlantic, he will always be remembered as Jack Buchanan – a star of the first magnitude.

Act 1 ~
The Performer

'And his Mother Came Too'
– The Early Years

'I LOVE THE LITTLE women, ol' boy,' Jack Buchanan would often say to his Gang. His devotion was returned.

In the history of the theatre, there can have been few leading men who aroused such affection in the women with whom he worked. This applied not only to the stars who played opposite him, but also to the old friends for whom Jack would always try and find a place in his show as well as his many discoveries from the ranks of the chorus. Outside the theatre, adoration came from the 'Gallery Girls' and Jack's many female fans of both his stage and screen work.

Although Jack's special gift for comedy made him equally popular with men – and he always had a gang of close men friends – this feminine influence explains why, even today, he is remembered with great affection by so many women. Since many of them were Jack's leading ladies, there must inevitably be a theatrical quality in their entrances and exists in this account. But pride of place goes to two women without whom there would be no story – the wife whose memories enrich much of this account and his mother, Patricia Purves McWatt.

She gave birth to Walter John Buchanan – henceforth known as Jack – on 2 April 1890 and, until her death forty-six years later, they were inseparable. It was in the revue *A to Z* in 1921 that Jack introduced Ivor Novello's 'And Her Mother Came Too'. It was to become his personal signature tune and, with the change from 'her' to 'his', neatly summarised not only Jack's successful early revue career but all the struggles which preceded it.

The popular image of Jack Buchanan as a glamorous West End star in top hat, white tie and tails has created a picture of unbroken glittering success. The reality, as so often in the theatre, was much harsher.

Certainly his early life was comfortable enough. Born in a distant branch of the 'Whisky' Buchanan family in Helensburgh, Scotland, his father Walter was a well-to-do auctioneer who provided Jack's mother and his older sister Jessie with a comfortable home in what was then Glasgow's fashionable seaside resort. There was no theatrical tradition in the family and when Jack was taken by his mother to dancing classes at the age of nine, he stamped his foot and howled until he was taken home. The strongest influence in Jack's early life was his home on the edge of the Firth of Clyde where great liners – which were to play such a great part in his future travels – were built and launched at Greenock just across the water. In the garden of the family house in Helensburgh, Jack's father installed a deck cabin from an old Scottish fishing boat in which Jack and Jessie spent many happy hours of make-believe. It was here, and during the family holidays on the Isle of Arran, that Jack acquired his lifelong love of the sea and it was taken for granted that he was destined for a Naval career.

On a visit to Helensburgh many years later he recalled:

> I remember every inch of the Loch front and all the streams that feed it. I used to go out with school friends in our little boat and fish in the early mornings and evenings. From time to time we even poached a few trout. Then we were afraid to take them home and answer questions as to where they'd come from.
>
> I remember very little about my father because he died when I was twelve. But he must have been a bit of a lad. He was supposed to specialise in auctioneering paintings and antiques but he liked to have a flutter on the side as my mother found out after his death. Evidently he bought several horses, or had an interest in them, and wasn't too successful in the racing game.
>
> I do remember that he had a great sense of humour although he sometimes made me angry with his practical jokes. In the evenings, when I was very small, I used to stand between his knees telling him the happenings of my day, and he would empty my pockets of all my little treasures – fishing weights, bits of string, boiled sweets, and so on without my knowing it – and I used to fall for it every time. And then he used to stretch out his foot and gently raise the marmalade cat, where it was snoozing in front of the fire, and turn it over. That used to irritate me, because it was my cat, and I didn't see why it should be teased.
>
> I remember something else about my father. It was during Sunday Service at the Scottish Presbyterian Kirk in Helensburgh, and I was very small, I couldn't have been more than five. During the sermon, a bluebottle flew in through the open window and got caught in the flowered hat of the lady in front

of me. It struggled to get free, and I watched fascinated. It buzzed, the woman twitched, and I got the giggles. Without a word, or glance around, my father picked me up and shoved me under the pew until the giggles subsided and the sermon was over. I remember it so clearly and most of all that my father was laughing too as he pushed me under the seat.

It was originally intended that Jack should go to Fettes, Edinburgh's leading Public School and the 'Eton of Scotland'. Meanwhile, he attended Larchfield School in Helensburgh where his closest friend was the local Rector's son, John Logie Baird, the future inventor of television. Their houses were only a few hundred yards apart and the two boys were inseparable.

John and Jack rigged up a telephone system which linked their homes by direct wires laid along the roadside. They were able to conduct private conversations after dark and make the usual mischief which small boys enjoy, including the use of the telephone lines as a trip wire.

In appearance and character, Jack and Logie Baird were entirely different. The Baird family recall Jack as a neat and tidy boy, always well dressed and extremely fond of music (indeed, at an early age he showed promise on the violin). John Logie Baird was a 'head in the clouds' character with the appearance of one who had been drawn through a hedge backwards. Both boys had much influence over their contemporaries. Their gang was based on two local interests. In the summer they would play cricket at the Argyle Street Cricket Club and, throughout the year, they met regularly as members of the local Photographic Society. This Society was not connected with the school but included many schoolboy friends. Baird was President and Jack was one of the Society's leading lights. Others in the gang included Jack Bruce and Neil Whimster, future Scottish shipowners; Bony Wadsworth, later a leading London accountant; and two who would be cut down in their prime in the First World War, Jimmy Bonner and 'Mephy' Robertson.

At first, the Photographic Society took itself seriously and Logie Baird showed himself an adept pioneer in early experiments in enlargement, flash light and delayed exposure work. One of the examples of his work was the flash portrait he took of Jack then aged about ten. But Jack's serious expression belies the fact that he was the established 'Court Jester' of the group. It was his enjoyment of practical jokes and generally playing the fool which produced the nickname of 'Chump' Buchanan which was to remain with him through his school days and into his early stage career.

Logie Baird, in some autobiographical notes, later recalled a typical 'Chump' Buchanan episode. Jack had been involved in some horseplay with Sonny Forbes, another member of the Photographic Society, as a result of which the boy's father had boxed Jack's ears. Jack and the gang borrowed a builder's ladder and removed the pigeons from the Forbes's loft and sold them to a local fishmonger for fourpence each.

The joys of this comfortable middle class Scottish life ended suddenly when Jack's father died. The change was immediate and painful. Jack's father's racing debts were substantial and, having assumed that he had many years of earnings ahead of him in the auctioneering business, he had made little provision by way of pension or insurance. The family had to sell the house in Helensburgh and move to Glasgow. Mrs Buchanan rented a house large enough to take boarders or 'paying guests' as the more 'refeened' Glaswegians preferred to call them. There began a long and worrying period for the family. Jessie was old enough to help her mother in looking after the house but for Jack the problem of completing an education remained. Fettes was no longer a possibility. Instead he was entered for Glasgow Academy.

While lacking the social cachet of Fettes, Glasgow Academy had a good solid reputation for scholarship and, during Jack's time there, produced a number of notable scholars, including John Reith (later Lord Reith) the first Director-General of the B.B.C. and Walter Elliot, a future Secretary of State for Scotland. Jack also found a kindred spirit in Eric Woodburn, who would later become well known for his dramatic monologues. Jack's own school career was not outstanding.

One of his schoolfriends, John McGregor, recalled that he was not particularly good or particularly bad at anything. His career plans seemed vague. He talked of becoming a barrister, but when pressed by his mother, confessed that this idea appealed to him because it involved eating dinners at one of the Inns of Court and family hardships meant that his eating habits tended towards the frugal. Nevertheless, it was perhaps an interest in the oratorical side of the lawyer's work which, in later years, stood him in good stead when he became a most effective impromptu speaker.

Gradually his ambitions became clearer. There was no doubt of his ability to make people laugh but he worried about his height. By the time he reached his mid-teens, he was almost six feet tall and most leading British comedians were small men like Harry Lauder, George Robey or Little Tich. Years later, Jack said 'God gave me a pair of long legs and a croak and I decided I might as well do the best I could with them.'

But these theatrical inclinations were hardly comforting to Mrs Buchanan. She worked long hard hours looking after her guests with practically no help. Once when Jack came home from school, she confessed that she had been forced to give up her part-time cleaning help and this made it necessary for her to scrub the front door step at night when she would be unseen by her neighbours. This so incensed Jack that he decided to approach his father's cousin, Sir James Buchanan, the head of the Buchanan whisky firm, for a loan. The approach was totally unsuccessful.

It was therefore decided that Jack should leave school and join his father's old auctioneering business in Glasgow. The failure of this career was almost entirely predictable. He later said, 'I couldn't tell the difference between a nod and a wink and I spent most of my time planning my future theatrical career. When I told the manager about this he said "You'll have to learn to survive on practically no food." How right he was.' Undaunted by this prophecy, Jack channelled his immediate theatrical ambitions into after-office hours when he began to appear regularly with the Glasgow Amateur Operatic Society.

This Society, one of the largest in Britain, was later to stage its own versions of some of Jack's most successful shows. In the years 1909 to 1911, Jack made his mark in a number of concert-party performances with his version of well known musical numbers such as Lionel Monckton's songs from *The Arcadians*.

In 1911, Jack made his first appearance on the professional stage when he was engaged for a week at Pickard's Panoptican. This splendid sounding professional baptism meant that, in reality, he was thrown in at the deep end. Pickard's Panoptican in Argyle Street was one of Glasgow's toughest music halls and famous as a graveyard for aspiring comedians. Its format was non-stop variety with four performances a day.

Jack went to immense trouble in preparing his début. Assisted by his friend, John McGregor, he answered an advertisement in *The Stage* and visited London specially to obtain West End material. The authors enquired where he would be working. When Jack replied 'Glasgow', they immediately reduced their prices. The material he obtained was two comic songs and patter of a highly bawdy variety.

Jack tried out his songs and patter on a somewhat unlikely audience while staying the weekend in Cheshire at the house of a girlfriend and her Curate father. The vicar actually laughed and, thus encouraged, Jack prepared to launch his act on the critical audience of Pickard's Panoptican.

His début paralleled the equally disastrous first appearance of Maurice Chevalier on the Paris music halls only a few years earlier. The notion of fresh-faced, innocent looking teenagers singing suggestive songs in a nervous – indeed terrified – manner was not apt to commend itself to the usually inebriated audiences of Pickard's Panoptican. His fate was virtually sealed even before he went on for, when the notice 'Extra Turn' denoting a newcomer went up on the side of the stage, the audience began baying for blood.

At a dinner given in his honour by the Gallery First Nighter's Club in 1928, Jack wryly recalled the full horror of the occasion. He described the upturned faces catcalling and drowning the orchestral accompaniment. When he attempted 'to patter', his voice was lost in shouting of which the most polite was 'Get off' and he finally 'dried'. 'Such is habit,' he added, 'that I sang verse and chorus unaccompanied before I went off.' He was greeted by the manager who said, 'You mustn't let them catch you at that song again!' Rather more comfort came from one of his fellow performers standing in the wings who said, 'Cheer up, wait till you see what I get when I go on – and I'm top of the bill!'

Fortunately, or unfortunately, for Jack, the management of Pickard's Panoptican regarded this kind of reception as something which kept the audience vastly entertained. He was therefore retained for the week and given an additional booking for a week at the Edinburgh Empire. Jack told the Gallery First Nighter's Club that his début must be a world record in 'getting the bird' at each of his four daily appearances or twenty-four times in his first week.

By contrast with this vigorous if totally destructive response from the audience in Glasgow, Jack was received in stony silence in Edinburgh. John McGregor has told how Jack appeared in front of the curtains while he stood immediately behind prompting at regular intervals. The audience heard more of the prompter than of the performer. Jack was greatly helped in overcoming his disappointment by the 'Top of the Bill' performers Lowenwith and Cohen, but when he went to collect his so-called 'treasury' of ten shillings for the week, the manager said, 'Honestly, I can't recommend you for the tour. You're young and seem a decent enough sort of chap; isn't there some steady line of work you could take up?'

Despite this discouragement, Jack decided to seek his fortune on the West End stage of London. After one more brief and unremarkable appearance on the stage at the Grand Theatre, Glasgow in a play called *The Elder at the Plate*, he returned to the Glasgow Amateur Operatic Society to play the leading role in the comic opera *Veronique*. Encouraged by the success of this production and, perhaps forgetting the vast gulf between amateur and professional theatre, Jack, with his mother and sister, moved to a small rented house in Brixton, South London.

Soon after they arrived in London, Jack had gone round to the

Apollo Theatre and requested an interview with the manager, Tom B. Davis. The great man had evidently had a good lunch for he consented to see him and asked what he could do. Jack, knowing of Tom Davis' interest in comic opera, went through the last scene of the first act of *Veronique*. Mr Davis promised to keep Jack in mind for his forthcoming production of *The Grass Widows*.

Meanwhile, Mrs Buchanan was obliged once again to take in boarders to support the family budget, for it took Tom Davis three months to send for Jack. Even then, he was faced with the prospect of seven weeks' unpaid rehearsals. As it turned out, the show only ran six weeks, and he would have been better off if he had accepted payment for rehearsals and made his West End début free of charge.

The Grass Widows was translated from a German production and featured music by Gustav Kerker, the composer of *The Belle of New York*. It starred a number of well known West End names, including Alfred Lester, Thelma Raye and Constance Drever. Jack played Monsieur Deschamps, a dancing master of the Snowdrops Academy in St Petersburg. After his brief appearance in the first act, most of the action switched elsewhere and Jack was given little opportunity to shine. Certainly press reviews of the time make no mention of his name and Jack's earnings from the six-week run were soon dissipated in the months of unemployment which followed.

Often after leaving home and Mrs Buchanan's breakfast in the morning, his only meal would be an 'All Rounder' (a bread bun with bacon) and a cup of coffee purchased at a stall in the West End before he returned to Brixton late at night. This insubstantial diet was to lay the foundation for Jack's early ill health when he suffered from both colitis and dysentery.

Jack's limited if hungry appearance in *The Grass Widows* had at least given him two advantages. He gained a first-hand knowledge of Alfred Lester's work which would prove useful later and he began to work on his dancing technique.

This was almost entirely self-taught, since Jack at this time was unable to afford lessons. He evolved his method by studying many of the great performers then appearing on the West End stage, from the cheap seat in 'The Gods' in which he spent most of his out-of-work evenings. He was particularly impressed by the work of Eugene Stratton, who appeared on the bills as 'The Dandy Coloured Coon'. Stratton was an American who came to England with a black-face minstrel show in the 1880s and stayed on to become one of Britain's best-loved variety performers. Then nearing the end of his career, he was nominated for the first Royal Command Variety Performance in 1912. Roy Busby,

9

Britain's leading music-hall historian, tells us:

> He had neither a powerful nor especially good voice, but he projected his songs by sheer artistry and natural acting ability. He stood on the stage lighted by a single spot, a slight figure in a black frock coat, silk top hat and bow tie. Seemingly oblivious of the audience, he sang softly at first, and slowly rising in pitch and volume, declared that Lily of Laguna was his lady love, or that little Dolly Daydream was the pride of Idaho. Towards the end of his song, he would drift into a soft-shoe dance, full of delicate grace.

It was this style which was to exert a powerful influence on Jack's own evolving technique. Indeed, Roy Busby's description of Eugene Stratton almost exactly fits the Buchanan of the 1920s and 1930s and it was this recognition of the early influence of the great American artist that, many years later, made Jack perform Eugene Stratton's signature tune 'Lily of Laguna' on radio and in variety shows.

Jack's study of Eugene Stratton had its apparent reward when, some months after his short-lived experience in *The Grass Widows*, he went to audition for a variety show at the Camberwell Empire. He had read an advertisement for 'A smart young man to do a song and dance between variety turns'.

On arriving at the Camberwell Empire, Jack found himself among the usual vast crowd of hopefuls. There were over a hundred – old as well as young – all after the same spot as Jack. When his turn came to perform, he was conscious of his competitors in the wings on either side of the stage, staring with jealous eyes and willing him to perform badly. His heart sank at the listless way in which the rehearsal pianist took his sheet music and played with apparently little enthusiasm or suggestion that this might be a continuing partnership. Jack went into the song and dance routine which he had developed in the 'Eugene Stratton' manner but felt in the deathly silence of the Camberwell Empire, lit only by the rehearsal light, that he was not 'going over'. The pianist was banging out his music in the wrong tempo. Jack's voice sounded flat and, in his nervousness, he forgot most of his dance steps and had to improvise. Thinking that he had better get off as fast as he could, he was leaving the stage with almost indecent haste when a voice called out 'Mr Buchanan, I said that would be all right. You will open first house on Monday. Band rehearsal at ten o'clock in the morning.'

His hundred-to-one chance had come off and he was booked for a week's trial work and a possible three-week engagement at a pound a week. He determined to work up his song and dance routine to perfection before the 'band call' on the following

Monday. He even got additional material from Hugh Wright in the hope that he might build up his spot.

Jack later recalled the sequel:

> Monday morning came and I made up my mind to rehearse with the band for at least an hour so that the music should be perfect. I got rather a shock when the musical director barely took any notice of me. 'That's all right; one verse, one refrain vocal, three dance refrains schottische time – next number' he said.
>
> I need not have worried. Music-hall orchestras were used to young men doing song and dance numbers and, that night, I could find nothing wrong with the accompaniment. I had felt very nervous before going on but now – with the make-up on my face and the lights on me – it all seemed to be going very well. The orchestra was just right and I remembered every step. I even wondered if I'd 'stop the show', perhaps have to make a speech and be offered a long contract.

What Jack was too inexperienced to notice at this time was the growing restlessness of the audience. It was only when there was a metallic clink at his feet that the penny literally dropped. The coin was followed by a bombardment. This only ended when – with a resounding crash – he reeled under the impact of the curtain roller as the stage manager rang down the curtain on what was by then almost a riot.

As he staggered off, Jack was aware of laughter and cheers from the audience. As he made his way to his dressing room, he heard the stage manager calling his name. 'All right, I know,' said Jack. 'You don't have to tell me.' 'You were a flop all right,' the Manager replied, 'but look here if – and only if – you let us drop the curtain on you every night, you can stay.'

The postscript was even sadder. For at the end of the first week, Jack's engagement was terminated and he was deprived of the possibility of being almost brained twice nightly for two more weeks.

There now began a really bad time for Jack. Always desperately nervous before going on – even in his later successful years – his confidence was badly shaken by the Camberwell Empire experience and this affected his attempts to land work at other auditions. Apart from this one brief variety appearance, he was out of work from October 1912 to April 1913. Even then, he was compelled to abandon his immediate ambitions as a solo performer.

He was offered a job in the chorus of the new revue at the Empire, Leicester Square, *All the Winners*. To make up for his disappointment, Jack was made understudy to two of the principals, the show's leading dancer Lionel Mackinder – who was the first 'theatrical' to be killed in 1914 – and the impressionist

11

Vernon Watson – who was shortly to change his name to Nosmo King on the sound theory that he would always be up in lights whenever 'No Smoking' signs were displayed. Vernon Watson's best-known 'take off' was of Alfred Lester with whom Jack had worked in *The Grass Widows*. It was also thought that Jack looked somewhat like Alfred Lester and, as an amateur, he had performed some of his numbers including the 'Lugubrious One's' best-known song from *The Arcadians* 'I've got a motter – always merry and bright'.

All the Winners was a typical Empire revue. The show had what *The Times* described as 'an unequalled cast'. In addition to Lionel Mackinder and Vernon Watson, the stars of the show included Seymour Hicks, Ida Crispi, Maidie Hope, Barry Lupino, Unity Moore and an up-and-coming actor called Eric Blore, who was also developing his talents as a revue writer and who would subsequently become the permanently worried butler in almost all the early Fred Astaire and Ginger Rogers pictures.

The content of the show was much influenced by the current craze for jazz which was typified by the Anglo-American revue *Hullo Ragtime* then playing at the Hippodrome where the Broadway star Ethel Levey was introducing 'Alexander's Ragtime Band' to London. At the Empire, in addition to the all-star cast and a chorus of over a hundred, the programme in 1913 concluded with 'Bioscope pictures of the Grand National' thus showing an early example of the theatre coming to terms with its new rival, the cinema.

For Jack, the opening night on 10 April 1913 offered only one small opportunity. Towards the end of the first scene set in Brighton at the Hotel Metropole, Ida Crispi had a song called 'Running Wild' with the chorus boys. In the audience was the young Douglas Byng, who was himself to achieve enormous success as a revue artist and comedian. He recalls:

Ida Crispi was singing the number dressed in black in the centre of the stage. All the boys were sitting round – it was a sort of cabaret scene – and they were in full evening dress but beige coloured, which was very unusual then. Suddenly, one of them seated on the right got up, walked to the centre of the stage and went on past Ida Crispi. She stopped in the song and looked back and then went on. And we all said 'My God, who was that?' This gorgeous looking young man, beautifully dressed in immaculate evening clothes – that was Jack Buchanan.

In recognition of the stir which Jack's appearance had caused, the later editions of the Empire programme showed the 'Running Wild' number performed by 'Ida Crispi – assisted by J. Buchanan'. However, his main hope of achieving real West End recognition lay in the possibility of standing in for either Lionel Mackinder or Vernon Watson. In this ambition, he was joined by the other principal understudy in the show, Stanley Lupino, who hoped to go on for his cousin Barry Lupino. Stanley Lupino, who was later to achieve great success in both musical comedy and revue, has described the nervous excitement which both he and Jack felt at this time. To be an understudy is by definition one of the most frustrating jobs in the theatre. Night after night, Jack and Stan would look anxiously at the principals, and, without wishing them real harm, pray that they would be unable to go on. At the same time, both felt the stomach-tightening nervousness of wondering whether they would be capable of taking the place of such well-known stars.

By chance, both Barry Lupino and Vernon Watson were unable to appear at one performance. Stanley Lupino tells in his autobiography how they exchanged 'Good luck, Jack' and 'Good luck, Stan' before going out to take their big opportunity.

In Jack's case, the result was a great success. He 'stopped the show' but, possibly because of this, Vernon Watson made a speedy return and Jack was unable to capitalise on his first appearance as a principal. Indeed, when *All the Winners* finished its two-month run, he was not offered a part in the succeeding bi-monthly Empire revue.

Once more, there followed the agonising round of agents' offices and Jack became entirely dependent on his mother and her small income from lodgers in the house at Brixton.

It was almost six months later when Jack got his next break. Johnny McGregor suggested that he try for a part in *Little Miss Muffet*, the pantomime at the Theatre Royal, Birmingham, which was due to open just before Christmas 1913. At this time the Theatre Royal, under the outstanding management of Philip Rodway, was famous for putting on all-star pantomimes which were unequalled in any other part of the United Kingdom and in this show the principals included Ernie Mayne as Simple Simon, Ella Retford as the principal boy and Maidie Scott – John Mac-Gregor's future wife – as the principal girl.

At McGregor's suggestion, Jack called on Philip Rodway and told him he was looking for a job. Philip Rodway's daughter described Jack at this time as 'a handsome young aspirant to the stage, full of an eager enthusiasm and charm of manner difficult to resist'. Jack was only offered a dancing role, but in a speciality tango with Maidie Scott on the 'Steps of the Monte Carlo Casino' 'he made,' according to the records of the Theatre Royal, 'a great success of this comparatively small part'.

Jack always said that he learnt much from Philip Rodway's management. A stern disciplinarian, 'P.R.' once found a snake backstage which had been brought in by one of his leading ladies. Consequently, he put up a notice which Jack found in his dressing room, reading:

> No animals, reptiles or relatives permitted in dressing rooms during times of rehearsal or performance.

After his Birmingham appearance it seemed that Jack's luck had at last changed, for he was asked to go straight into rehearsals for another revue at the Empire, Leicester Square. Despite the fact that it was almost a year since his previous experience at the Empire, it seemed that his good work was not entirely forgotten. Jack was no longer in the chorus and was given fourth billing.

The show, entitled *A Mixed Grill*, opened on 31 March 1914. It was a combination of revue and burlesque which gave Jack an opportunity of doing good work in several comedy sketches. His growing versatility was rewarded when *The Times* described him as 'A very clever young comedian who does everything with a taking air of nonsense.'

For Jack the future seemed set fair. He was now in an established hit at the Empire with good prospects of continuing to play in succeeding editions of the revue. His hopes, along with those of many other aspiring actors, suffered a total setback on 4 August 1914 with the outbreak of the First World War.

For Jack the outbreak of the war was to provide several opportunities and a major disappointment. Although later stories of his contracting tuberculosis were untrue, the years of early struggle and malnutrition had taken their toll. Jack failed his medical test for military service. His exemption was bound to give him opportunities denied to other actors already serving in the forces, but Jack – who was intensely patriotic and deeply sensitive – was much distressed.

These feelings were heightened in the early part of the war when Basil Hallam, the leading matinée idol of the day, was killed in an observation balloon over France. Hallam had made his name with his theme song 'Gilbert the Filbert – the Kernel of the Knuts' and had thus given to the language of musical comedy the term 'Knut' to describe the sophisticated man-about-town. Jack, whose style was evolving in precisely the same way, was deeply saddened when he heard that Basil Hallam, who had one leg shorter than the other, had talked his way into the Air Force only to meet an early death. Hallam had become a victim of the vicious 'white feather' campaign that was put at its crudest by the Gallery Girls who shouted 'Why aren't you in the Forces?' and musically by the current hit song 'We don't want to lose you but we think you ought to go'.

As the war went on, Jack, too, lived in constant dread of the 'white feather' treatment. To add to his worries, the financial pressures on the family began to mount as, at the outbreak of the War, many new productions were postponed and Jack was once again 'resting'.

Jack's mother, and sister, Jessie, decided that they must return to Scotland where there were better opportunities of running a boarding house which could pay its way when their own living expenses were modest. This was a heavy blow for Jack who, until then at the age of 25, had virtually never left his mother's side. She promised to return when he was firmly established and their decision was made easier by the kindness of the owner of a small private hotel in Coram Street, Russell Square. This lady, Mrs Mills, was active in local charities and had a daughter, Elaine, who was training to become a ballet dancer. Both of them sympathised with the aspirations of struggling West End performers. It was agreed that Jack could have one room in the hotel on the basis of 'Pay when you can' and, as the weeks of unemployment turned into months, Jack's landlady turned a blind eye on his debts.

Her daughter, who was to achieve considerable success as the ballet dancer, Elaine Genée, recalls how Jack, despite his poverty, would spend most of his infrequent earnings on being well dressed. He was to remember with gratitude the kindness which Mrs Mills showed to him, which he was later able to repay when he was established. Meanwhile, Mrs Mills insisted that Jack shared family meals and generally took the place of the mother who Jack missed so much.

It was through Mrs Mills that, early in 1915, Jack's personal life was to undergo a dramatic change. Her daughter, Elaine, tells the story:

> At the same time as Jack was staying, we also had with us my agent, Mr Spizzi, who was later to become the agent for the Metropolitan Opera House in New York. One day, he told my mother 'I'm bringing a lovely girl over from Milan to stay here.'
>
> She was going to sing at the new London Opera House in the Kingsway and she was the most beautiful thing you ever saw. She was simply lovely. She looked like Hedy Lamarr and her name was Saffo Arnau, or Drageva as she was known professionally. Mr Spizzi thought he had discovered a great star and, as well as her lovely voice, she was the kind of girl who, when she went out on the street, all heads turned.
>
> Well Jack met her at my mother's house and fell passionately in love. It was only a matter of weeks before he came to my mother and asked her to the wedding. They were married from the hotel and stayed with us for another four or five months.
>
> Later, Saffo had trouble with her voice and Jack told my

15

mother that she had just disappeared during one of her concert tours. He was touring himself and, later, when they were divorced, he asked my mother to forget that there had even been a marriage.

For most of his life, Jack Buchanan was known as 'the eternal bachelor' and the secret of his first marriage was maintained virtually until his death. No doubt Jack's reasoning was that the bachelor image was enormously helpful in building up his West End success, but other friends recall that there was another side to the story which led up to the wedding in a St Pancras registry office with Drageva Saffo Arnau in November 1915.

Although Drageva had trained for opera in Italy, she was a Bulgarian national. In October 1915 Bulgaria joined the Ger-alliance in declaring war against the United Kingdom. Saffo told Jack that unless he married her, she would be interned as an alien and their marriage followed almost immediately.

After all these years, it is unreasonable to speculate on whether or not Jack's first marriage was purely a love match or a marriage of convenience. It may be that the truth is somewhere between the two. What is certain is that, at the end of 1915, his life was about to change from one of continuing professional struggle to that of an established West End star.

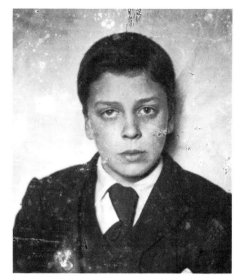

Above, *Jack's mother, Patricia Purves (McWatt) Buchanan. Above right, Jack photographed at the age of 12 by his school friend, the T.V. and photographic pioneer, John Logie Baird. Right, Jack with his first great partner, Phyllis Monkman, in the 'Pom Pom' dance from* Tails Up *at the Comedy Theatre in 1918.*

B

'Bubbly' – Enter Phyllis Monkman

BUBBLY WAS THE WARTIME revue which was to bring Jack his first opportunity as a leading man in London. His progression to this show, as so often in the theatre, was a mixture of good luck and hard work.

His first piece of good fortune came towards the end of 1915 when he joined the touring company of *The Cinema Star*. This show, which Jack Hulbert had translated from German, had originally opened at the Shaftesbury Theatre in June 1914. It was now going out on the road while the London theatre adjusted to wartime conditions. Jack Buchanan was offered a small part in the company as well as understudying Jack Hulbert's leading role.

J.B. later recalled the significance of that tour:

We had been on tour for some time (and altogether I toured nearly two years during the First World War) and Jack Hulbert was fit and fine. I despaired as understudies always do of ever getting on and doing my stuff. Jack Hulbert's a very nice chap – we later became great friends – but my God I thought he was a bastard in those days, at least as far as I was concerned.

Several times during the tour, Jack hadn't arrived at the fifteen-minute call, and I would be rushed into his dressing room, made up and dressed in his clothes (or my approximation of them), going through my lines, trying to get the pipes warmed up to sing the big numbers, and thinking 'This is it, finally I'm going to do it'. With my nerves, I was in a panic that I wouldn't be able to do what I had planned and rehearsed and eaten and slept for in all the previous nights of touring. As the call boy said 'Beginners please', Jack Hulbert would invariably dash in, look at me, nod his head at the door and say 'out'. Of course, I realise now that probably even he – great star that he was – could have been just as nervous and tensed up as I was but that's all he said. And out I would go in an agony of frustration and disappointment.

This had happened several times during the tour when, before the Saturday matinée at Cardiff, I was once again in his dressing room, made up and ready to go on, and when 'Beginners please' was called and he didn't turn up, I was out in front of the lights before I realised it. But I got my chance, and I suppose somehow I thought he would turn up before the show was through, and so I did my damndest. And it worked. I stopped the show three times. I had 'got' the audience, and I was in heaven.

After the matinée as I sat shaking with relief and reaction, taking off the 'slap', there was a knock at the door and in came Ivor Novello. He had already 'arrived' and was well on his way both as an actor and composer of the great First World War song 'Keep the Home Fires Burning'. He had come home for the weekend to see his mother, Dame Clara Novello Davis, and thought he would see Jack Hulbert in the show. Ivor was very kind and complimentary, and said he would get in touch with George Grossmith and next time I came to London I should go to see him.

There was an amusing sequel. When Jack Hulbert met Ivor Novello at a party that evening, he apologised for being away. Ivor, who had a dry sense of humour, said: 'Oh, you mustn't worry. I saw your understudy go on and stop the show three times.'

Immediately after his Cardiff appearance, Jack returned to London and, following Ivor Novello's suggestion, called on George Grossmith. He found that Ivor had been as good as his word and George Grossmith immediately auditioned him for the leading role in his touring company of *Tonight's the Night*. As Jack himself said: 'This was the real turning point of my career.'

Nevertheless, the leading role in the number one tour of *Tonight's the Night* was an immense challenge. The show was already one of the biggest British musical-comedy successes of all time with music by Paul Rubens and Jerome Kern. Unusually it had been given its first performance by an all British cast on Broadway in 1914 and George Grossmith played the lead then and again when the show opened at the Gaiety Theatre in London in April 1915.

Following 'GG' was a daunting prospect. Although he was no 'Knut', he had built up a tremendous personal following. George Grossmith did not have Jack's good looks but he sang and danced

19

with great panache and his dress sense made him the 'Beau Brummell' of the London stage. His relaxed style and gift for comedy would be hard to follow. Moreover, the Number One touring company had already been on the road for six months and Jack would be replacing Gerald Kirby who had already established himself on the West End stage.

At early rehearsals, 'G.G.' realised Jack's anxiety. On one occasion, he went up on stage and taking Jack by the arms, led him through a series of steps and movements. As Jack himself said later: 'It was an eye opener to me in showing how to appear completely relaxed on the stage, even if, inside, you are scared to death.'

It is one of the more satisfying pieces of theatrical history that there is such an obvious and direct link between George Grossmith and Jack Buchanan.

Grossmith, who had been in at the birth of musical comedy and who had taken over the management of the Gaiety Theatre from George Edwardes, was now paving the way for his logical successor in Jack Buchanan as Britain's future leading musical comedy actor/manager.

In *Tonight's the Night* Jack had, at last, an opportunity to work up a leading role in the best musical-comedy tradition. The number one tour played for over a year to large and enthusiastic audiences up and down the country – audiences which were progressively filled with the boys on leave from France. For such audiences, this kind of show presented a tuneful and romantic evening which was precisely the kind of escape they sought. For Jack, the show presented many opportunities to shine, whether it was introducing the 'Chicken Trot' with Elsie Paton (who had succeeded Peggy Kearton in the role of 'Lady Pussy Preston') or in the show's biggest hit when he sang to Maidie Andrews one of Jerome Kern's most memorable songs:

> And when I tell them
> And I'm certainly going to tell them
> That I'm the man whose wife you'll one day be,
> They'll never believe me,
> They'll never believe me
> That from the great big world
> You've chosen me.

Recalling those wartime touring days some sixty years later, Maidie Andrews said:

> The tour was nearly two years. It was so different to the limited tours of today. In those days we ran to three touring companies red, white and blue. We were the red company which played all the number one towns. We did six weeks each in Edinburgh,

20

Newcastle, Birmingham, Liverpool, Manchester, Cardiff and Glasgow where we opened the enormous new Alhambra Theatre. Sometimes we had a return date and everywhere we packed the place with queues waiting to book.

If Maidie Andrews was to give Jack his first experience in playing opposite a leading lady in an extended run, it was another member of the cast, Dorothy Monkman, who was to be the link in Jack's first great West End partnership. For her sister, Phyllis Monkman, was then the toast of London and the sweetheart of every 'Tommy' after three years as André Charlot's principal dancer at the Alhambra and the current star of his revues at the Comedy Theatre.

Phyl (who, until her death in 1976, remained one of the most popular and generous members of the theatrical profession) recalled her first impression of Jack:

My older sister had been on tour in *Tonight's the Night* and she had said to me 'There's a young man in the company who I think you ought to see – come to Richmond and have a look at him.' It was Jack Buchanan. Of course I realised at once he had got the lot – he looked wonderful, he had charm, he could dance, he could do everything.

We were having problems with my new show at the Comedy, *Bubbly*. Jack Hulbert was likely to be called up at any minute and the understudy was absolutely terrible. Charlot came into my dressing room and my sister Dorothy happened to be there and he said 'Phyllis, what are we going to do? The understudy can't wear clothes, he can't sing, he's terrible, he's awful – what are we going to do?' So Dorothy said 'What about that boy I told you to come down and see at Richmond?' So I said 'Darling, what a wonderful idea.' Then Charlot said 'Where is he?' and Dorothy replied 'I haven't the faintest idea.' But Charlot just said 'Go out and find him' and by God she did. She found him at the Trocadero lunching with one of the girls he had been on tour with and with whom he was having a ding dong at the time. Dorothy said 'Drop everything, drop everything – come at once to the Comedy Theatre, you'll be on with Phyllis as soon as they can get you on.' And he was on in three days.

In three hectic days of rehearsal, he was installed as a member of the *Bubbly* revue cast. This company, led by Phyl Monkman's outstanding artistry as a dancer, comedienne and singer, was already a well-established team.

Their success was measured by the fact that Columbia had already issued seven twelve-inch records which included a selection from the show as well as its eleven most popular songs. This virtually unique gramophone coverage of a wartime West End show was also a tribute to the high quality of the music of Philip (Pa) Braham – the future composer of 'Limehouse Blues' – who until then had composed only a few concert-party numbers but who, as Charlot's musical director and conductor of the Comedy Theatre orchestra, was now receiving his first chance to write the score of a complete revue.

It was an enormous challenge for Jack to fit into this highly successful all-star company at short notice. As Charlot himself later recalled:

> When I first met Jack he was so terribly shy that he was really one of the worst rehearsers I have ever had to handle. All the assurance that was later so much admired had been acquired. No one was less self-assertive by nature than this languid, elegant man with the natural aristocratic manner.
>
> His shyness must have been a great handicap for him and there is no wonder that he had to struggle for success. If he was rehearsed by people who did not understand him, he went right back into his shell, right out of sight. Luckily, we got on well together and the twelve guineas a week I offered him was probably the biggest money he had earned until then.'

Despite the good understanding which existed between Jack and André Charlot his début as a West End star was almost a disaster. Part of the trouble was that there were only three days for rehearsals and, even worse, his first big number – a terrible tongue twister called 'I'm Reckless Reggie from the Regent Palace' – was ruined by the comings and goings of an inebriated party in one of the Comedy's stage boxes. They kept banging the sliding door of their box so that, half way through the number, a terrible expression came over Jack's face and he dried up completely.

He still had enough presence of mind to signal to Phyl Monkman to come on for their dance routine. The first night audience realised that something was amiss but was clearly sympathetic to Jack, who was known to have taken over the lead at short notice. So, at the age of twenty-seven, after the hard grind of a seven-year theatrical apprenticeship, almost all in the provinces, *Bubbly* was the start of a long period of work for Jack under the Charlot banner which, during the next seven years, was to bring him fame and outstanding success both in the West End and on Broadway.

Much of this success was based on Jack's partnership with Phyl Monkman. Duggie Byng's professional assessment of their partnership at this time is typically crisp and witty:

> They both looked as though they had been out all night and they probably had. But in any case it was a lazy sort of tap dance they did together which was very nostalgic. It wasn't the usual

'full of zip and pep' type of dancing, it was almost languid and it was very attractive.

In its way it was quite sensational because they even had a finale which wasn't a finale. It was a sort of 'the party's over now' number. That was most unusual then because I don't think anybody else had ever tried this before.

Towards the end of the run of *Tails Up*, the show which followed *Bubbly*, Jack and Phyl had developed two speciality dance routines. The first, a number called 'Have You Forgotten', was an acrobatic dance in which Jack literally threw Phyl all over the stage. The second 'The Pom Pom Dance' involved stunning costumes with Phyl in a daring slit skirt and a massive osprey feather head-dress, while Jack wore the grey top hat and cravat of a Georgian dandy.

These two numbers aroused such audience enthusiasm that, when the run of *Tails Up* ended in 1919, André Charlot was able to book Jack and Phyl for a season at the Casino de Paris.

This was not their first appearance in France. Shortly before the War ended, they had been members of probably the greatest West End cast ever assembled when Leslie Henson's wife, Madge Saunders, had taken a company to Wimereux to entertain the troops. Jack, on that occasion, made his first and last truly drunken appearance. As he was to appear as 'The Officer' in a sketch called 'The Disorderly Room', the waiters in the Officers Mess 'fixed' the drink which was pressed on Jack before he went on. As a result, he kept falling off his chair in the comic military court martial scene he was playing with Stanley Holloway and others.

The service audience were almost hysterical with laughter when Jack went down for the third time. However, he profited from the experience as he never again had an alcoholic drink of any kind before going on but he made a point of working some kind of simulated drunken routine into most of his future shows.

Jack found that performing in post-war Paris was also not without its problems. Phyl Monkman later recalled:

When Jack and I arrived at the theatre one evening, we were told there was a musicians' strike on and there'd be no orchestra. There was, however, a lady pianist on the stage who'd go through our routine with us. I remember at this particular performance – it was that ghastly Sunday matinée they have in France – when it was our turn to go on, someone connected with the strike tried to stop us and we made our entrance by dodging under his arm and dashing onstage before he could catch us. The trouble was that, although the lady pianist had been perfectly splendid when she was on the stage with us, when she got down into the orchestra pit she couldn't see what we were doing – and she just wasn't with us any longer. Jack said we must begin all over again and I said 'Well, how shall we manage?' 'We'll just have to "la-la" it', Jack replied. But it was an incredibly strenuous acrobatic dance and, having stopped the pianist, pretty soon Jack hadn't any breath left and I had to hold myself rigid for the throws and so neither of us could 'la-la-la' any longer. The dance ended with Jack throwing me all over the stage in absolute silence. The audience didn't seem to notice. We got exactly the same round when we'd finished as we did with a big orchestra going full out.

Part of Monsieur Volterra's interest in importing foreign principals for his revue at the Casino de Paris which was then competing strongly with the Lido and other French revues, was that it gave an International flavour to his shows. It also gave him an opportunity to arrange for his 'in house' stars, Maurice Chevalier and Mistinguett to meet Jack and Phyl for lessons in the 'Have You forgotten' number which they were to use for later editions at the Casino. Phyl Monkman later described the problems in coaching the most volatile theatrical partnership in Paris:

Charlot knew that Maurice and Mistinguett would probably pinch our number anyway. So he said 'I advise you to rehearse with them – that way you'll at least get recognition'. But I got the best of the bargain. I worked with Maurice who wasn't bad as a dancer but Mistinguett was terrible. She had no idea of time or rhythm. Later, though, they worked up quite an effective copy of our acrobatic dance which ended in their famous roll across the stage inside the carpet with romantic results about which we all know.

Following their return from Paris, Jack and Phyl went into a new Charlot show *Wild Geese* which opened at the Comedy Theatre on 12 January 1920.

Charlot was departing from his traditional revue format for a musical comedy in which the numbers were staged by Phyl Monkman's future husband, Laddie Cliff. This Charlot diversion proved a failure. The theme, daring in the extreme in those days long before women's lib, involved the establishment of a women only colony on an uninhabited island in the Pacific by members of the 'down with men' sect of the Junior Jumper Club. Although romance was eventually allowed to have its way, it took too long to overcome the audience's resistance to this theme and some of the more obvious shortcomings of the lyrics and book which included such gems as 'the shocking waste of raw material of a crowd of virgins on a desert island'.

This failure brought Charlot's usual reaction. When in difficulty, he had a simple recipe. He took to his bed at home in

St John's Wood and would refuse to budge until he found some sign of encouragement which might persuade him to begin all over again. In this situation, Phyl and Jack would call at the house to find him unshaven and looking sorry for himself. They would express their willingness, if necessary, to work for nothing, whereupon the great impresario would rise from his sick bed as if totally refreshed and decide the time was ripe for a new production.

After *Wild Geese*, Jack and Phyl joined the revue which Charlot had already put on at the Prince of Wales, *Bran Pie*. Jack and Phyl's main number was 'The Talky Trot' which was an obvious skit on the currently fashionable 'Turkey Trot' ballroom dance. In one sketch, Jack appeared with his admirer, Phyllis Titmuss, in 'Une tasse de thé'. In this scene which Jack was to use on many subsequent occasions, he meets a girl who he has assumed is French. They conduct a long and tortuous conversation in fractured French before it eventually dawns on them that they are both English.

During the next year, Jack was involved in three shows which were largely unsuccessful but which certainly got him away from any charge of 'type-casting'.

In the first, he accepted Charles B. Cochran's invitation to appear in *Her Dancing Man* at the Garrick. Although this was entitled 'A Topical Farce' Jack's role was an unsympathetic one since he played a gigolo – or as the programme more coyly described it 'A Dancing Man' – opposite the dramatic actress Viola Tree. After only a short run in this show, Jack went to work once more under the George Grossmith and Edward Laurillard management. The idea was to bring back burlesque somewhat updated, to the Gaiety Theatre.

The result *Faust on Toast*, involved some of the best musical comedy talent in the West End. George Grossmith supervised the production; Leslie Henson produced the show and wrote much of the book, Melville Gideon, on the eve of his Co-optimist success, wrote the music and the outstanding cast included Tom Walls, Maisie Gay, Heather Thatcher and Maidie Andrews. Jack as Faust sang 'I love to sit and look at you' to Maidie Andrews – described as 'the world's lump of cuddle'. Despite its all-star cast, *Faust on Toast* did not succeed.

Jack's third consecutive short run was a non-musical part in August 1921 in a farce at the Strand Theatre entitled *The Trump Card*. Jack played opposite another glamorous dramatic actress, the Canadian, Margaret (Bunny) Bannerman. He failed to please all the critics, but *The Times* said that in a show which fizzled out in the Third Act 'the palm must be given to Mr Jack Buchanan. He played a wildly improbable character who for a whole act pretended to be someone else but he never struck a false note and fully deserved the good reception he received.'

These three comparative failures had, nevertheless, given Jack an opportunity of widening his experience. He decided, therefore, that the time was ripe for a return to work with Charlot. This time he would be without Phyl Monkman for *Bran Pie* had marked the end of their partnership. Although they were to appear together again briefly under Charlot's banner some years later – and although they remained lifelong friends – Phyl was soon to marry Laddie Cliff and join 'The Co-optimists' while Jack was on the verge of his greatest revue successes.

Charlot and Broadway

A Cup of Coffee, a Sandwich and You
A Cosy Corner – A Table for Two
The Things I long for are seldom and few
A Cup of Coffee a Sandwich and You

'A CUP OF COFFEE, a Sandwich and You' was the famous duet which Charlot produced for Jack and his new leading lady Gertrude Lawrence. Their partnership was one of the chief reasons why Jack was delighted to return to the Charlot fold when, in October 1921, 'The Guv' put together perhaps the most successful of all his London revues – *A to Z* at the Prince of Wales Theatre.

As the title implied, there were twenty-six items in the revue running from A to Z. *The Times* described its component parts as 'Charlot, charm and Chinatown'. André Charlot had assembled an unusual galaxy of creative and performing talent. Dion Titheradge and Ronald Jeans had written the book and Ivor Novello the music; Jack himself was responsible for the dance routines; and the performers included the famous American Trix Sisters.

Helen and Josephine Trix (who composed most of their own music and lyrics) had established a reputation for an exciting kind of close harmony singing at the piano which was part of the American post-war invasion of the London stage. Off stage they were regarded as daring in the extreme when they wore beige stockings (considered suggestive of flesh) when lunching at the Ritz. They also established a reputation as a temperamental pair who were constantly at each other's throats but whose good looks and snappy style fitted perfectly with Jack's comedy routine in numbers like 'Dapper Dan' which was introduced with such throwaway dialogue as:

Trix Sisters: 'Hullo Jack, can you sing an American song?'
J.B.:   'Sure, I know all three of them'
Trix Sisters: 'Do you know "Dapper Dan"?'
J.B.:   'No, but I'll lay you 6–4 he comes from Dixie'

The Times reference to Chinatown meant 'Limehouse Blues'. Over the years, Gertrude Lawrence's recording of Pa Braham's music and Duggie Furber's lyrics have obscured the fact that this number was introduced in *A to Z* as a duet. Jack and Gertie were dressed in Chinese silks. Gertie had sapphire-blue fitted trousers and turned-up black shoes. Jack had a very long pigtail with the slit eyes and heavy make-up of the Chinese landlord who terrorises the 'Limehouse Kid'. This was typical of Jack's versatility in going from comedy to drama in revue. When he sang:

> Poor broken blossom
> And nobody's child
> Haunted and taunted
> You're just kind of wild

he hardly moved his lips at all and the audiences loved this new 'menacing Jack' appearance.

But for Jack, undoubtedly, the principal moment in the show came when he embarked on item 'L' in the first half entitled 'Too Much Mother'. This was a new song called 'And Her Mother Came Too' with lyrics by Dion Titheradge and music by Ivor Novello.

Years later, Jack told Alan Melville how Ivor, who had spent the £18,000 earned by his First World War hit 'Keep the Home Fires Burning', would drop in at the stage door of the major West End theatres. On one such occasion, he had produced 'And Her Mother Came Too' and Jack, who knew a good thing when he saw one, persuaded André Charlot to put it into *A to Z*.

The song had an interesting history. Ivor Novello had written it with Elsie Janis and her mother in mind. Elsie, then America's leading woman revue artist and a brilliant writer, was later to make her name as a producer of early Hollywood film musicals. During the First World War, she became the 'Sweetheart of the American Forces' when she appeared in many troop concerts in France and in Britain. At this time, she became very friendly with Jack, helped in part by the fact that they were both devoted to their mothers.

Elsie's mother, a formidable lady, was well known as a doughty performer who would take on the most hard-boiled theatrical management in defence of her daughter's rights. It was also said that if you wanted a date with Elsie Janis, you had to accept the fact that 'her mother came too'. Jack who would often adopt the same family routine was not only fond of Elsie and her mother, but also of the theme which was to become his personal signature tune.

Over the years, the magic of this number has remained for all

Buchanan fans. Jack put over the song in a simple straightforward manner, giving full vent to the ironic humour of the lyrics as he launched into the verse:

My car will meet her
And her mother comes too,
It's a two seater,
Still her mother comes too,
At Ciro's when I'm free
For dinner, supper or tea,
She loves to sit on my knee –
And her mother does too.

Wyn Clare, who was then appearing in the chorus of her first Charlot production, still recalls the number vividly:

He used to wear midnight-blue tails. They looked perfect in the hard white spot. Then, of course, he had his silk top hat and a beautiful black malacca cane. He sang the song without a movement holding the stick in front of him with his hands folded over the silver top. He sang it very, very quietly until he came to the last line when he gave that little breath giggle of his on the words 'and her mother came too'. Then he went into a lovely soft shoe dance. Not a tap dance – a lovely soft shoe which fitted perfectly with his image.

This number almost always stopped the show towards the end of the first half and one of its keenest fans was the Prince of Wales. The Prince had been a long-standing devotee of Charlot's revues which he had first come to see as a soldier during the War. At that time, he had shown his interest in befriending Jack who, with his usual shyness, had not allowed himself to be 'taken up' by the Royal Set.

Now in *A to Z*, Jack found it easier to fit in unobtrusively to the pattern of Royal patronage. His friend, the young Lord Lathom, was one of the show's principal backers and both he and Gertie were on easy terms of friendship with the Prince of Wales.

It was almost as though 'H.R.H.' (as he was referred to informally) regarded the Prince of Wales Theatre as his own. Night after night, he would bring his party which often included his brother, Prince George (The Duke of Kent) and his A.D.C., Lord Louis Mountbatten.

There were parties afterwards in the private room upstairs at Rules Restaurant in Maiden Lane (the same room where Edward VII was said to have entertained Lily Langtry) or in the Prince's apartments in St James's Palace. So far as Jack was concerned, those were occasions for quiet enjoyment. Never one to seek the 'centre of the stage' at parties, he left that to Gertie who would sing and dance the Prince's favourite numbers.

The same was true of backstage parties when 'H.R.H.' and his friends would drop in for drinks with Jack and Gertie. They would chat, play gramophone records and Jack would teach the Royal brothers how to tap dance. Lord Louis Mountbatten remembers these as 'quiet and enjoyable occasions'. Sometimes the Royal party would come behind during the interval since it was rumoured that Queen Mary had expressed her disapproval of the Prince of Wales making visits after the show. It was thought that visits during the interval – by definition of short duration – might be less likely to cause Royal censure. In fact such visits often went on far longer than intended.

When Gertie remonstrated with the Prince of Wales, he would just say 'Oh, but you and Jack told me that your dressing rooms had an ever open door'. Jack would later recall how one of the girls in the *A to Z* chorus – anxious that the show should finish on time so that she could get to a party – devised an ingenious way of getting the better of 'H.R.H.' His brother, the Duke of Kent, had asked her to get some theatre tickets and seeing that the Prince was disinclined to let the second half of the show get under way, she said 'Your Brother owes me a lot of money' whereupon 'H.R.H.' beat a hasty retreat back to the Royal Box.

A to Z opened on 21 October 1921 and ran for 428 performances. In so long a run, Charlot was able to introduce new material and new performers. Jack therefore worked alternately with Gertrude Lawrence and Beatrice Lillie. He had become an indispensible anchor man and it was the establishment of this trio that encouraged Charlot in his plans for taking intimate revue to the United States.

In making these plans, Charlot knew that he could count on Jack's personal regard and loyalty despite two incidents during the run of *A to Z* which, in a partnership lasting for almost a decade, were among the few major rows between the impresario and his leading man.

The first happened when, as Robert Coote has recalled, he and André Charlot's son, Philip, were given the stage box for a matinée while both were on holiday from school. During Jack's big number 'And Her Mother Came Too', he found his dance routine more hazardous than usual when young Philip Charlot persisted in pelting him with chocolate creams.

Jack's anger on this occasion was heightened when he found that the whole incident appealed to André Charlot's somewhat bizarre sense of humour. It was this same humour which led to the Guv himself playing one of his more elaborate practical jokes on Jack.

One of the sketches in the show was entitled 'Fate'. This involved a good deal of audience participation which meant planting someone for the sketch to be effective. It also required Jack, as the link man, to memorise several alternative plots. As he had difficulty in remembering one of these, he arranged that the stooge in the audience would be his old schoolfriend John McGregor. It was even agreed that John would travel with the company to America to carry out this task on Broadway.

One night during the last few weeks of the London run Charlot, realising Jack's problem, invited John McGregor for drinks in the interval. He refused to let McGregor return and planted his own stooge in the audience. When the sketch started, Jack found to his horror that a complete stranger kept feeding him lines from the audience to which he could not reply. After desperately ad libbing his way through the rest of the sketch, Jack sought out Charlot and, scarlet in the face, showed as Charlot later recalled 'that even the most charming of all my performers could get into a towering rage.'

Jack's appearance on Broadway was not accomplished without extensive horse trading. As Charlot himself said 'So highly did I value Jack that, when I arranged to take my show to New York in 1923, I decided that I must have him at any price. He had just started working under his own management and his price had gone up a long way from the twelve guineas I first paid him, but he was worth every penny.'

Jack's later account of the same story was slightly different. 'When I made my first success with Charlot, I was offered five times the salary by Charles B. Cochran and the New York boys. The Guv called me in one day and said "I know you can write your own ticket for next season but you will stay with me, won't you, my boy?" The extra salary he had in mind was ridiculously small but he offered me one of my first chances to produce and direct as well as appear in his revue and we had something entirely new to offer the American public.'

On Broadway at this time, revue meant the great big spectacular 'girlie-girlie' shows of the Ziegfeld Follies, George White's Scandals or the Earl Carroll Vanities. The New York impresario, Archie Selwyn, had seen *A to Z* and some of Charlot's early revues. It was therefore decided to mount a production for New York which would incorporate the best numbers from all the shows to be entitled *André Charlot's London Revue of 1924'*.

In theatrical terms, this was a major gamble. The British musical had done well when transposed to America in the years before the First World War. But, with the War and its aftermath, there had been no British theatrical invasion of any consequence on Broadway for almost ten years. In those days before talkies and television, the stars of one side of the Atlantic could only make themselves known on the other by personal appearances and, at this time, the names of Buchanan, Lawrence and Lillie meant nothing to American audiences.

Conscious of this, André Charlot set out to arouse an interest in the special qualities of intimate revue. Interviewed in New York during the negotiations with Archie Selwyn, he told the American Press:

> When the American theatre-going public is given a chance to see my London Revue, they will understand the difference between this type of show and revue in America, which in some ways, is too subtle to put into words. Over the years, we have developed an intimate understanding between players and the audience, such as you do not know in this country. The mixture is hard to define since it depends not only on a company in which everyone – and not just the principals – can sing, dance and act, but also on lighting and scenic effects which are simple but artistic. I intend to offer outstanding melody, humour, good taste and distinctive charm.

Conscious of the 'soft sell' approach implied in his comments, Charlot, who was never slow to take advantage of free publicity, now began an intensive campaign to ensure the success of his first New York production. For this purpose, he and Archie Selwyn engaged as their press and public relations man Walter Wanger, who was later to achieve fame both as a Hollywood film director and as the man who shot the agent who represented his filmstar wife, Joan Bennett.

Walter Wanger, on seeing the quiet civilised style of the Charlot revues – in which all the girls in the chorus were not only expected to sing and dance but also to play character roles – felt that there was still a need to inject at least an element of 'oomph'. He therefore suggested that a suitable gimmick would be to run a beauty competition and announce that the winner would become a member of Charlot's famous chorus for the New York production. The competition was in fact rigged since Walter Wanger had his eye on a statuesque blonde who worked in the bar at Rules Restaurant where the Charlot company would often dine after the show. The lady's name was Bobbie Storey and the American press were soon enthusing over the impending arrival of Charlot's all star revue team, together with 'Britain's most beautiful blonde barmaid'.

The British Press, too, was intrigued by the forthcoming invasion of Broadway by Charlot's team. At this time, the traffic was mostly in the other direction, typified by Fred and Adele Astaire, who had just opened with enormous success in their first London performances of *Stop Flirting*. The *Sunday Times* said: 'Americans are already talking of the great success which Jack Buchanan, Gertrude Lawrence and Beatrice Lillie are likely to

Above, *Gertrude Lawrence, André Charlot, Beatrice Lillie and J.B. arrive in New York on the* Aquitania *on Christmas Eve 1923. Below, Publicity photos of 'The Big Three' in André Charlot's 1924 Revue at the Times Square Theatre.*

make in *André Charlot's London Revue of 1924*. Indeed, Mr Buchanan who is expected to have as big a success over there as Fred Astaire has had over here, may well not return. One of his American friends said yesterday "He is sure to be offered $1,500 a week since we have no one with such a fine appearance who can sing and dance like Buchanan does".'

Jack did not share this happy self-confidence. Ever the first night worrier, he knew that the 'American friend' in The *Sunday Times* report was Charlot's P.R. man, Walter Wanger. Jack also had one great drawback for his fellow artists. His nervousness before putting on a show could reach almost frenetic heights. During the London try out of the Charlot American revue and, during the entire voyage from Southampton to New York, he kept muttering 'Thank God there's a ship sailing home every Saturday'.

Despite Jack's professional gloom, public interest in the show was enormous and it was given a Royal send-off. Charlot announced that there would be a one week try out at Golders Green, which would be attended by the Prince of Wales. One reviewer noted that the Prince of Wales 'laughed as heartily as anyone' and 'afterwards the Prince and his party went backstage and personally wished every member of the company good luck on their first American venture.'

André Charlot and his Company sailed to New York on the pride of the Cunard fleet, the 45,000-ton *Aquitania*, on the last sailing before Christmas 1923. The whole of 'B' deck had been reserved for the company. Most of the company's fellow passengers were wealthy American or British travellers heading for Christmas in New York or Palm Beach. Among them were Alistair MacIntosh and Max Aitken.

Allie MacIntosh was a former Guards Officer and the current glamour boy of Anglo-American society who would later marry the film star Constance Talmadge. He already knew America well and made himself Jack, Bea and Gertie's unofficial adviser on the potential hazards and excitements of New York. Max Aitken, the future Lord Beaverbrook was the host of much of the entertainment on the *Aquitania* where he christened Jack, Bea and Gertie 'The Big Three' – a collective title which was taken up by the Press throughout their American appearances during the next three years.

However, when the *Aquitania* docked in New York on Christmas Eve, it was not The Big Three for whom the American Press made. Almost to a man, they descended on 'Britain's most beautiful blonde barmaid', Bobbie Storey. Perhaps it was as well that she was able to enjoy her brief moment of glory for the adulation of her American admirers was to prove too much and, only a few months later, she was found dead in a gas filled hotel bedroom in New York.

The pressmen did not confine their enthusiasm to Bobbie Storey. They also waxed with horticultural lyricism over the other members of the chorus, one reporter enthusing:

> With cheeks that the mist and fog of London had tinted the colour of English roses and with appearances as neat as the hedgerows in springtime, with eyes that glowed as brightly as the lights that illuminate Big Ben at night, and lips that laugh merrily, twenty-five beauties from the tight little isle across the sea who are due to appear in the André Charlot revue at the Selwyn Theatre, tripped lightly down the gangplank of the *Aquitania*.

The Big Three moved into the Algonquin Hotel which then, as now, had minute bedrooms but a lobby cum sitting room which, with its well worn settees and armchairs and the stately grandfather clock, have made generations of British actors feel at home.

This 'home from home' feeling helped the trio to settle down during the two weeks of strenuous rehearsals. They were helped too by new found friends. They went 'on the town' with the English-born Hollywood film director, Eddie Goulding, and his friends Billy Reardon and the debonair Clifton Webb, who, long before his film career, was an established Broadway musical and revue star. With this gang, there was a party every night and prohibition was regarded as a joke. Jack had brought over a specially fitted trunk which opened out into a fully stocked dressing room cocktail bar. This was soon to be installed in Beatrice Lillie's dressing room which was affectionately christened the B.B.C. – Bea's Bottle Club'.

The theatre going experiences of the three, although enjoyable, brought home the immensity of the challenge which faced the Charlot Company. In her autobiography *A Star Danced*, Gertrude Lawrence recalled:

> Before our New York opening, Jack, Bea and I were taken to see all the shows on Broadway. We were very much impressed and rather frightened by the obvious lavishness of the productions in comparison with our intimate revue. As Jack said 'It seemed to us that what New York wanted was hundreds of girls dressed in feathers, with tons of scenery studded with diamonds and ten dollar bills'. We saw Grace Moore sing 'Orange Grove in California' for which song the entire theatre was perfumed by orange blossom. We wondered if we could compete with our tiny show and our British humour.

The first test came at Nixon's Apollo Theatre in Atlantic City where the show opened for its week's try out on 2 January 1924.

First reactions were far from promising. The audience seemed mystified by the proceedings and Archie Selwyn when asked by Charlot for his reaction replied 'Geez. It stinks.' Jack later recalled:

> The American side of the management apparently had cold feet having got our show into their own atmosphere and they felt that it would be rather a doubtful success on Broadway. They wanted me to alter a lot of the stuff that I had already done. Well I said I really couldn't see that. I was going to open as I played that night or not at all and André Charlot supported me in no uncertain terms and said his revue must not be touched.

On 9 January 1924, André Charlot's Revue opened at the Times Square Theatre on 42nd Street before a glittering first night audience. The New York *Evening Telegram* described their reaction:

> When André Charlot's Company stepped out on the stage last night with their opening 'How do you do?' number there was an immediate response between actors and audience. That cordial relationship continued throughout the evening and when the curtain fell, the fact was established that in Charlot's Revue, Broadway has something new in the way of musical comedy.

Jack's personal success was twofold. His quiet mannered talent, his good looks and his English tailored clothes made him attractive to the female half of audience. But also he was successful in winning the applause of the American male who not only admired his stylish work but his gift for comedy. It was this rare combination of romantic appeal and the ability to make the audience laugh that now made Jack, literally, as one reviewer said, 'The most popular British visitor of this or any year'.

Jack also showed an ability to put over Noël Coward's more cynical contributions to the show. In a song called 'Sentiment', Noël hit out at British hypocrisy. When the author had performed it in London, it fell flat. Now on Broadway, 'The Master' described how he 'experienced the mixed pain and pleasure of seeing Jack Buchanan bring the house down in top hat, white tie and tails singing "Sentiment", watching to see why he should succeed so triumphantly where I had failed, and finding at first no adequate reason, except perhaps that it was because he made no effort at all. It wasn't until later that I acknowledged to myself in secret that the truth of the matter was that his whole technique was superior to mine.'

This effortless quality of Jack's was one that carried through the entire show. Indeed, its charm was so potent that it disarmed even the most hardened New York critics who were usually known as 'The Butchers of Broadway'.

Yet Percy Hammond, describing the magic of Jack's partnership with Gertie in 'You were meant for me' enthused: 'The gloom was at once dispelled. The music was velvety, the steps graceful and different and the acting was full of subtle charm.'

Heywood Broun said: 'For the most part, the success of the entertainment rests upon the three principals. Costuming, settings and so forth are quite secondary. From our point of view, Beatrice Lillie, Gertrude Lawrence and Jack Buchanan are worth a good deal more than their weight in gold cloth and velvet hangings.'

Alexander Woollcott took up the same theme: 'It is fair to suspect that Mr Ziegfeld and Mr George White must have fairly laughed themselves into a coma at the innocence of this London manager for thinking that any revue so airy and so unpretentious would not be trampled underfoot in New York. Why the chorus was not half so populous as that of the Follies and there wasn't so much as a yard of gold cloth in the whole thing.'

Heywood Broun and Alexander Woollcott were not alone in reflecting on the way in which the brilliance of the performers offset the simple sets. In one of the boxes at the first night performance, Jack's old friend, the American revue star Elsie Janis, had organised a party which included Irving Berlin and Walter Pidgeon then an up-and-coming young musical comedy performer. When the show ended amid enormous enthusiasm, Irving Berlin was seen to be sitting silently without showing the least sign of appreciation. Walter Pidgeon recalled: 'Elsie said to Irving "Come on now, What's this? Sour grapes?" Irving replied: "No, I'm simply thinking how this entire production has cost less than the finale of one of my Music Box revues!"

Gertie and Bea soon moved from the Algonquin, and took a duplex apartment on West 54th Street in which they maintained virtually open house for many of those connected with the theatre. The piano was played non stop since the regulars included composers Oscar Hammerstein II, Howard Dietz, Arthur Schwartz, Jerome Kern, Bert Kalmar, Harry Ruby, Richard Rodgers and Larry Hart, George and Ira Gershwin, Irving Berlin and Vincent Youmans and Irving Caesar who composed most of *No, No, Nanette* including 'Tea for Two' in Bea and Gertie's living room. They also welcomed actors like Richard Barthelmess, Laurette Taylor, Jeanne Eagels, Estelle Winwood and impresarios such as Charles Dillingham, Alex Aarons and Vinton Freedley.

Earlier during their stay at the Algonquin, The Big Three had also been taken up by 'The Round Table' where New

York's most famous group of writers including Dorothy Parker, Robert Sherwood and Alexander Woollcott dined regularly. They were entertained, too, by Jules Glaenzer, the head of Cartier, who gave New York's most lavish theatrical parties.

Perhaps as a result of all this adulation, Jack and Bea found they had some difficulty in controlling Gertie. The Canadian comedienne and the Scottish revue artist shared a somewhat basic sense of humour. Thus, soon after they had first met, Jack began pulling Bea's leg about her problems in wearing tails and other men's clothes in her numbers. On one occasion he said:

'Tell me, Beattie, how do you dress – left side or right?' Bea misunderstanding the question and missing the twinkle in his eyes, looked puzzled. 'Come on, Beattie, don't be shy. On which side do you dress?' Suddenly the light dawned and Bea replied: 'Oh yes, In number five dressing room. Stage left.' Jack roared with laughter at what he took to be a brilliant riposte.

With Gertie, the de-bunking process was sometimes harder work. For she was inclined to get up in the morning and decide on which part she would play on that particular day. Sometimes it would be tomboy Gertie, sometimes hard-working trouper Gertie, but sometimes it was 'Duchess' Gertie. On these occasions, Gertie's illusions of grandeur were out of all proportion to the money difficulties which were her usual lot.

For the moment, however, none of The Big Three seemed likely to have any problem about their future earnings. *Charlot's London Revue of 1924* which had originally been booked for six weeks was so successful that the Selwyn Brothers took it out on tour to Boston, Toronto, Baltimore and Chicago. They left without Jack who had to return to London because of his musical comedy commitments, but the Three were soon to be reunited as André Charlot was already planning to cash in on his Broadway success by putting on his company in London before taking it back to America for a new production in 1926.

The London reunion on 30 March 1925 has gone down in the history of British revue as perhaps the greatest gala event of all time. So many of the Charlot Company's fellow performers wanted to pay tribute to them that The Guv arranged two first nights on the same evening, the first at 8 p.m. and the second at midnight. The midnight show was the first of its kind. The pictures taken on this occasion on both sides of the footlights include almost every well known West End performer of the day. In the front row, Noël Coward sat between Gladys Calthrop and Lilian Braithwaite; further back Jack Hulbert and Cicely Courtneidge were with Violet Loraine and Isobel Jeans; Lady

Diana Cooper was with John Barrymore and Ivor Novello, Joe Coyne and Leslie Henson were in the same party as the Duchess of Rutland and up in a box sat George Grossmith and Heather Thatcher, both sporting monocles. Beatrice Lillie adds: 'Zena Dare wore black and Tallulah Bankhead a mammoth bunch of orchids. There sat Fay Compton and Leon Quartermaine, Phyllis Monkman all in pale pink and gold tissue and Fanny Brice in the flesh.'

During the interval, Jack came round after his show at the Empire and led twenty-seven stars in the audience to join the stars on the stage for a special tribute to André Charlot.

The Guv was much moved but – ever practical – announced that since it was now three in the morning, he had arranged for a number of restaurants to stay open all night with transport provided.

Jack interviewed by the press after the midnight matinée said:

It was a wonderful experience for which there is no parallel in the history of the theatre. Gertie and Bea showed no nerves at all despite the pressures involved in performing before their professional peers. And yet, I remember how much terror we felt when we opened the same show on Broadway last year. I'm looking forward to joining the team again in July when we can work up some new material before returning to the United States at the end of the year.

Once more The Big Three were preparing themselves for the challenges of Broadway. They took advantage of Charlot's current policy of producing a monthly edition of his revue at the Prince of Wales Theatre. As a cartoon by Nerman shows, he was able to call on the finest talent available in London and Jack was briefly reunited with his old co-stars Phyl Monkman and Maisie Gay. He worked with Gertie in the July edition and Bea in the August version and took his holiday in Scotland in September before leaving for New York.

The Company's arrival in New York in November 1925 was given full press coverage as a major Scottish occasion. Mistakenly, a mass band of pipers came to the quayside to welcome the new Lady Peel (Beatrice Lillie) and her husband, Sir Robert Peel. When it was pointed out that they had no Scottish connection, Jack diplomatically reminded the American reporters that he was not English but Scottish and, with Mr McIntire, the Cunard Purser, showed every sign of enthusiasm as the local Caledonian Society Pipers did their best to make the company feel at home.

On this occasion there was little fear that the principals would be filled with the same uncertainties as in 1924. Jack's salary was

André Charlot's Midnight Matinée at the Comedy Theatre, London on 30 March, 1925 to celebrate the success of his revues in America. Above, The audience.

Jack, Gertie and Bea are joined on stage by the stars from the audience:
Front Row: *Rosaline Courtneidge, Irene Brown, Tallulah Bankhead, Beatrice Lillie, Gertrude Lawrence, Dorothy Dickson.* Second Row: *Cicely Courtneidge, Gwen Farrar, Norah Blaney, Isabel Jeans, June, Heather Thatcher, Ivy St Helier.* Third Row: *Fay Compton, Phyllis Dare, Phyllis Monkman, Maisie Gay, Lilian Braithwaite, Vi Loraine, Zena Dare.* Back Row: *André Charlot, Joe Coyne, Herbert Mundin, Peter Haddon, Jack Hulbert, Leslie Henson, George Grossmith, Noël Coward, Laddie Cliff, Henry Kendall, Jack Buchanan, Morris Harvey.*

The Charlot Revue back home again – Nerman's impressions of the principal artists dancing to André Charlot's tune (From J.B. clockwise, Bea Lillie, Phyllis Monkman, Morris Harvey, Gertrude Lawrence, Herbert Mundin and Maisie Gay.)

a guaranteed $2,500 per week plus ten per cent of profits from the run. Archie Selwyn had already obtained $200,000 worth of advance bookings at his theatre. He had also guaranteed sell-outs for the first few weeks of the run by making the theatre available for New York's leading charities, including Mrs William K. Vanderbilt's Gala Night (for which tickets were $25 a head). For Jack, Gertie, and Bea, who were so dear to New York socialites after their last Broadway appearance, this presented an arduous task as they were obliged to appear night after night at the parties which preceded and followed their performance.

The opening at the Selwyn Theatre on 11 November 1925 aroused audience and critics alike, and press reports reflected the social cachet of the occasion in which the audience was reported upon almost as fully as the performers. That night, it included parties brought by Condé Nast, Ralph Pulitzer, Otto Kahn, Herbert Bayard Swope, Henry F. Dupont, George Roosevelt, Elsie de Woolf, Frank Crowninshield, Gloria Swanson, Elsie Janis, Adolph Zukor, Neysa McMein, Hassard Short, Ring Lardner, Samuel Goldwyn, Norma Talmadge, Franklin P. Adams, Irving Caesar, Jules Glaenzer and Ruth Gordon.

The *New York Times* reported:

> For more than half an hour before the *Charlot Revue of 1926* opened a gauntlet of quite common citizens of this vicinity lined up on 42nd Street gazing carefully at the ladies and gentlemen passing into the Theatre. When the principals walked on the stage for the opening number, each was greeted in turn for a few moments while the music obediently stopped. It was a first night of good feeling on both sides of the footlights.

Robert Kellman in the New York *Daily Mirror* struck a slightly sourer note in criticizing the late curtain time of ten o'clock adding:

> In the old days the idea of a first night was so that the newspaper reviews could pass judgement on the show. Now, in this case, the idea of a late curtain was simply to suit the dinner engagements of the 'Four Hundred' and make sure that the socially prominent could have an extra dinner cocktail. Certainly this was the most brilliant theatrical gathering of the year and the most enthusiastic and appreciative array of playgoers seen and heard in this or any other season.

For the performers, Robert Kellman had nothing but praise although, in keeping with the populist slant in his report, this was translated into American football comparisons. Thus Gertie was described as the Red Grange of the musical backfield, Bea as 'Five yards' McCarthy and Jack 'As lithe and fascinating as a grid-iron greyhound'.

To a man the Press was taken with Jack's new versatility. As a result of the musical comedy experience he had gained since the American visit two years earlier, he was now the unquestioned master of ceremonies and director of all the show's dance routines and ensembles. As to Jack's performance, Alexander Woollcott summed it up this way:

> Much of the success of the show has to do with the person of Mr Buchanan, probably the only living person who can fall all over the stage like Mr Leon Errol, still keep on an even keel and yet look like one of the incredible Gibson men of yesteryear.

Jack's elegant British clothes aroused much public interest. Apart from his Hawes and Curtis suits, while in America he introduced New York society to such innovations as the backless evening-dress waitcoat and matching piqué shirts. Such sartorial splendour required an infinite attention to detail. For example, evening-dress shirts in America were always starched and Jack sent his soft white piqué shirts, collars and waistcoats back on the weekly Cunard sailing so that they could be laundered by Hawes and Curtis in London.

American tailors were not slow to cash in on Jack's elegant image. They were soon offering 'Buchanan' ties, cravats, shirts and socks. Jack was unhappy about an obvious commercialisation in which he had no financial stake. He was later to rectify the situation but for the moment, he had to accept the old saw about imitation being the sincerest form of flattery. Indeed his name even entered the American dictionary. A well dressed New York male would greet another with 'Say, you're looking very Buchanan today'.

This elegant image was part of the reason why Jack was so taken up by New York society. Gertie and Bea were old hands at this following their long stay in the city during the previous year. But for Jack it was a real opportunity to enjoy the full impact of his Broadway success.

He moved in two main circles which constantly intermingled. There was the social set of Willie Rhinelander Stewart, Allie MacIntosh, Bert Taylor, 'Doc' Holden and the New York Society hostesses. There were also the writers, composers and actors who Jack met again through the Cartier chief, Jules Glaenzer, Max Dreyfuss, the head of the music publishers, Chappells and at the home of new friends such as the owner of the Blomingdale department store.

While Jack enjoyed some aspects of the social scene, he was most at home in the company of his fellow artists. He would spend weekends in Bronxville with Max Dreyfuss where he met

Joseph Meyer and Irving Caesar, who were responsible for the two biggest hits in the Charlot Revue, 'A Cup of Coffee' and Jack's big solo number 'Gigolette'. Now both in their eighties, they still recall Jack's dedicated interest in their work. To Joseph Meyer, Jack was 'a great humanitarian . . . a good man.' Irving Caesar is even more fulsome in his praise:

> Jack was fascinated by a song Joe Meyer and I had written called 'When I Go Home'. He made us play it again and again and I know he tried for years to fit it into one of his shows. But then Jack was deeply interested in musical composition and he was very generous in his appreciation. There was no envy in him. He was a true artist. He rooted just as hard for the other fellow. His soul was in the thing and he had great empathy. This reflected itself in his work. He had a simplicity about him – it was almost naïvety – and yet he had that marvellous sophistication. He remained unspoiled – forever unspoiled. A dear fellow.

Despite these off stage friendships, work was never far away. André Charlot, quick to exploit his success, had taken a lease on the Rendezvous Club in West 45th Street. The opening in time for Christmas 1925 was described by the *New York American*:

> One of the most brilliant gatherings of the night club season was at New York's newest 'Gin' club when Jack Buchanan, Gertrude Lawrence and Bea Lillie made their cabaret début. The scene was reminiscent of some New York millionaire's private party. Some of those present were Harpo Marx, Ethel Barrymore, Irving Berlin, Edmund Goulding, Elsie Janis, Marilyn Miller, Clifton Webb, Grace Moore and the William K. Vanderbilts.

Also in the first night audience at the Rendezvous was Noël Coward. Writing in his autobiography *Present Indicative* he recalled the way in which success had given The Big Three an extra star quality:

> It was thrilling to see them hailed as great stars by the whole of New York. It invested them, for me, with a new glamour as though I was discovering them too, and had never seen them before in my life. The appreciation of American audiences certainly gave an extra fillip to their performances. There was a shine on all of them, a happy gratification bursting through. I could swear that none of them had ever been so good before.

The appearances at the Rendezvous Club had to be limited to a four-week season as the Charlot Revue was due to set out on a nationwide tour in February. Charlot had committed the Company to give the opening performance in Hollywood at the new El Capitan Theatre on 19 April 1926 following two weeks in

Detroit and three weeks in Chicago. A three-month run was planned at the El Capitan followed by four weeks in San Francisco and a tour of Canada and the rest of the United States which would delay Jack's return to Britain until the beginning of 1927. While in Hollywood he was expected to appear in films and, following the renewed success of the Charlot Revue, the British press began gloomily to predict that Jack might not return to Britain for at least seven years (which was the length of the normal Hollywood silent movie contract).

Perhaps fortunately for the British public, the proposed tour proved over-ambitious. Nevertheless the initial reaction was a continuing triumph. In Detroit the Press talked about 'the great triumvirate'. In Chicago, Ashton Stevens, doyen of the local critics, said 'The trio of Buchanan, Lawrence and Lillie is matchless. I haven't seen Jack Buchanan's like since the early George Edwardes' Gaiety days. He has manner, looks, smartness and youth. He is funny when it needs to be and has a pleasant dignity too.'

On their travels, the Company experienced the full pleasures – and indeed in those days they were pleasures – of travelling by train across the American sub-continent. They left New York at 6 p.m. on the famous Twentieth Century Limited train after railway officials had escorted the principals over a red carpet to their sleeping compartments. This took them as far as Detroit and then on to Chicago. In Detroit Jack took a photograph of Gertie with Eddie Cantor and others when they visited the Ford Motor Company's head office. In Chicago, they picked up another famous American train, the Santa Fé Chief, which was due to reach the Union Station in Los Angeles after two days' time. Once again, a stop was made *en route* – this time at the Grand Canyon – where a local photographer took a picture of Jack and Gertie on a trek to the foot of the Canyon. Their guide on this excursion was the self-appointed host to visiting notables to the West, Will Rogers. The cowboy movie star with his famous quiff and sombrero had recently become the unofficial mayor of Los Angeles and took it upon himself to look after the Charlot Company when they reached the West Coast.

On arriving in Los Angeles, the Company found that the construction of the El Capitan Theatre was well behind schedule and so they took up many of the invitations to parties on the beach in Malibu and in the homes of Beverly Hills. At one such party, Jack looked up his old friend the Scottish born comedian, George K. Arthur, who was now well established as a Hollywood feature player.

Jack returned hospitality in the exotic house he had rented from its equally exotic owner, the Russian tragiedienne, Alla

Nazimova, who had created a sensation in her art nouveau appearance in *Salome*. He was quickly taken up by the British colony in Hollywood and made a 'Three Musketeer' friendship with Richard Barthelmess and Ronald Colman. Through them, he became friendly with Marion Davies and visited the Hearst Ranch where he took more snaps of Bea Lillie with his two pals as well as a solo study of the legendary star of the silent cinema, John Gilbert.

The delayed opening of the El Capitan Theatre was typical of some of the planning failures which marred the end of the Charlot Revue's tour. Apart from the financial squeeze imposed on the company by the idle time before the opening, the twelve-week engagement was much too ambitious for an area which was still backward in theatrical terms. Hollywood was still engaged in rivalry with Broadway and the legitimate stage. Each side looked down upon the other. Thus, while the early performances at the El Capitan Theatre attracted many of the acting community, there was little possiblity of forming the kind of large sophisticated 'in group' from the general public who would come again and again as they had done in New York.

As a result, the Selwyns began to lose money on the show and Charlot, who was now back in England having obtained his guaranteed earnings, felt unable to intervene. Plans for the extensive tour of other American and Canadian cities had to be cancelled.

Despite the somewhat sad financial note towards the end of the tour, the Company found many attractions to life in Hollywood. Jack and Bea were approached to appear in the silent classic *Corporal Kate* while the Charlot girls worked as extras in *What Price Glory*. But uncertainties about the future of the show made Jack reluctant to commit himself to a long stay.

Whatever the problems with the general paying public in Los Angeles, the Charlot team had made many friends among their fellow performers. If they could not get a seat, they stood in the wings. The last night of the show was a gala occasion. For Gertie and Bea however, the evening looked like ending in disaster. When they came on for the famous Scottish finale, they were mortified to find that all the big names in the audience had apparently left and they gazed out on row upon row of empty seats.

What they did not realise was that Jack had given his friends Dick Barthelmess and Ronald Colman the key of the pass door from the auditorium to the back of the stage. Suddenly the stage began to fill with their particular men friends all trying to add a contribution to the Scottish theme. Charlie Chaplin appeared with his trousers rolled up and performed in mime, Rudolph

Valentino was carrying a ladder for no special reason, Douglas Fairbanks, Senior, was enwrapped in a bedspread while John Gilbert and George K. Arthur were all cheer leaders in the huge ovation which followed when the curtain came down.

Then the artists bridged the audience across the orchestra pit, joined crossed hands and sang 'Auld Lang Syne'. The stars wept. The girls in the chorus wept. As Wyn Clare remembers: 'We could have gone on playing there for ever, they loved us and we loved them.'

This tremendous send-off was a fitting climax to the Charlot Revue in America. Although Jack was never to return with The Guv, he had made many friends and acquired a deep love for the United States which, from this time onwards, made him determined to divide his time between London, Hollywood and Broadway.

Dancing Honeymoon – The Great Musical Comedies from *Battling Butler* to *This'll Make You Whistle*

I hated dancing
Till I met you,
It never found me
Until I felt your arms around me

'DANCING HONEYMOON' WAS JACK'S first really popular musical comedy number. It was typical of the many romantic duets which he was to use in the nine musical comedies which he put on under his own management in London during the twenties and thirties. Although 'Dancing Honeymoon' dated from the first of these shows, *Battling Butler* in 1922, it was only when Jack returned from the United States in 1926 that he was able to establish himself as London's pre-eminent musical-comedy actor-manager.

Jack's decision to go into management was based on two main considerations. First, during his early years of struggle, he had vowed that he would never again put himself in the hands of those who found it difficult to accept his particular shyness and the nervous tension that had put him at such severe disadvantage when auditioning. Second, as a Scotsman and one who was 'careful with money' Jack, confident in his own producing skills, saw the entry into management as a way of ensuring financial independence.

In all his musical comedies, there were certain common features. The plot was always secondary to the requirements of providing a vehicle to show off Jack's versatility as a comedian and romantic leading man. The book and lyrics were usually by his friend, Duggie Furber, who had a feel for the kind of material which Jack could use effectively. For the music, Jack used a wide variety of talent taking full advantage of both his British and American music publishing connections. Thus from the pens of Pa Braham, Philip Charig, Max Darewski, Vivian Ellis, Ira Gershwin, Sigler, Goodhart and Hoffman, Johnny Green, Oscar

Hammerstein II, Otto Harbach, Hugo Hirsch, Jerome Kern, and Joseph Meyer came a stream of hit songs which Jack used in his shows and recorded.

Beginning with 'Dancing Honeymoon', they included 'This Year, Next Year', 'Who', 'Two Little Bluebirds', 'Fancy Our Meeting', 'There's Always Tomorrow', 'Oceans of Time', 'Weep No More My Baby', 'I'm in a Dancing Mood', 'There isn't any Limit to My Love for You' and 'This'll Make You Whistle'. In putting over these romantic numbers, Jack almost invariably used the same formula and over the years, he sang and danced with glamorous *ingénues* like Phyllis Titmuss, Peggy Kearton, June, Binnie Hale, Anna Neagle, Roma Beaumont, and Jean Gillie.

There were other features common to his shows. Jack would usually be involved in comedy scenes with character actresses playing either the 'older woman' or the 'large lady' as personified by Sydney Fairbrother, Veronica Brady, Kate Cutler or Vera Pearce. There were also the girls who played 'the other woman'; Ethel Stewart, Maidie Andrews, Lalla Collins and Sylvia Leslie and the men who took the 'heavy' or character parts: Duggie Furber and Fred Groves in the early shows, followed by Jack's particular chums, Bill Kendall, Fred Emney and Dave Hutcheson.

These players became Jack's repertory company – most of them appearing with him on a number of occasions. Only one performer appeared in all but one of Jack's nine musical comedies between the Wars – Elsie Randolph (for which reason she deserves the separate chapter which follows).

In Jack's first venture into musical comedy management, *Battling Butler* which opened at the New Oxford Theatre in London on 8 December 1922, he made his entrance in the traditional driving gear of the day; cap, leather coat and huge fur gauntlets. As he pulled off the gauntlets, his first line was 'Take these out and give them each a saucer of milk'.

This business of Jack's first entrance was to become an intriguing feature of all his shows. In *Battling Butler*, he also showed the attention to detail which was to characterise all his productions.

Thus, when playing the hen-pecked husband, who pretends to be a boxer in order to get away from home, he took coaching lessons from the French world light-heavyweight champion, Georges Carpentier.

He also took enormous trouble over the costumes for the show. He ordered over three hundred elaborate dresses for scenes set at a garden party, a ball and the Albert Hall. His choice of couturier fell on the then unknown Norman Hartnell who has recalled that

50

Above, *A typical J.B. entrance in*
Battling Butler *at the New
Oxford Theatre in 1922. Above
right,* Jack with June *in* Toni *in
1924. Elsie Randolph's first big
number with Jack 'Don't Love
You', in* Toni *in 1924.*

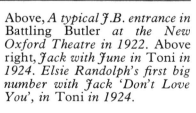

'fortunately Jack was as nervous as I was and, at that time, didn't know the difference between Scottish wool and French tulle'.

As well as being one of the first to discover the future Royal dressmaker, Jack was also instrumental in bridging the long established gap between the theatre and London Society. In the early twenties, there was still a tendency in aristocratic circles to regard actors as 'rogues and vagabonds'. Yet Jack's leading lady, Sylvia Leslie was a débutante – the daughter of 'Spy', the greatest Victorian and Edwardian cartoonist of his day.

She and Jack were witnesses at one of the most sensational weddings of the year when he gave away Vena Galt – who played the maid in *Battling Butler* – to a City merchant at Princes Row Registry Office in May 1923. The merchant concerned had seen over a hundred performances of the show and proposed seven times before the London press ran banner headlines reading 'Actress Weds Rich Man'.

The Prince of Wales was almost as regular a visitor. The late Sylvia Leslie has recalled:

> Our big duet was 'Dancing Honeymoon'. We used to take a lot of liberties with the plot in those days because I played someone else's wife and yet I had this flirtatious number with Jack. We were all very intrigued by the fact that the Prince of Wales virtually made it into a trio. He used to come and sit right in the front of the stalls or in the second row. He came many, many times and he just loved the song and you could see him singing as we did the number.

The Prince of Wales also became a keen fan of Jack's next show *Toni* which opened at the Shaftesbury Theatre on 11 May 1924. One of his particular interests was in the double-breasted dinner jacket which Jack had brought as the latest American fashion to London. The Prince came backstage and asked Jack where he could have the same style made and some tailoring experts date the rise of the dinner jacket and the decline of tails in London society from this time.

Toni was, in its own way, a Royal occasion. It had a typical *'Prisoner of Zenda* – set to music' theme of which *The Times* said:

> We are on familiar soil in a land addicted to brilliant military uniforms and the unlimited consumption of alcohol. Mr Jack Buchanan was taken post-haste to the Continent to save the political situation. He does so in a characteristic British way by displaying a continual sense of humour. He never allowed anyone to be serious while he was on the stage and as he was there nearly all the time, it may confidently be stated that he saved from ruin not only the land of Mettopolachia, but also the fortunes of the musical comedy itself for in addition

52

to showing his ready wit, he sang with spirit and danced admirably.

Part of the show's success was undoubtedly due to the fact that London audiences were delighted to see Jack again after his success in the Charlot Revues on Broadway. He made the most of his personal popularity in his first entrance. The girls of the chorus came on with their backs to the audience, dancing a cross-over step, hand in hand. As the last of the twenty girls came on it was seen that Jack was the last link in the chain. All this aroused the audience so that, as *Punch* said:

> The audience was in a mood of enormous goodwill towards Jack Buchanan for coming back from America and certainly his delightful dancing, his deft strokes of mimicry, his pleasing voice, with its not unpleasant transatlantic flavour, his resource in providing engaging variations on a simple theme, deserved the applause they won. And when we applaud our musical comedy heros, we don't merely clap, we roar over them as the Spurs are roared over when they kick the winning goal on their own ground.

In recalling the show in later years, Jack said that it had an unusually strong plot for a musical comedy (and it was for this reason that he was later to star in an almost straight dramatic film version of the play). This meant that Jack, himself, had to be on the stage almost throughout the play to inject enough comedy to make sure that the actions of the revolutionaries and pompous military men were not taken too seriously by the audience. In one number 'Blotto', Jack performed one of the first of what was to become a standard routine in his shows by dancing while 'under the affluence of incohol' with a large lady, in this case Veronica Brady. Silly jokes abounded as when June, trying to persuade Jack to show some backbone, said 'But even a worm turns, Toni' to which our hero replied 'I don't see why it should – it's the same all round'. Or when Jack, asked to define 'fortifications' replies 'two twentyifications'. As one reviewer said, Jack's style and delivery made even this corny dialogue seem witty, adding: 'Does the reader deem this unfunny? He should have heard it in its time and place.'

In *Boodle* which opened at the Empire, Leicester Square on 10 March 1925, Jack – the most superstitious of men – defied the old theatrical warning against putting on plays with a circus theme. They rarely do well but, on this occasion, he was no doubt optimistic about the possibility of a follow-on success from *Toni*. He brought virtually the same company to *Boodle* and Jack collaborated with Duggie Furber in writing several of the musical numbers. He had also taken enormous trouble with the

Left, *Jack sings 'Some Unfortunate Child' to Jenny in* Boodle *in
1925*. Below, *Jack and (for no
apparent reason) hunting chorus
in 'The Big Tune gets me going
every Time' from* Boodle *in 1925.*

dances and ensembles and had brought in Carl Hyson (who with his wife Dorothy Dickson was then London's leading cabaret dance act) to help in producing the big number with June, 'This Year, Next Year'.

Such was Jack's confidence that he made a record of this and the other big romantic number, 'Garden of Lies', for release on the assumption that the show would have a long run. Certainly the failure of *Boodle* could not be blamed on the score but the short run meant that a number of other songs received less airing than was their due. In 'The Big Tune' Jack sang – for no particular reason – as elegant as ever in a lounge suit with the chorus behind him resplendent in full hunting attire:

I croak a small cadenza
Like a goat with influenza
There's no reason, there's no rhyme,
The song is just sublime
The big tune gets me going every time

Notwithstanding the failure of his last show based on a circus theme, Jack's next production *Sunny* – the story of a circus bareback rider – was a much safer bet. The show had already played on Broadway with enormous success where the tuneful score by Jerome Kern, Otto Harbach and Oscar Hammerstein II, was outstanding.

The London production which opened on Thursday, 7 October 1926 was to be the first of four smash hits for Jack at the London Hippodrome. For his leading lady he engaged Binnie Hale, who had just made an enormous reputation as the *ingénue* in *No, No, Nanette*. Jack also brought into his company Jack Hulbert's younger brother, Claude, who was then emerging as one of the West End's most effective comedians and whose stammering and diffident manner contrasted well with Jack's own on-stage assurance.

Sunny as produced in London was, as *The Times* described it, more a revue than a musical comedy. Apart from Jerome Kern's famous score which included 'Two Little Bluebirds', 'Let's Say Goodnight till the Morning', 'When We Get Our Divorce' and 'Who', there were a number of *avant garde* features. The sets were elaborate, allowing the action to wander freely from the circus opening sequence to scenes on board ship and in the countryside of both Britain and the United States. This 'spare no expense' theme was reflected in the presence of Alfredo and his band who played on stage during the intervals to supplement the work of the Pit Orchestra. Jack estimated that the cost of band payments, staff wages, dresses, scenery and lighting amounted to almost £45,000, an enormous sum in the twenties.

Binnie Hale has two particular memories of Jack in *Sunny*. From the first she learnt his professional weak spot and from the second she appreciated his quick wittedness and skill in handling an audience. She recalls:

> I always remember Jack as a highly-strung performer. The only thing which broke him up was a nose blow. It always seemed to happen after a line like 'Shall I tell you what I think of you?' And he couldn't speak. It floored him.
>
> Another very funny thing I remember. There was a cue and my father was supposed to come on. Jack gave the cue and nobody appeared. There wasn't a sign. And Jack just went to the footlights and said to the audience 'You'll have realised that Sunny's father is off. Now, if you just listen, we'll hear him.' The audience started to giggle and we heard running footsteps tearing down the stairs. The audience started to laugh and Nicholas Adams, who was playing my father, had to dash along behind the backcloth to make his entrance completely out of breath. He got the biggest round of applause he'd ever got and he couldn't think what he'd done. It was so clever of Jack to turn the situation to advantage like that.

Towards the end of the show, Jack added a typical revue touch which had no relevance to the plot – but which always stopped the show – when he took part as a member of 'The Famous Dud Singers Quartet' in 'The Fox has Left its Lair'. This Quartet was to become part of Jack's standard repertoire for cabaret appearances and was made into a film short by Warner Brothers only three years later.

The sequence began with the arrival of a Glee Club Quartet apparently intent on singing in totally straight-forward fashion. The fourth member of the Quartet fails to appear and Jack, as a last minute substitute, joins the group. As soon as they begin singing, it is obvious that he is ill prepared, having written the words of the song on his starched cuff. Inevitably, the cuff becomes detached from his shirt and Jack's frantic looks and antics in trying to retrieve the cuff and maintain his place in the intricate Glee Quartet singing invariably caused waves of laughter in the audience.

Jack used a similar comedy routine in his next show *That's a Good Girl* when, in a cod Grand Opera finale, 'Parting Time' he ruined the proceedings with constant interjections such as 'I shall take Bovril to pull me through the winter'.

That's a Good Girl opened on 5 June 1928 and was one of Jack's biggest Hippodrome successes. Elsie Randolph took the lead opposite him for the first time. Kate Cutler played the maiden aunt on whom – as in so many musical comedies of the period – the hero depends for finance.

Jack gave a lot of thought to his first entrance. The show opened with the boys in the chorus line coming on in top hat, white tie and tails with their backs to the audience, tap dancing to the tune of 'Let Yourself Go'. When all twelve were on the stage, they turned and the audience invariably gave an enormous roar of appreciation as the figure in the middle was revealed as Jack Buchanan.

One of the twelve 'gentlemen of the chorus' was Richard Murdoch who recalls:

> The critics were very complimentary about the chorus which was described as 'manly'. This was no accident for Jack (who typically involved himself in every facet of the show) had chosen them so that he could eliminate some of the more delicate contenders. In this, he was largely successful but one of our number who was probably the oldest chorus boy in the business – and certainly one of the most fragile – got wind of Jack's screening process. At the audition, after he had finished the dance routine, he pulled in his stomach and marched off the stage with the most 'butch' exit ever seen.
>
> As he got into the wings, he said to one of the other chorus boys: 'That ought to fool the old bastard'. Elsie Randolph overheard this and told Jack. It made him laugh so much that 'the oldest member' kept his place in the chorus.

The first night at the London Hippodrome saw a demonstration of what the Press called 'Buchananism'. One report said: 'The Gallery Girls gave a demonstration of the cult last night, one of them calling out, at the final curtain, "Jack you're wonderful" again and again.' Jack had to make a speech almost every night from the first performance onwards and his presence in the show was so crucial that when he injured his leg and went to the South of France for two weeks holiday in August, the takings dropped by a thousand pounds a week. One critic said that, at this time, only Gladys Cooper, Gerald du Maurier, George Robey and Sir Harry Lauder had comparable 'pulling power'. The *Theatre World* illustrated Jack's popularity by quoting a conversation between two autograph hunters outside the Hippodrome: 'What? You've got Jack Buchanan twice?' 'Here give me one and you can have Bobby Jones, Paul Whiteman and Flanagan and Allen.' 'No deal' Lengthy pause. Then: 'All right, I'll chuck in Davy Burnaby as makeweight.'

Stand Up and Sing, which opened its out of town tour on 2 December 1930, was typical of the many shows where Jack shrewdly ensured that his personal following would yield a guaranteed profit before the West End opening. After the first week in Southampton, Jack and his company toured for twelve weeks at Manchester, Glasgow, Edinburgh and Birmingham.

They then played thirty-nine weeks at the London Hippodrome before Jack once more took the company out on the road for twenty-one weeks at Golders Green, Liverpool, Edinburgh, Glasgow, Newcastle, Manchester, Leeds, Birmingham, Southsea, Southampton, Streatham Hill and a final week at the Kings Theatre, Hammersmith.

This meant that the show ran for a total of 604 performances covering seventy-four weeks until 14 May 1932.

The show is remembered with special affection by a number of those who appeared in it, several of whom were making their first major West End appearance. In this respect, pride of place must go to Anna Neagle:

I had been with Jack in New York but only in the chorus when I was Marjorie Robertson. I took singing and dancing lessons there and worked very hard on 'tap' routines in a style which would be new to British audiences.

Through Jack's stage director, Frank Smythe, I got the chance to audition for the *ingénue* lead in *Stand Up and Sing*. I thought I might fool Jack with my new name but he said 'Aha – so it is you. I thought I recognised the face, but I couldn't place the name. Well let's see what you can do.'

I was terribly frightened and somehow my dance routine just didn't seem to go over. Then, when I tried to sing, nothing came out. 'Come on, we'd better start all over again, hadn't we?' said Jack. I tried again but I was so nervous and conscious that this was my big chance and if I failed, my career might never take off. So the second attempt wasn't much better than the first.

We went back to Jack's office at the Prince of Wales Theatre. He sat down behind his desk. 'Well, you're the best I've seen for this part so far but, frankly, I don't know whether you could quite manage it. I must look for someone but if I don't find her in the next few days, I'll give you a chance and I'll let you know by the end of the week.'

I thought the week would never pass and I couldn't believe that Jack would fail to find someone else. At the end of the week his secretary asked me to see him again. Jack was smiling. 'I'm not quite sure whether you can do the part or not but we'll take you out on tour and if you manage there, you'll get a West End contract.'

Jack couldn't have been kinder or more patient in helping me in those prior to London weeks. Our big number together was 'There's Always Tomorrow', and I never hear the song without thinking of dear Jack, sitting centre-back, perfectly relaxed, smoking a cigarette, humming a little and smiling at me encouragingly. He helped me enormously and I'm sure it was because he had suffered so much when auditioning himself.

When *Stand Up and Sing* opened at the London Hippodrome on 5 March 1931, the audience response was massively enthusiastic. Jack had not appeared on the West End stage for almost three years owing to his film commitments and this added to the poignancy of his first appearance. Certainly the British press made much of this, almost every report referring to 'Jack Buchanan's triumphant return'. There was only one carping critic who referred to the show as *Sit Down and Shut Up*. The majority view was summed up by one report which said 'There is only one Jack'.

The *Sunday Times* singled out his traditional inebriated dance routine saying 'Jack Buchanan was marvellously supported – almost literally – by Vera Pearce who combines the majesty of Boadicea with a native impishness. In their dance, Miss Pearce, taking the stage like a battle cruiser, overbore her partner by sheer weight of metal, and the building rocked literally as well as metaphorically.'

In this number, 'When It's Hiccup Time in Burgundy', Jack had a typical piece of comedy dialogue with Vera Pearce, who played the part of an Egyptian Princess. Jack asked her 'Are you really a Princess?' To which she replied 'Of course, what else could I possibly be?' To which Jack's punch line was 'Oh, I don't know. I thought you might be a hammock tester.'

At the end of the show, when the usual misunderstandings of the plot had been unravelled, he staged a scene which might have been taken from any of his earlier revues. In this, all the principals, Vera Pearce, Elsie Randolph, Anton Dolin, Richard Murdoch and Richard Dolman joined Jack in full evening dress with all the girls of the chorus for a big finale. Jack, interviewed after the show, said simply: 'It has nothing to do with the show, I just put it on as a kind of afterthought to send everyone away with the feeling that they had value for money.'

Jack's next show *Mr Whittington* reflected the same lavish theme. In addition to the normal programme, audiences at the London Hippodrome were also given a 'Glowgramme' in which the cast and the synopsis of scenes were printed in white phosphorus print on a red background which could be read in the dark. The main programme was itself a work of art with many scenes from the play as well as pictures of the principals.

Mr Whittington was a modern musical version of the traditional Dick Whittington theme and this gave Jack the opportunity of appearing in a number of dream sequences. He was seen on stage as a policeman, as a prospective parliamentary candidate, as a boxer at the Albert Hall and winning the Derby. In addition, a cinema screen was lowered which allowed the audience to see Jack winning a Test Match, the World Billiard Championship, and the Schneider Air Race Trophy. These scenes – to say nothing of a minstrel show which was mounted in the unlikely setting of the Greater London Council Chambers – made *Mr Whittington* lavish in the extreme.

Jack had his usual regulars with him in the company. But, once again, he repeated his discovery act in taking one of Mr Cochran's young ladies, Kathleen Gibson, at the age of eighteen to play the *ingénue* role. He also brought into the company someone who was to become one of his regulars and a close personal friend, Fred Emney, who recalls:

> Jack went into partnership with Jack Waller for this show. Greatorex Newman was writing the book and lyrics and recommended me and I got the part of Lord Leatherhead – an apt title for this silly ass part – when Jack Waller put me on a contract at twenty five pounds a week.
>
> When we took the show out on the road, Jack took a great fancy to me and this was the start of a lifelong friendship. After a few weeks, he said to me: 'Why don't you stay at my hotel. You'd be much more comfortable.' I told him I simply couldn't afford it and anyway my digs were quite reasonable.
>
> Next week, he turned up at my digs and said to the landlady: 'I've come to take Mr Emney to stay at my hotel.' When I started to protest, he said: 'Fred. You're coming.' and then to the landlady: 'It's not that you don't make him comfortable here. Of course you do. But you see I need him near me at my hotel where we can discuss the show and make plans.'
>
> I explained to him again that I couldn't afford his hotel. 'What are we paying you?' Jack asked. I told him and he said: 'O.K. Well, you'll soon be earning much more than that and I'll pay your hotel bill.' He did, too, *and* he doubled my salary.

Jack was also able to keep another long-standing commitment to another old friend when he brought Johnny Green from the United States to compose most of the music in *Mr Whittington*. John W. Green (as he now prefers to be called as a serious musician and conductor) was then an infant prodigy who Jack had first met and encouraged when he was in the Charlot Revue on Broadway. Since then, Green had made his name as the composer of such standards as 'Body and Soul'.

Certainly the score for *Mr Whittington* was one of the best in any of Jack's shows and in 'Weep No More, My Baby', 'Like Monday Follows Sunday', 'Oceans of Time', 'Who Do You Think You Are', Johnny Green wrote four smash hits which had enormous record sales for Columbia.

In *The Flying Trapeze* at the Alhambra in 1935, Jack took a major gamble. This was the first London show he had put on anywhere but the Hippodrome for almost ten years. In addition, the show, as its name implied, was entirely based on a circus theme in which Jack himself played a high wire artist, René, King of the Air. Perhaps even more significant, this was the only show in all his own musical comedy productions in which Elsie Randolph did not appear.

This combination of changed circumstances and, once again, defiance of the theatrical superstition against plays based on the circus, proved ill-fated. Yet the show had many qualities. It was sumptuously staged with scenery and costumes designed by Professor Ernest Stern, then considered Europe's most advanced stage designer, and had a lovely score.

Many of the Gallery Girls who had become so devoted to Jack had come to take it for granted that his partnership with Elsie Randolph was a permanent feature. When they demonstrated their displeasure, David Fairweather, then editor of the *Theatre World* said:

> When, I wonder, will it be realised that these Galleryites know less than nothing about the quality of a new play? They are actuated by personal bias, and in this case their complaint seems to be that Jack Buchanan dared to present himself in a play out of the ordinary, with a change in leading ladies. The publicity given by newspapers means that these stupid over – or is it under – sexed girls wrongly imagine that their shrilly voiced opinions really count for something, whereas they are really a pest and a menace to the theatre.

Fred Emney recalls that Jack was philosophical about this failure, his first in London for over ten years. 'We must give the public what they want,' he said. His next show *This'll Make You Whistle* at the Palace Theatre on 15 September 1936 was very much the mixture as before with Jack and Elsie together again, with support from Bill Kendall and Sylvia Leslie. To this team was added Jack's pal Dave Hutcheson who, together with Bill Kendall, played Jack's best friends, a role which they also occupied in private life. For the *ingénue* role, Jack, yet again, brought in another of his discoveries from the ranks of Mr Cochran's young ladies, the enchantingly pretty Jean Gillie.

He had also sought musical help from the United States and in the team of Sigler, Goodhart and Hoffman, he found three composers who in this show and in a series of films in British studios in the thirties, produced just the right kind of light catchy tunes ideally suited for Jack's style. With the title song 'This'll Make You Whistle', 'There isn't any Limit to My Love for You', 'I'm in a Dancing Mood' and 'Without Rhythm', Jack had four big hits which boosted his earnings from the sale of gramophone records.

Another factor in the show's success was the exceptionally long tour both before and after the West End opening. Jack's old friend, Bill Kendall, who had now established himself as almost a permanent fixture in supporting roles, recalls the tour and Jack's generosity:

> We were playing the Manchester Opera House when the 1936 Grand National was on at Aintree. Some of us dropped the hint that we'd like to see the race. Suddenly, it was announced that the entire company – and that was probably eighty or more – were being taken to the National at Jack's expense. He had a special train and everything was on Jack – champagne, lunch, admission fees – and he even gave the boys and girls in the chorus something to bet on the race.
>
> On the way back, we had somehow picked up a ten percenter – an agent – called Alf Zeitlin. He was busy drinking Jack's champagne. Suddenly when the train was just outside Manchester, he called for silence, and said: 'This is a wonderful thing Jack has done for us today. I can think of only one other management that would treat its company so well'. Jack bridled a bit at this and said 'Who's that, ol' boy?' and Alf said 'That well known solo artiste, Ruth Draper'.

It is perhaps appropriate to leave this account of the last of the musical comedies which Jack Buchanan staged in the twenties and thirties with a vision of Jack's happy family enjoying his champagne and good nature. The *Observer* caught the mood of Jack's reunion with old colleagues in saying: 'Mr Buchanan's new musical show is like a house party of old friends. His smooth style masks the watchful care of the artist who is also the host, eager to amuse, while concerned that the fun should be communal.'

Elsie Randolph

Fancy our meeting
For this one fond greeting,
When days are so fleeting
And few
Paradise seeming
With no thought of scheming
A dream worth dreaming come true

'FANCY OUR MEETING' WAS the big hit song in *That's a Good Girl* and this haunting tune is played and sung whenever Jack and Elsie's long partnership is recalled. One of those who remembers this number with special affection is the playwright Alan Melville. He was later to become one of Jack's pals but when he saw 'Fancy Our Meeting' it was as a schoolboy at the Alhambra in Glasgow. He recalls:

> 'Jack and Elsie sang with the full chorus. They were all dressed in the palest of silver grey and the palest of silver blue. Glasgow thought it the last word of chic. So did I. For me this number sums up the magic of their partnership. There was some strange feat of levitation . . . their feet never seemed actually to touch the stage, or if they did, it wasn't for long. You could hardly hear a sound except the quiet pizzicato of the strings or the occasional, very occasional, tap of Jack and Elsie's shoes.'

That's a Good Girl marked the start of full partnership between Jack Buchanan and Elsie Randolph since, in doubling up in two major parts as the pert detective Joy Dean keeping an eye on our hero and, as Wilhelmina, the constantly sniffing Swiss post girl, Elsie was recognised on merit as Jack's true leading lady.

She achieved this position by sheer hard work and, above all, by her willingness to fit in with the needs of Jack's musical comedies. It could not always have been easy for her to see Jack performing many of the best musical numbers in his shows with whichever glamour girl was chosen for the *ingénue* parts while, by contrast, Elsie's role would normally provide a foil for the comedy scenes with Jack. As the *Theatre World* said about one of the early shows in which Elsie worked with Jack (*Boodle* in 1925): 'It is surely very noble of Elsie Randolph to go through the evening with her hair scraped back in playing the unsympathetic part of Clinging Clematis since she is, in reality, so very handsome.'

Elsie's first show with Jack was a tiny role in *Battling Butler* in 1922. They had first met when she was appearing in the chorus at the Queen's Hall Roof Follies Cabaret (in the old building which is now an annex to the B.B.C.). Jack was, at this time, producing the dance numbers for Jack Hylton and he would, from time to time, appear himself as a speciality turn. On this occasion, Jack had brought his current leading lady Sylvia Leslie to perform their famous 'Dancing Honeymoon' duet from *Battling Butler*. Elsie had just been taken out of the chorus to replace the leading girl in solo numbers in the supporting cabaret (in view of that lady's habit, as Elsie has described it, of 'dipping too freely into the trifle'.). Jack, unaware of this, suggested that she should come and see him about a possible part in *Battling Butler*.

When Elsie presented herself after the next matinée performance at the Adelphi Theatre, Jack, who had by now heard of her improved standing at the Queen's Hall, said: 'Oh my dear, I had no idea you'd got a lead part. I have really nothing suitable for you here. There's only a tiny part as a flapper asking for autographs in Act I, doubling up with a maid part in the Second Act.'

Elsie later said: 'I didn't want to stay in cabaret all my life. I wanted to play in full length productions – comedy parts and roles with character in them.' So she readily accepted when Jack suggested that she might like to try working both at the Adelphi Theatre and at the Queen's Hall late night show. This was risky, since Jack Hylton, a very tough Lancastrian employer, as well as brilliant pianist and band leader, did not allow the girls in his shows to work elsewhere. Sure enough, Elsie's double act was discovered and Jack Hylton gave her the sack.

However, by then, she had made her mark in *Battling Butler*. Soon afterwards, Sylvia Leslie's mother wanted her daughter to be presented at Court and, as the first understudy was ill, Elsie went on and performed 'Dancing Honeymoon' with Jack. She also had the opportunity of performing a solo number. Jack, watching her from the wings, was impressed when the stage manager, Frank Smythe, said 'Look at those kicks. That girl will go a long way.' At the end of the performance, Elsie received a message from Jack saying that he was taking up the option on her contract and from that day in 1923 began a musical-comedy partnership which lasted for over twenty years.

Although Elsie was only a teenager, she made rapid progress. In *Toni*, (1924) she had the second lead part, and her first regular

Jack and Elsie in unsympathetic disguise as the barmaid and 'Clinging Clematis' in Boodle *in 1925.*

song and dance number with Jack, 'Don't Love You', was the
first of many gramophone records they were to make together. In
Boodle (1925) and *Sunny* (1926) Elsie continued her work as a
second lead to Jack while the lead roles went respectively to June
and to Binnie Hale.

After *That's a Good Girl* in 1928, Elsie's place in the lead
opposite Jack was firmly established, and in *Stand Up and Sing*
(1931) she had what was described as 'the longest part ever
produced for a musical comedy actress.' Charles Lefeaux's
assessment of Elsie's work in this show is interesting. 'Because
of her piquancy, she was more of a soubrette than a romantic lead.
And she was a brilliant foil for Jack. She could tackle the broadest
comedy – even burlesque.'

Although they concentrated on comedy work together, Elsie
was progressively able to take over most of the big duets with
Jack. Since he was still expected to 'get the girl' playing the
ingénue role this usually meant that Jack and Elsie's number
treated the romantic theme in a light-hearted way, and almost
invariably involved the theme of rejection. At its most obvious,
this was reflected in 'The One I'm Looking For' in *That's a Good
Girl* when Jack ungallantly sang to Elsie (made to look as un-
attractive as possible as a snivelling Swiss post girl):

You're figure's gone
You look like sin,
What was pushed out
Is now caved in . . .
I'd as soon be on my ownsome
When you're near me
I feel lonesome
No, I don't think you're
Quite the one I'm looking for.

In Stand Up and Sing, Jack used the – by now – classic device of
a praise section leading to the punch line. So, seated on a couch
in a front scene, he sings to Elsie:

Oh, her nose
What a prize
Realised
It is no Bridge of Sighs
. . . It's not you

This theme gradually became more sophisticated so that in the
later shows like *Mr Whittington* in 'Who Do You Think You Are'
the contest was pitched in more even terms and:

Loved you, lost you
Darn you, who do you think you are?

was posed as a mutual question.

But above all the success of their partnership was based on the marvellous rapport of their dancing. Binnie Hale describes it thus: 'Jack so tall and elegant was marvellously contrasted with Elsie – just the right height for him, so pert, lively and vivacious.' When they danced together, the most hard-boiled dramatic critics went into raptures. Of Jack and Elsie's partnership in *Stand Up and Sing* even *The Times* said:

> As we listen to the slow flip, flop, flap of two pairs of shoes caressing the stage in harmony, it seems that the dancers are diversifying the silence with an exquisite pattern.

The *Observer* summed up their success by commenting:

> There are in all their shows many pleasant tunes and these allow a great deal of tap dancing by Mr Buchanan and Miss Randolph. They dance very fast, they dance very slowly but always they dance hard and often. Miss Randolph taps a five minute number, Mr Buchanan tap-taps a slow rythmn for limbs and shoulders that lasts twice as long.

In their last big pre-war musical *This'll Make You Whistle*, Jack sang to Elsie:

> I'm in a dancing mood
> A gay romancing mood
> Whenever I'm with you.

Apart from the enjoyment of this dancing partnership, the general theme of the 'elusive Jack' was much to the taste of the Gallery Girls. Jack was for so many years 'Britain's most eligible bachelor' that the fans built up an almost excessively possessive view of his partnership with Elsie. It was this which led to the demonstration on the first night of *The Flying Trapeze* when Jack, for the first time in his life as a star, faced a hostile reaction when leaving the theatre from the Gallery Girls, who wanted to know 'Why have you got rid of Elsie?'

This was never the case (and in this particular show, Jack had been meeting the wishes of the show's backers in the choice of a leading lady). For Jack was the first to acknowledge his dependence in musical comedy on Elsie. She was and is extremely clever and a quick study. She was able to help Jack greatly when he began the early part of a tour ill-prepared because of his many other commitments. In these circumstances, Elsie, who would know his lines as well as her own, was able to help him gain the necessary breathing space until he worked up the part into its own inimitable J.B. performance. She also showed the patience which was often necessary in waiting for Jack to appear. His reputation for elegance was not lightly achieved and Elsie would sometimes say: 'Oh, The Master will take at least an hour to get ready.'

Elsie, in turn appreciated the way in which Jack was receptive to any of her suggestions for improvements to the show. She was also grateful to him for preserving her own distinctive role. For the finales, he laid down a general rule that none of the other girls could wear white. This was to ensure that Elsie's final appearance in white would be in striking contrast to Jack's top hat, white tie and tails. He also showed himself particularly solicitous whenever Elsie was away from the show. She has told how, when she was too ill to appear, he would ring up her hotel and arrange for half a bottle of champagne to be sent up with her dinner. He would also telephone every night during the interval of the show to say 'How are you, dear?' His generosity on first nights was legendary. For Elsie there would be enormous bottles of perfume and once even a mini piano. The trust in their relationship was so complete that they never had a contract in writing which, as Elsie has said, made it much more binding.

As to the romantic link, Elsie Randolph today comments simply: 'He was like a father to me. He confided in me and I could go and talk to him about anything. He had a certain puritan streak and, when I was very young and first joined him, he would stress the importance of taking care to dress well, to go out with the right boyfriends and to be seen in the best places.'

In this respect, Jack was urging upon Elsie the philosophy which he sought to encourage in all members of his company. He believed passionately that the public had a right to expect exemplary behaviour and dress from its stars. Elsie recalls that he would often say:

'If you want to wear your old woollies and slacks, go home. But you must always dress up both to go out on the town and when going to and from the theatre.'

Looking back on the shows she did with Jack over a twenty-year period, Elsie Randolph recalls that J.B. and his company were more like a family than a group of actors. They were sad when the shows came to an end, although, in most cases, they knew that there would soon be another big success to look forward to – except when Jack went off to America. It was a way of life which had, for the theatrical profession, an unusual degree of stability, coupled as it was with the extensive provincial tours which Jack regarded as essential in maintaining his following and financial support for his shows. On most days when touring, there would be golf in the morning, a snooze in the afternoon and everyone would meet up in a relaxed and friendly way in the evening so that, as Elsie Randolph describes it, they never went on stage cold.

It was this way of life that makes Elsie Randolph even today say that nothing – despite her current television, radio and film commitments – can replace the glamour, the elegance and the happiness of the days when she was working with Johnnie B.

Films in Britain – From
'Bulldog Drummond's Third Round'
to *'Goodnight Vienna'*

BETWEEN 1917 AND 1939, Jack made twenty-five films in Britain. His film career in that period developed in four phases.

First came the silent era from 1917 to 1928 when Jack was established as a leading film star. Then came his partnership with Herbert Wilcox in the early thirties which was part of the talkie revolution. In the mid-thirties, Jack mounted a major attack on the American film market and, in the last part of the decade, he achieved his great personal ambition of forming his own film company and acquiring the Riverside Studios at Hammersmith.

Jack made his first film appearances as an extra for the old Neptune Film Company in 1913 and 1914 when he was working in the chorus of the Empire Leicester Square. The company had a runner, Brian Daly, who was responsible for finding good looking extras for society scenes in the films which were shot in the daytime on the outskirts of London. Jack was paid at the rate of ten shillings with an extra ten shillings if he brought his own evening clothes. This frequently meant smuggling his top hat and tails away from the Leicester Square Theatre for unofficial use.

Jack's first efforts to build up his film parts met with a curious rebuff. Noticing that Neptune's director, John East, kept pictures of unknown actors and actresses round the walls of his office, he suggested on one of his calls to collect his daily pay that it might be appropriate to put up a picture of himself. 'Oh no, I don't think I'll do that' said Mr East. Jack enquired why he was not so favoured, adding 'I thought you liked my work'. To this, Mr East replied 'Oh yes, I like your work but the pictures I have on my walls are my rogues gallery of 'orrible types who have worked for me in the past and I keep them up there to remind me never to offer them work again.'

Jack's first starring role in films came during the First World War and it is interesting that in this and his first few films, his work, unlike his stage roles, almost invariably required him to play the villain or a heavy dramatic role. In *Auld Lang Syne* (1917) he played a peer married to a Hoxton shop girl who takes the blame when her brother steals a necklace. Theft was again the theme when Jack worked with Phyllis Monkman (in an obvious attempt to cash in on their successful stage partnership) in *Her Heritage* (1919). In this film he was an artist who helps to steal letters from a blackmailer. In *The Audacious Mr Squire* (1924) Jack was again involved in a plot about robbery in which he is mistaken for a thief.

From 1925 onwards, Jack began to establish a major reputation as a silent film star. He made four films that year, two of them with Fay Compton. In the first, *The Happy Ending*, he played what *Variety* described as a 'Cur of the first water' and said that Jack, 'departing from musical comedy, shows he can do fine work as the blaggardly husband'. But it was in *Bulldog Drummond's Third Round* that Jack had his first real film star success. In this film, he played the classic British detective hero. The part involved the usual far fetched nonsense in which Jack saves his fiancée (Betty Fayre) and her uncle (the inventor of a process in which real diamonds can be made from a few cheap raw materials) from the kidnapping attempts of the villian Carl Peterson and his exotic vamp partner, Irma, played by Juliette Compton.

The film was notable for an opening sequence in which Jack was seen sparring with Phil Scott (a genuine boxer) in a gymnasium. Once again he had been given training and advice from Georges Carpentier who said that Jack at 160 pounds could make, with a little more application, a useful middleweight.

In 1927 and 1928 he made his last two silent films. In the first, *Confetti*, Jack played a Count who was in love with an older woman. He is 'saved' by his Aunt – played by his old friend from *Battling Butler* days, Sydney Fairbrother. Much of the film was shot in the South of France where another old friend, the Gaiety Girl Ruby Miller, joined the party.

However, as the Theatre World said:

'This tale of the Carnival in Nice might as well be set in Wigan for all the use that is made of the Riviera scenery.' The report went on to list some of the unconscious humour of the film as, for example, when the old confetti maker was seen grinding away on his machine with the caption 'Purple for passion, grey for strife, confetti is tears on the street of life' or when the 'older woman', the glamorous Annette Benson, was, at the age of 30, supposed to be in the last stage of decay.

Duggie Furber, who had written the script, was also criticised for being 'the first person to make Jack Buchanan play a romantic role' and the report goes on: 'But who in hell's name wants him to? Here is a comedian of brilliant versatility, condemned to moon about in a nebulous tale without a vestige of redeeming humour.' This dilemma for Jack as to whether he should be used for heavy romantic roles instead of his usual comedy parts was to be repeated many times in his film career. It was probably why, at the première of *Confetti*, he told the audience: 'I suffer torture seeing myself on the screen'.

Expanding on this 'reluctant romantic' theme afterwards, Jack said: 'It has always been my desire to make out and out comic films, but it has been my fate when approached by British film companies to be persuaded to enact the sentimental hero, which candidly has never appealed to me. I have yielded and endeavoured to introduce as many smiles as possible. I have noticed, however, when the picture has been screened, that these have been carefully cut out. During the last year I have refused at least a dozen offers to make this kind of "romantic" picture. Invariably, I have asked to be supplied with a broad farcical subject and I have at last succeeded in persuading a film company to make a comic film.'

The company in question was British International Pictures and the picture – which proved to be Jack's last silent film – was *Toni* which was adapted from Douglas Furber's musical comedy play of the same name. There was little resemblance between the two although the screen play by Dion Titheradge tried to live up to Jack's comedy ambitions with limited success.

Thus, Jack, as the playboy who is reformed when he takes over a detective role from his double, is described in one of the early captions as 'Toni O'Farrell, son of an Italian Count and an Irish colleen, born on an Italian liner, weaned on Scotch whisky and has been in a muddle ever since'. The opening sequence – which involved a good deal of play with champagne, Alka Selzer and other signs of dissipation – and the subsequent change, when Jack begins his detective work, was captioned: 'So a liverless wreck becomes a reckless liver'.

Jack's first British talking film was for Paramount's multi-lingual version of *Man of Mayfair* which was produced for both British and French distribution in 1931. Supporting Jack, the film starred several of the West End's most distinguished actresses including Nora Swinburne, Ellaline Terriss, Lilian Braithwaite and the current glamour girl of the theatre, Joan Barrie, who was shortly to leave the stage to become the wife of the

International Banker, Henry Tiarks. This range of talent was wasted in an inane plot and the film was notable only for its two hit songs which Jack recorded 'Alone With My Dreams' and 'You Forgot Your Gloves'.

It was with *Goodnight Vienna* in 1932 that Jack began his long and successful partnership with Herbert Wilcox. Strangely, their first collaborative venture in the days of silent films had been completely unproductive, as Herbert Wilcox later recalled:

> In 1919, I was making my first pictures at Kew in a tiny studio built like a glasshouse in the days when we had to use as much natural light as possible. One day, Jack – even then a popular matinée idol – came along to this tiny edition of the Crystal Palace to make a film. At the end of the first day's shooting, I regretfully decided that he was not photogenic. We had a discussion and Jack agreed that it would be sensible for him to drop out of the cast.

In 1931, Herbert Wilcox had no reservations about making a film with Jack as his star. His worry was who should be the leading lady. Evelyn Laye was approached but was unavailable. So too were various continental stars. With this problem on his mind, Herbert Wilcox went to see Jack during the run of *Stand Up and Sing*. He recalls:

> Late one night, I wandered into the Hippodrome about half an hour before the final curtain. I hadn't seen the show, and someone asked me if I'd care to stand at the back and watch the last half hour. I saw Anna Neagle performing with Jack and, at the curtain, I went straight to his dressing room and said 'What are we worrying about? She's here – the girl in the show'. I didn't even give her a test – I knew.

The result lived up to Herbert Wilcox's expectations. Not only was he subsequently to marry Anna Neagle but, in *Goodnight Vienna*, she was launched on the start of a successful cinema career in what was perhaps the best of Jack's British musical films.

The film was not without its technical hitches. Because of Jack's and Anna's commitments on tour in *Stand Up and Sing* it had to be shot in four weeks – much of it at night. Anna Neagle recalls:

> When we made the big restaurant scene for the title song which ends the film, all the crowd players, extras and technicians had been at it for about twenty-two hours. By the time Jack and I got to the studios from the theatre and were ready to play the scene, it was around three in the morning.

Herbert Wilcox later completed the story:

All through rehearsals, everyone had been drinking toasts in the usual ginger ale. I decided that – at that hour in the morning – the real thing was called for. It very nearly ruined the scene which was supposed to be a quiet and tender one. You see, my dear Anna's tummy made such extraordinary rumbling noises and the microphone picked them all up – I thought we were never going to get the scene shot.

Set in Austria in 1913, Jack played a General's son who is engaged to the Emperor's niece, but who falls in love with a girl in a flower shop (played by Anna Neagle) who – true to form – becomes a great opera star while he is away in the War. After the usual misunderstandings, all ends happily but not before Jack and Anna had enjoyed some charming scenes together.

These were enhanced by George Ponsford's tuneful songs 'Just Heaven to Know that You are Mine' and 'Living in Clover'. Jack's treatment of the title song 'Goodnight Vienna' was typically individual. It was so successful that he had to record it after the film was finished while on tour with *Stand Up and Sing*.

Goodnight Vienna was a smash hit on release in March 1932, and this despite the fact that the critics were somewhat churlish about yet another Viennese operetta. Once again the *Theatre World* took up the theme of it being 'a criminal waste to have Jack in a romantically yearning role with comparatively few opportunities for his own special brand of fooling.' Nevertheless, the film ran for many weeks at the Capitol Cinema and did good business in America when it was re-titled *Magic Night*. In both countries, it effectively launched Jack Buchanan's partnership with Herbert Wilcox.

As a result of this partnership, Jack became progressively more involved in the distribution side of his films. Through Elsie Randolph he got to know Jack Prendegast, a Yorkshire distributor with wide-ranging cinema interests. Jack Prendegast was to play an important part in Jack's business and private life. Their friendship grew from an occasion, soon after *Goodnight Vienna* was released, when Jack rang up 'Prendy' and asked him how the film was being received in Huddersfield, only to receive the laconic reply 'Probably as well as "Good Night Huddersfield" would be received in Vienna'.

In their next venture *Yes, Mr Brown*, which was released in January 1933, Jack and Herbert Wilcox were joint directors of a film which was obviously produced with the American distribution in mind since it was based on the ill-fated Haymarket comedy *Business with America*.

Once again, the film was set in Vienna and one wonders where British scenario writers would have been without that city in the

Above, *Jack, Anna Neagle and Herbert Wilcox celebrate their decision to go into films together in 1931.* Below, Goodnight Vienna (*British and Dominion 1932*) *– from right Jack, Bill Kendall, Anna Neagle, Gibb McLaughlin and the Girls.*

thirties. Jack was the manager of a factory who had to get his secretary (Elsie Randolph) to represent his wife (Margot Grahame) when she walked out in a huff over Jack's dislike for her pet dog – all this on the occasion of the visit by the big boss from America.

The result, according to the *Theatre World*, was the best British film Jack Buchanan had made so far, if only because it gave the film-going public an insight into his work as a comedian and not as a romantic lover, a role to which the *Theatre World* still thought he was unsuited.

Jack's new glamour girl partner in *Yes, Mr Brown* was the South African born Margot Grahame, who was then at the height of her success as Britain's answer to Jean Harlow. She recalls Jack found, once again in his career, that there were hazards in performing with animals:

> In the picture, Jack, playing the part of my husband, loathes the little dog I dote on. This would normally have been hard for him as he adored animals. But this particular dog had one major drawback. It had the most appalling bad breath. So when you see Jack with the fork poised over the dog and a maniacal look in his eye, he was playing for real – he loathed that dog.

That's a Good Girl was the third British and Dominion film in a row which Jack made with Herbert Wilcox. This was more or less a straight version of his musical comedy which had been such a success at the London Hippodrome. It was filmed at the Eden Roc Hotel in the South of France. There he reassembled most of those who had played the original leads, including Vera Pearce, Elsie Randolph, Kate Cutler and Bill Kendall.

For the *ingénue* role, Jack had engaged his old friend Dorothy Dickson's daughter, Dorothy Hyson. She was in France at finishing school at the time. She had made one brief film appearance but Jack decided to bring her in although she was only seventeen. She recalls how Jack and Bill pulled her leg:

> One night they took me out to dinner in Nice. We dined very well and on our way back driving along the Grande Corniche, Jack and Bill were full of giggles. Eventually, Bill pointed to the local French radio mast which towered over the Riviera hills with its red navigation light blinking and said to Jack 'I say, old boy, that must be the highest brothel in the world'. I was so innocent at the time that I asked Jack what Bill meant and they both had near hysterics.

The resulting film is a faithful expression of what a 1920s musical comedy was really like. One reviewer said: 'The plot is a knock about farce compounded of ripe old jokes about legacies and match-making, private detectives and aunts who must be impressed.'

It went on to make the comparison which was increasingly drawn in the thirties between Jack Buchanan and Fred Astaire:

> Like Astaire, Jack Buchanan is the debonair man about town, but his svelte is acquired from British musical comedy, not, like Astaire's, from American Vaudeville and cabaret. The difference in tradition is apparent in their presentation of numbers in films where Fred's incredibly hard work and technical precision, contrasts with Jack's apparent 'throwaway' style, which disguises the many hours of work which have gone into its preparation.

It was with *Brewster's Millions* in 1935 that Jack began his major assault on the American film market. When he returned from Hollywood in 1930, he had told the press of plans for making British films which could compete with those from America. He was conscious of the great wealth of British acting talent which Hollywood lacked and he felt that superior American technical and financial resources could be matched.

Although *Goodnight Vienna* and *Yes, Mr Brown* had some success in America, Jack felt the need to import American skills if he was to compete on equal terms. For his next four films, he brought over American directors, stars and songwriters. This did not mean the end of his partnership with Herbert Wilcox who, as one reviewer said, 'Always got the best out of Jack's sensitive temperament as a performer by his persuasive approach'. But Herbert was branching out with many of his own films and was also building up Anna Neagle's career. He therefore worked as a producer in Jack's next two films, encouraging him to recruit the best outside directorial talent.

For *Brewster's Millions*, Jack brought Thornton Freeland over from America. 'T' Freeland was then at the height of his success following his direction of Fred Astaire in *Flying Down to Rio*. As his co-star, Jack signed on one of Hollywood's current glamour queens, Lili Damita. This exotic French actress had begun her career at the Casino de Paris (where she succeeded Mistinguett). David Niven has described her as 'A beautiful hour glass creature who epitomised the sexy French cover girls of *La Vie Parisienne.*' She was within a few months of marrying Errol Flynn who called her 'Tiger Lil'.

Brewster's Millions was the most expensive British film in which Jack had ever appeared and no effort was spared to give it the real Hollywood image. A mock Sicilian village was built at Pinewood for a carnival in which Thornton Freeland staged a dance called 'The Caranga' – an obvious attempt to recreate the Carioca sequence in *Flying Down to Rio*.

The film had a tuneful score from another section of Jack's American team, the songwriters, Sigler, Goodhart and Hoffman.

Their three big numbers in *Brewster's Millions* were the catchy theme song 'Never Forget that One Good Tune Deserves Another' in which Jack danced one of his more acrobatic Astaire type routines; 'The Caranga' which was supposed to be a Sicilian dance and which allowed Jack some good comedy moments as the rear end of a carnival dragon and 'I Think I Can' in which Jack, vowing to overcome his shyness, sang:

I've got to change my style
And then I'll learn to smile
And love a little while
I think I can . . .
I'll hear the voice of spring
And then I'll learn to sing
And make them call me Bing

At this point, he broke into his 'bu-bu-bu-boo' impersonation of Bing Crosby before ending on throaty chuckle 'I think I can'.

The result of all this extravaganza on the critics was that, as the *Theatre World* said: 'A heap of money has been spent on this production and although the spectacular scenes will no doubt ensure its success, we would have preferred less elaboration and more opportunity for Jack Buchanan's individual kind of comedy and burlesque. Nevertheless, he gives a fluent and easy performance in his best vein.'

The film did well in the United States on both its first showing and in a later reissue. Maud Miller said that 'the film has certainly secured some of the real Hollywood "sparkle" thanks to Jack's performance and the able direction of Thornton Freeland.' She went on to suggest that this pointed up the weakness of some of Jack's earlier efforts where he tried to do too much by both starring and directing. She added 'Jack, clever as he is, should allow himself to be directed as he was with Lubitsch in *Monte Carlo* and Herbert Wilcox in *Goodnight Vienna.*'

Perhaps Jack was acting on this advice for, in his next film, *Come Out of the Pantry*, the direction was entrusted to one of British and Dominion's staff directors, Jack Raymond, who had first worked with Jack as an assistant director in the silent film *Bulldog Drummond's Third Round*.

The attack on the American market was continued. After an opening sequence which – for sentimental reasons – allowed Jack to show his departure on the elegant as ever four funnel Cunard White Star *Aquitania*, the rest of the film was almost entirely set in New York where Jack, as an impoverished English peer, restores the family fortunes before he can honourably marry a rich American heiress. The heiress in question was played by Fay Wray who had achieved screen immortality only a year or two earlier, as the blonde girl who was King Kong's playmate.

This lustrous dark haired beauty (as she was in real life) was currently one of Hollywood's most popular actresses and this was the first film she was contracted to appear in with Jack as a result of arrangements made by the Hollywood agent, Myron Selznick.

The American influence was also evident in the music, as Jack had retained the team of Sigler, Goodhart and Hoffman. Their two numbers for Jack, 'Everything Stops for Tea' and 'From One Minute to Another', were big record hits.

Jack's next picture, *When Knights Were Bold*, released in February 1936, was based on the well known play of the same name by Charles Marlow. Jack as the heir to a title finds he has to overcome the opposition of an extremely stuffy family before winning the hand of his cousin (played by Fay Wray) largely as a result of dream sequences which allow flashbacks to Medieval days. This allowed Jack to perform a charming song called 'I'm Still Dreaming' – another Sigler/Goodhart/Hoffman effort. To the amazement of all those clad in armour during the Medieval sequence, he appeared in white tie and tails to give this song 'The Sand Dance' treatment.

After making several films with Hollywood stars, it was almost a family reunion when Jack made *This'll Make You Whistle* in 1936. Elsie Randolph, Dave Hutcheson and Bill Kendall were with him and for the *ingénue* role, he chose the 19 year-old Jean Gillie. The music was once again by Sigler, Goodhart and Hoffman, who had written four catchy numbers including the title tune. The photography as for many of Jack's films in the thirties was skillfully handled by F. A. Young, and Herbert Wilcox returned to take over full direction of this, his last film in partnership with Jack.

There was also a reunion with Anna Neagle for, while preparing *This'll Make You Whistle*, Herbert Wilcox was finishing off a film called *Limelight* on an adjoining set at Elstree. He needed a scene which would give some punch to the end of this film and hit on the idea of a party which would involve various visiting celebrities including Jack, the dancer Tilly Losch and the theatre historian W. Macqueen Pope. When Jack and Anna were introduced to each other in *Limelight* they recreated their original dialogue of the audition for *Stand Up and Sing* when Anna said 'I don't suppose you remember me – I was in the chorus of one of your shows in New York' and Jack replied 'Oh yes I do, you were third from the left in the front row'.

Although Jack was delighted with the commercial success of *This'll Make You Whistle*, he had, for some time, been keen to branch out on his own. This film had been the first of seven which Herbert Wilcox was making through his recently formed company. Although he and Jack had an excellent business and personal relationship, Jack was effectively under contract to him. This had meant, for example, that Jack had been unable to accept an offer to play for another director in the screen version of *The Scarlet Pimpernel*.

Early in 1937, it was announced that Jack Buchanan Productions Limited had been formed with capital of £100,000. Jack's fellow directors included two of the principal architects of the successful modern British film industry, J. Arthur Rank and Charles Woolf. Throughout the thirties, British film making had been through one financial crisis after another, culminating in the fire which totally destroyed the British and Dominion studios at Elstree where Jack had made most of his talkies. There was, therefore, a widespread welcome for Jack's expression of confidence in the industry – a confidence which was geared to development of the splendid new studios at Pinewood. On one of them, Jack's personal insignia was painted in green – the thistle of Scotland with the letters 'JB' on either side of it.

In announcing the formation of his company, Jack told the press that he was planning – even in the first year – to make at least four films in seven months. He went on: 'I have two reasons for wishing to have my own film production organisation. One is that I want to produce films with other people playing the leading parts. The other is that I want to appear myself in something other than the musical comedy type of film.'

A few weeks later, over a press lunch at the Savoy Hotel – with what one reporter described as 'an easy manner and clarity of statement that many a City chairman might envy' – Jack announced the details of his company's production schedule. The first four films would have a budget of £400,000 and eight to ten films would be made in the second year. The first film would be a comedy drama for Jack and Elsie Randolph. The second was to star Jack and his pals, Dave Hutcheson and Bill Kendall. The third would be a starring vehicle for Jean Gillie and in the fourth, John Gielgud was contracted to appear in a Technicolor film version of his current theatrical success *Richard of Bordeaux*.

In making these announcements, Jack was living up to his promise to exploit British talent. But the attack on the American market was to be maintained. For this, Jack had decided to go beyond the usual importing of American talent. This was well represented in the initial film schedule. Two of the films would have American directors. Tim Whelan, who Jack had first interested in working in Britain when they met in Hollywood, would direct one film. The other would be directed by Lee Garmes who had made his name as the cameraman with the gift for bringing out Marlene Dietrich's cinematic glamour. The last

Above, Yes, Mr Brown (*British and Dominion 1933*) – *Jack threatens Margot Graham's dog while Vera Pearce raises a protective hand.* Below, '*Jack Buchanan Productions Limited presents*' ... *J. B. and Maurice Chevalier in* Break the News.

two films in the 1937 list would be entrusted to France's leading director, René Clair, who had just made a great impression on both sides of the Atlantic with *The Ghost Goes West*.

For his leading ladies, Jack, after his first appearance with Elsie, would play opposite Maria Loseff, the Russian born Viennese opera singer. For his third film, Jack had planned a double coup. His leading lady was to be Lady Charles Cavendish – better known as Adele Astaire – who was coming out of the retirement which had followed her marriage in 1932. In the same film, Jack was to work with his old friend from the Casino de Paris days, Maurice Chevalier.

This ambitious programme meant an enormous load for Jack. His personal appearances in these films had to be completed by September when he was due to go to America to appear on Broadway. As he told the press: 'If I am successful in my show there and on the air, it will help to publicise the products of my film company and we may get more of the American film market. If our quality is comparable with Hollywood as regards treatment and tempo, I cannot see why we should not do very well over there. The head of Universal has assured me that if any of our pictures are suitable for the American market, he will definitely make us firm offers and I intend to take him at his word.'

Much of the press interest centered on Jack's proposed partnership with both Maurice Chevalier and Adele Astaire. There was widespread satisfaction at the prospect of teaming together Europe's two greatest musical comedy men. But the idea of bringing Adele Astaire to the screen prompted the question as to whether Jack intended to try and match Fred Astaire in working with his sister. Jack's response was typically modest as well as generous: 'Fred's the greatest dancer in the world today and I know what I can't do even if I'm not sure what I can do. If Adele and I do dance, it will be a burlesque. Her film tests were magnificent and her personality doesn't need dancing to put it over on the screen.'

As so often in the entertainment world, the clear cut intentions which Jack had announced to the press came somewhat short of fulfilment. Jack's first film *Smash and Grab* with Elsie Randolph was made according to plan. In this film, Jack and Elsie obviously attempted to follow *The Thin Man* theme of William Powell and Myrna Loy. They played John and Alice Forrest, a husband and wife team in which Jack, as an insurance inspector, has the classic private detective part. Set in Dublin where the Forests combine to unmask a crooked jeweller who is head of a smash and grab team, the film did so well that Ralph Spence who was responsible for the screenplay was commissioned to write a sequel.

The Sky's The Limit which was released in November 1937, had some unusual casting for which Jack himself was responsible since he wrote the screenplay with Duggie Furber. Jack played a serious figure, an aircraft designer working for a stuffy and insensitive boss, Bill Kendall. Dave Hutcheson in the traditional comedy part as Jack's composer flatmate was allowed to show off his singing and dancing talents – although Jack was still able to put across one or two musical numbers in trying to sell his friend's songs to Maria Loseff as the opera singer.

Jack's starring vehicle for Jean Gillie was *Sweet Devil*. This story of a playboy who falls for a typist, was based on a French play and, as the director, Jack replaced René Clair with René Guissart to give the film the right kind of Gallic flavour. For Jean Gillie's leading man, Jack chose Bobby Howes whose 'Little boy lost' routine on stage made him one of Jack's few British musical comedy rivals.

The ambitious plan to film *Richard of Bordeaux* never materialised. Although Jack had made only a verbal agreement with John Gielgud, he had been so much impressed with his stage performance in the part that the project was held in abeyance for many months in the hope that conditions might still allow the film to be made. By the middle of 1938 the threat of war made film financing uncertain and Sir John Gielgud recalls:

> We had dinner at the Savoy to discuss the project and another meeting later in Jack's office over the Leicester Square Theatre. I was too shy to ask if he had seen the play himself and I was delighted to learn later that this was the case because I had always been a great fan of his own work.
>
> Jack bought the rights of the play and, after our meetings, Miles Malleson made a skeleton film scenario. Eventually, after two years delay the whole project was shelved. I thought I should hear no more about it but to my great surprise, Jack paid me £2,000 not to make the film – the only time I have ever been given such a sum for nothing!

It was typical of Jack to regard an unwritten contract as binding despite the difficult financial climate. This situation now began to affect the future of Jack Buchanan Productions Limited and the plans for René Clair to make two films had been reduced to one. This was *Break the News*, in which Jack and Maurice Chevalier were due to appear together with Adele Astaire.

Jack was bitterly disappointed when, after two days of filming, Adele Astaire dropped out. He had had insufficient time between films to ensure that the comedy in her part predominated and, as she recalls today, 'I thought "Oh boy, if my brother Fred sees this – I'm gone!" I knew I'd be awful and thank God I got out'.

Fortunately, the Buchanan/Chevalier partnership worked

well. They played a couple of chorus boys who, in order to get star billing, plan a fake murder. Jack disappears and Maurice appears at the Old Bailey and almost on the gallows before his partner – who has been delayed in a middle European revolution – returns to prove his innocence.

Jack and Maurice worked well together in the film. They built up a nice line of cross talk which made fun of Maurice's English pronunciation and Jack's Scottish burr. In their big number together they were seen in top hat and tails singing and dancing a Cole Porter song 'It All Belongs To You'. It was, as one critic described it, 'A historic moment when the cognac baritone of France mingled with the British tenor to show just what is meant by star quality. Each in their way represents the finest in musical comedy technique in Europe and each has done more to show this to advantage before American audiences than any other performer from our two great countries. They are the best thing we have had since the Entente Cordiale.'

The high regard which the two great stars had for each other was reflected in the picture taken during their top hat and tails number upon which Maurice wrote: 'To Jack, hoping this is just the start of something' and then added hastily – 'Please don't take this the wrong way – you know what I mean! Maurice'.

Break the News, which was released in July 1938, was the last of the four films made under Jack's own Scottish Thistle emblem. With the threat of war, the programme for the rest of the year was held in abeyance and it was almost a year later when Jack completed work on the 'Thin Man' sequel to *Smash and Grab*.

This was released in June 1939 under the Associated British Picture Corporation banner in which Jack had merged his interests. The film *The Gang's All Here* was made when it seemed as though the threat of war might have receded and there were ambitious plans to release it in America under the title of *The Amazing Mr Forrest*.

Once again, Jack played the private detective part. Elsie Randolph was not available and his wife on this occasion was played by the up and coming Googie Withers. She recalls how Jack was not entirely amused by her consciousness of their age difference:

He was a wonderful man but on the business of age, he was a bit vain. Even so, he could laugh at himself about it. For example, he told me that in one scene in the film, just before going on, he was checking himself in the mirror. He looked tremendously handsome but he was checking up to see that his make-up was right. He had rather wonderful shading to bring up his cheek bones. Suddenly, he looked up and saw one of the old chippies standing behind him with his hammer in his belt going 'Tut, tut, tut'.

For what proved to be his last film before the outbreak of war, Jack made an Ian Hay classic *The Middle Watch*, in which a bevy of beautiful girls are accidentally taken to sea in a Royal Navy battleship. The complications of the plot follow naturally from Jack's problems, as Captain Maitland, R.N., in hiding the glamour girls from his Admiral. Chief among them were Jean Gillie, Kay Walsh and Greta Gynt. Jack also found parts for other members of 'The Gang' in Dave Hutcheson and Fred Emney.

In *Bulldog Sees it Through*, Jack worked with many of the same performers in a drama which was designed to reflect the outbreak of war when, as the blurb put it 'A test pilot and his secret agent Butler unmask his ex-fiancée's husband as an armaments saboteur'. Jack played the test pilot and Greta Gynt and Googie Withers provided the glamour. The eye rolling Robert Newton, played the butler. This marked the start of a life long friendship.

Jack showed an extraordinary patience and understanding which was often necessary in getting a performance from Bobby Newton, who was a colossal imbiber and led a Rabelaisian life. One evening, after they had completed their day's work on the film, Bobby invited 'The Master' back for drinks at the elegant house he had rented in Cheyne Row. There was no furniture and no light. Bobby invited his guest to sit on one of the mattresses which were his only creature comfort. He lit a candle in one of the many bottles which surrounded them, exclaiming 'There, it's a lovely light, isn't it?' A moment or two later, he started a fire by the simple device of tearing out a large section of the superb Regency bannister.

Jack appreciated Bobby's 'larger than life' qualities as well as his drawbacks. In return, he received exceptional loyalty. On one occasion, Bobby – after one of his escapades in Cornwall – rode on his motor bike all through the night to be in time for filming with Jack on the Monday morning. 'Couldn't let you down, Marster', he said, as he arrived in a cloud of dust and gracefully passed out at Jack's feet.

But these carefree days – when filming with Jack's own company was a party as well as profitable – were soon ended. His last two films for Associated British Picture Corporation were released after the outbreak of war. Inevitably, they were produced on a shoestring and it is interesting to speculate what might have come of Jack's ambitions to put Britain high in the world film-making league in the forties if the War had not made this impossible.

His ambitions to conquer the American market had not been achieved, but, in Britain, Jack's popularity was such that even his low budget films were well received. This was particularly true in the Provinces where Jack's films from 1932 to 1940 introduced him to a vast new public not all of whom were able to see his stage performances.

Jack's ambition to be seen on films at his very best in America was – as we shall see later – to depend on his Hollywood appearances. His greatest achievement in British films was to help in maintaining an industry which – in the years before the War – had often looked doomed. His confidence in forming his own company, in purchasing the Riverside Studios at Hammersmith just before the War and in his partnership with J. Arthur Rank and C. M. Woolf laid important foundations for the post-war growth of the British film industry.

The Gang's All Here

THE GANG'S ALL HERE was one of the many British films that Jack made in the thirties. The title is an apt summation of the many occasions on which he worked with his inner circle.

From the earliest days, his closest men friends had been Philip (Pa) Braham and Duggie Furber, with whom he had collaborated in his first big successes. Off stage, he would see Pa Braham and his wife in the country at weekends. Duggie Furber, although married, was more a 'man about town' friend and he and Jack would often meet after the show for supper at the Café de Paris.

Short, bald, bespectacled, Duggie was something of a bohemian and brought Jack into contact with his pals at The Savage Club. Here the great lyric writer held court in his poker school and, although Jack was never really a clubman, he was persuaded to join the Club. Duggie was also involved with Jack in some of the leg pulling on and off the stage which became a hallmark of his intimate friendships.

They would have a go at each other when they had a dull matinée audience in a long run. But as Wyn Clare recalls: 'Duggie Furber was a true friend to Jack and to all those in his companies. He was not only a brilliant writer, he was also a nice man who concerned himself with the welfare of all those around Jack. He was especially considerate to anyone in the company who might be in difficulty.'

Later, Fred Emney, whose generous girth matches his expansive nature, became another of the married pals who, like Duggie Furber, devoted much of his off-stage life to Jack. He also became perhaps the greatest and most fearless of the practical jokers in The Gang.

'The Gang' in the sense that most people thought of Jack and his bachelor cronies – consisted of himself, Bill Kendall and Dave Hutcheson. Together they formed a friendship which became one of theatrical 'Three Musketeers'.

Bill Kendall, short, dark with a dapper 'Ronald Colman' moustache, had started life as an oil company executive. He had drifted into the theatre in the footsteps of his brother, Henry, who was already an established star.

Dave Hutcheson became a close friend of Jack's in the thirties. A fellow Scotsman from the Isle of Bute, he was tall and fair, with piercing blue eyes and an infectious grin.

In their differing ways, the two other musketeers became an indispensable part of Jack's private life. So assured on stage, his 'little boy lost' air was a true reflection of his off-stage life. While Jack's mother was alive, she gave him a secure home base. Even on tour, he would usually return to spend the weekends with her in London. Bill Kendall with his *savoire faire* and ability to organise was usually called on to arrange whatever sporting or social entertainment might be required to supplement life with mother. He recalls:

> All through the twenties, Jack and his mother had a charming little house in Connaught Square, just off Hyde Park. Then in the thirties, they had a sumptuous flat which Jack built on top of the Leicester Square Theatre.
>
> I practically lived in both homes – and, indeed, I moved in with Jack after his mother died. But from the earliest times of our friendship, I would organise Jack's relaxation. He hated going to bed so, when we were playing in London, we would go to Ciro's or the Café de Paris. Jack insisted on having a table on the balcony at the back. He couldn't bear the limelight off stage.
>
> On Sunday mornings, we almost always played golf at Moor Park. I would go over to Jack's place where his mother would give us herrings cooked in oatmeal – delicious. We had them for brunch so that we could start our round at lunchtime when Jack wouldn't have to face a crowd on the first tee.

Bill Kendall never laid claim to great acting ability in the early days of his friendship with Jack although, over the years, he became a most effective performer. Dave Hutcheson, on the other hand, had much of Jack's 'fey' charm. Moreover, he could match many of Jack's professional skills as a brilliant dancer, he had a good singing voice and a generally *avant garde* creative approach to musical comedy work. Jack came increasingly to rely on Dave's judgment in theatre and film work and, meanwhile, relished his extrovert humorous qualities.

It was totally appropriate in *This'll Make You Whistle* when

Bill Kendall and Dave Hutcheson played the parts of Jack's best friends. In both the play and the film version, there were numerous sequences in which the friends embarrassed Jack by offering his future mother-in-law lockjaw chocolates and seated all visitors on cushions which let out suitable indelicate noises. As well as these jokes in the script, the musketeers frequently added bits of 'business' which were deliberately designed to make Jack fall about. Occasionally, if Jack felt that The Gang was getting above itself he would – as one of his stage directors George Cross recalls – restore order by saying in a conversation intended to be overheard: 'Just remind them who's boss, will you?' But although a strict disciplinarian and professional in every respect, Jack was willing to overlook and indeed to enjoy on-stage jokes with his closest friends once the success of his show and a long run was assured.

Bill and Dave learnt to judge when the moment was ripe to be disrespectful to J.B. At such times, they called him 'The Scottish Comedian' and tried to work on Jack's weakness for an on-stage giggle. In these activities, they were often supported by Elsie Randolph and Fred Emney.

Among the tricks they got up to was the passing round of the bawdiest postcards they could find. These would be used as part of the action of the play to see who would break up first. On one such occasion, Bill Kendall recalls how Jack had to retrieve the show from almost total chaos as all the principals collapsed with laughter: 'Eventually, Jack went right up to the footlights and said "Ladies and Gentlemen. It would be quite impossible to tell you the joke. I do apologise. It's unforgivable. If you'll bear with us, we'll try and find out where we'd got to and start again." Only Jack could have got away with it. What's more, we got a huge round of applause.'

Elsie Randolph was very much part of The Gang, even if – as sometimes happened – she was on the receiving end of some of their horseplay. This was literally the case on at least one tour. When *Mr Whittington* was playing in Glasgow, Fred Emney and Bill Kendall managed to get one of the racehorses used in the Derby scene into both Jack's and Elsie's dressing rooms. Fred Emney recalls: 'When we got the horse into Jack's dressing room, we put a sign up on the door which said "Horse and Mr Buchanan" giving the old man the worst of the billing. But when we got the horse to Elsie's dressing room, it ate a sofa and kicked down the partition. The management accused us of vandalism – extraordinary.'

Fred became something of an expert in planning off-stage jokes at Jack's expense. These were frequently designed to take advantage of some of his superstitions and personal vanities. For

Right, *J.B. with his oldest friend and professional collaborator Duggie Furber, while filming* That's a Good Girl *in the South of France, 1933. Below, Jack and 'The Gang' at sea. From left, Hollywood star Reggie Gardner, Golf pro Harry Fernie, J.B., Dave Hutcheson and Bill Kendall. Maiden voyage of* Queen Mary *in 1936.*

S. QUEEN MARY
DEN VOYAGE
BOUND)

example, Jack hated to be reminded of his age and ignored Christmas and birthday gifts. When he was living with his mother in a flat above the Leicester Square Theatre, a huge cupboard under the stairs was filled with presents which Jack refused to open. Fred, as his next Christmas present, sent Jack a huge Camembert cheese wrapped in many layers of brown paper. This joined the other presents under the staircase. After a few days, Jack was compelled to send for plumbers and sanitary engineers when he became convinced that his home was about to become condemned.

Jack's forbearance on these occasions was remarkable. In fact, he seemed to accept leg pulling as a normal occurrence and himself described the typical hazards of April Fool's Day:

> Some years ago, I was touring with my gang, all of whom are keen on playing practical jokes on one another. On 1 April, I came down to breakfast in my hotel to find a huge pile of catalogues and price lists awaiting me, containing details of everything from baby rattles to expensive cars. I thought this was relatively tame but I was soon to find that the real plot had not yet developed.
>
> Before I had finished breakfast, agent after agent began to call, thanking me for my letter, producing catalogues of goods I had never even thought of and asking for my esteemed favours. One man arrived to demonstrate a vacuum cleaner, another brought a special ice container and a third was armed with a peculiar looking hygienic dustbin.
>
> Finally, a gentleman arrived in clerical garb announcing how sorry he was to hear Jack Buchanan was so ill and asking if he might have a few minutes to chat with the sick man. It took me quite a long time to convince him that I was Jack Buchanan and he, like me, had been the victim of a practical joke.

On another occasion, Jack was being entertained by friends at The Spaniards Inn in Hampstead when he heard the familiar sound of Bill Kendall and Dave Hutcheson singing in the street outside. They were performing an appalling busker duet and passing round the hat to raise funds for what they described as 'The impoverished Scottish comedian inside'.

The situation was, in fact, entirely the reverse. Jack enjoyed the leg pulling of his pals and returned it with extraordinary generosity. He included Bill and Dave in many of his overseas trips and he did not forget his pals when he was away. Fred Emney recalls:

> After, *Mr Whittington*, Jack was taking Bill Kendall and Dave Hutcheson off to Nassau. He said to me 'I'd love to have taken you Fred but you've got your wife and the family!' I could have done with the trip – I was almost broke at the time. Anyway he

said 'Come up to the office tomorrow and say goodbye.'

So up I went. We had a drink and then he said 'Here's my address in case you need it.' On the way home I thought 'The mean old so-and-so, why couldn't he take me. I wonder where he's staying?' So I opened the envelope. Inside was a cheque for £400 and a note saying 'You may need this, Fred. See you soon, Jack'. You don't find them like that, do you?

If Jack was extraordinarily generous to his Gang, they, in turn, were expected to fit in with his mood. Sometimes he would become prey to a black depression. This usually coincided with the eve of his latest show. Working as he did, not only as a performer but also in producing, directing and writing, he would, if necessary, stay up all night to see that the lighting was right.

After one such session, an aspiring stage management recruit presented himself at Jack's office and asked his then manager, Gus Bingham, if he could see Jack, adding: 'It's because of some advice he gave me as a boy that I went into the theatre.' When Jack was told this, he replied lugubriously: 'What does he want to do – sue me?'

On another occasion, when Jack was suffering from jaundice – but determined to appear as he knew the success of the show depended on it – he was approached by Tony Smythe, the son of another of his managers, Frank Smythe. Jack had built up Tony Smythe from just another chorus boy into a juvenile lead and was upset when Tony asked if he could be released to appear in a better part elsewhere. He recalls: 'I shall never forget standing behind J.B. in his dressing room and looking at him in the mirror as I revealed what I now realise was a truly awful disloyalty. He sat there without saying a word for a long time and then said "Of course, if you must – go and good luck, but I wonder if you realize how tough it is at the top?" How right he was!'

Such incidents deeply depressed Jack. He gave – and demanded – total loyalty within his inner circle. Only his mother could guarantee to overcome those black moods but, over the years, Elsie, Bill, Dave and Fred learnt how to trade on his saving grace and dissolve these crises with laughter.

'The Boys' were also called on to perform the more delicate role of diverting the attentions of some of Jack's more ardent female admirers. This they achieved with a combination of personal dalliance and diversionary tactic. As Bill Kendall says: 'It may sound fun now but it wasn't always the easiest job in the world to keep Johnnie B. out of trouble. His absent-minded silences were often misinterpreted by the ladies who pursued him. So – if we were specially favoured in the Gang, we earned our corn as J.B.'s private bodyguard. But, looking back on it, we had a whale of a time.'

Hollywood – For 'Paris' and 'Monte Carlo'

IN 1929 AND 1930, Jack made three films in Hollywood. He was one of the first of the many stage stars who were part of the sound 'gold rush' in those early days of talkies. From the time when he had made one of the last of his silent films, *Confetti* in 1927, for First National in Britain, he had a standing invitation to make a Hollywood film for the same company who were in the process of merging with Warner Brothers. Early in 1929 he agreed to a picture deal with both companies. He invited Bill Kendall and Duggie Furber to accompany him on his visit to Hollywood where he was to make a screen version of the recent Broadway success *Paris* with the French star Irene Bordoni, while simultaneously taking part in Warner Brothers' all star spectacular revue *The Show of Shows*. It was intended that in this film revue, Jack would recreate 'The Glee Quartet'.

Paris introduced another chapter in the classic theme of show-business versus high society, the former represented by Irene Bordoni and Jack as revue artists and the latter by Louis Closser Hale and Jason Robards as the Sabbot mother and son (a thinly disguised representation of the famous Bostonian Cabot family). The plot required Jack to become engaged to the mother in order to break the son's engagement with Irene Bordoni.

Most of the musical numbers were written by Al Brown and Eddie Ward, whose best known composition was 'Brown Eyes, Why Are You Blue?' and whose work could hardly be said to match that of Cole Porter, who had written the original score for the Broadway show. The best known song in the film was a one-off contribution by Edgar Leslie and Horatio Nichols, 'Among My Souvenirs'. Otherwise Jack had to content himself

'*Two can play at that game in Hollywood*' – Above, *Irene Bordoni flirts on the telephone to make Jack jealous* (Paris – *First National 1929*). Below, *Jack does the same to Jeannette Macdonald* (Monte Carlo – *Paramount 1930*).

with such classics as 'I'm a Little Negative Looking For a Positive'. However, the director Clarence Badger made full use of Jack's famous routine with the chorus girls in 'Miss Wonderful'. This number is technically interesting because it had one of the first long technicolor sequences filmed in Hollywood. Jack recalled that this involved working through the night since the limited number of cameras available for Technicolor filming were then in use on several productions simultaneously.

In general, the film played up the romantic aspect of the Anglo-French partnership of Buchanan and Bordoni in which Jack's casual 'throwaway' style contrasted well with the Gallic exuberence of Irene Bordoni's 'You are a vairy, vairy naughtee boy'. In maintaining this Parisian sauciness, Clarence Badger arranged that in one scene there would be a fire at the theatre in which Jack and Irene are appearing. This allowed the entire line of chorus girls to exit hurriedly in various stages of undress, which was considered very daring at the time. It also led to a sequence in which Jack showed his willingness to sacrifice the romantic image of the immaculate top hat, white tie and tails by appearing as the dishevelled victim of a soaking from the fireman's efforts to put out the fire. It was typical of the humour in the film that Louise Closser Hale as Mrs Cora Sabbot in turn called Jack (as the hero Guy Pennell) Mr Pencil, Mr Panel, Mr Kennel and Mr Funnel and Irene Bordoni's best attempt at Massachusetts was 'Must-we-choose-it'.

Press reaction to *Paris* was generally favourable. Mildred Martin writing in the *Philadelphia Inquirer* said that Irene Bordoni was given an opportunity to display her delightful accent, her own particular eye rolling methods of delivering songs, but regretted that this made it all the more inexplicable that 'Let's Do It' and 'Babes In The Wood' had been excluded from the original Cole Porter score. She added that 'Jack Buchanan is pleasing as her partner in the revue.' Richard Watts summed up the film by suggesting that it suffered from the same loss that Hamlet would feel if it had no Danish prince by putting on a film version of the stage comedy without the Cole Porter score. He thought that Jack played the male lead 'so engagingly that he is sure to be in demand among the cinema magnates and with Louise Closser Hale quite steals the show away from Miss Bordoni.'

Jack was critical of the speed with which he had been rushed before the cameras in *Paris*, commenting: 'My personal feeling was that the whole thing was done too quickly and that it would have been better if more time was given to considering the production and building up the film.'

However, when it came to making the Glee Quartet sequence

'*Hollywood used him better than the British Studios*' – *Jack, the Girls and a typically lavish set* (Paris – *First National 1929*).

for the Warner Brothers' extravaganza *The Show of Shows*, Jack appreciated that time was money in Hollywood. As he said: 'When a company is paying artists at the rate of say £1,500 or £2,000 a week (I'm not thinking of myself here!) and a certain length of time has been scheduled for making one picture before getting on with the next, it is imperative that there should be no avoidable delay.'

Despite the pace of Jack's first film making experience in Hollywood, he had taken up with some of the friends made during the previous visit with Charlot. Now, before returning to England, Jack was able to make a new friend when he became a regular at the Montmartre Café. This nightclub on Hollywood Boulevard was near Grauman's Chinese Theatre and the film colony's big names would often come on to dance to the music of Roy Fox after film premières. Roy Fox, who used as his signature tune 'Whispering', recalls how he was introduced to Jack's current theme song:

> One evening, Jack came in with Duggie Furber. They sent the head waiter to me and said would I like to join them. I'd heard about Jack and his big success in *Paris* but I'd never met him. So I went over for a chat. They told me all about London and their plans in Hollywood. Then, Duggie Furber took out a song copy of 'Fancy Our Meeting' and asked if my band could play it. I said 'It's very difficult to play from one song copy'. Anyway, I had an arrangement made and, after that, every time Jack came into the Montmartre, we would play his signature tune 'Fancy our Meeting'.

Jack and Bill Kendall had a brief time to enjoy 'The Three Musketeers' rounds with his old friends Richard (Dickie) Barthelmess, Ronald Colman and John Gilbert. They were invited to join the 'All Men' club at Dickie Barthelmess' house. On one of Jack's last evenings in Beverly Hills, they returned at 5 a.m. to find the house full of other guests from London who, at various stages during the evening, the Three Musketeers had generously invited to share their home. John Gilbert who was nominally in charge of the party had been one of the first to succumb to the effects of good hospitality and Jack and the rest of the gang found him fast asleep with his evening clothes carefully placed on a suit of armour.

The party continued when Jack and Bill Kendall sailed home on the *Ile de France* only to find that John Gilbert was on board with his new wife Ina Claire. Bill Kendall recalls: 'John Gilbert had been going through a difficult time professionally when the great silent screen lover's voice was found unsuitable for talkies. He was therefore giving the bottle a bit of a bash and, coming from Prohibition, he really wasn't used to drinking the good stuff. As a result, Jack and I had to carry him to bed for three successive nights on his honeymoon trip.'

When Jack came back to Hollywood in 1930, life was somewhat less hectic, as he had been appearing on Broadway and was able to plan his return in a more organised manner. On this occasion, he had brought his mother out from England and they rented a house in Beverly Hills. They also brought with them their cook from New York, who together with the Japanese and Filipino servants they employed locally, provided Jack with a more settled home base.

Jack's enjoyment of Hollywood life was enhanced by his working partnership with one of the greatest of all Hollywood film directors, Ernst Lubitsch. In 1930 the German director was at the peak of his enormously successful Hollywood career and he intended to star Jack with Jeanette MacDonald in *Monte Carlo*.

Unlike his previous experience in making *Paris*, Jack found that Lubitsch took enormous trouble not only with repeated takes but also in rehearsals. He also had unusual skill in encouraging his artists, which appealed to Jack's sensitive nature. Thus, when trying to get a better take, Lubitsch would usually say 'That's marvellous. I enjoyed it so much that I want to see it again.' For his part, Lubitsch obviously found Jack's creative talent immensely appealing as he, too, had learnt his trade the hard way through the theatre. They also shared the same sense of humour and an enjoyment of practical jokes.

On one occasion, this succeeded almost too well, for as Jack recalled:

He and I happened to be standing on the set, and noticed that Jeanette MacDonald was in the sound booth. We thought it would be a good idea to stand under the mike and discuss her performance in fairly uncomplimentary terms, knowing that she could hear all this from where she was through the loud speaker in the sound booth. Unfortunately, we must have conducted our conversation in a very realistic manner, because in the next scene with Jeanette, there were obvious signs of tears. When we asked what was wrong, she wouldn't tell us. We had to own up to our gag but, by then, we'd come to the conclusion that our joke had mis-fired badly as she took a lot of convincing that we'd only been fooling.

The critics were enraptured by the film which has now taken its place among the classics of early Hollywood film musicals. Mordaunt Hall writing in the *New York Times* in August 1930 said that both Jack and Jeannette were able to give a far better account of themselves than they had hitherto in other film vehicles adding 'It is sophisticated entertainment in which the merriment is like the bubbles in Champagne which keep constantly rising to the surface.'

For Jack the enjoyment in making such a big success in *Monte Carlo* was heightened by his friendship with Lubitsch. He called him 'Mr Loob' and Lubitsch called Jack 'Mr Book'. Ernst Lubitsch's fractured English was a source of constant amusement to them both. He told Jack that this was not quite as bad as another of the middle European colony of film directors in Hollywood who caused considerable concern to one of his leading men when he kept insisting 'Take your balls in your hand and chuckle' until this was finally translated as 'Take your balls in your hand and juggle'.

Jack's general impressions of Hollywood are well documented. In articles written for the British Press in the early thirties, as well as in notes he made at the time, it is clear why he could not be persuaded to settle for the traditional seven year contract. In 1931, he said: 'Hollywood for a holiday – yes. As a place of permanent abode – definitely no! To act as a breather between stage engagements – yes. Film acting as a permanent career – emphatically no!'

Jack's principal objection to a film career was simply that it lacked an audience. It was this kind of immediate measure of success or failure which appealed to him as to perhaps all the greatest performers. He went on:

> To overcome the lack and indeed the handicap of no audience, the most thoughtful Hollywood producers employ at very high rates of pay, professional 'watchers'. Harold Lloyd, for example, has never fewer than twelve 'gagmen' on his pay role. Primarily, their job is to create 'sure fire' funny situations but no less important is their function as an audience and they are present from the beginning to the end of all his films. He allows them to sit there watching every move and if they are not enthusiastic, the scene is repeated until they agree that it is right.
>
> Charlie Chaplin, the greatest comic genius in the film world, uses half a dozen high-salaried gagmen for each of his pictures. He really does not need them but because he is a genius, he employs these gagmen in the same way as Harold Lloyd to act as his audience. Until they express their satisfaction, he frequently remakes scenes over and over again.

At a personal level, Jack was much taken with life in southern California in 1929–30, which he described as 'the place of lovely blue skies and magnificent green trees and scrub'. He spent much of his time in pleasant domestic gatherings at the homes of his friends Charles Chaplin, Pauline Frederick, Elsie Janis, Harold Lloyd, Mary Pickford and Douglas Fairbanks. Jack found a common bond with Chaplin who he described as 'rather a lonely man who does not care for mixing much, preferring to entertain at home'. He thought him 'an exceptionally good and amusing conversationalist who is extremely well read'.

Despite his many friendships with this aristocracy of Hollywood, Jack could not be unaware that, among them, were many personal tragedies caused by the 'talkie revolution' in which stage actors like himself had been urgently required to take the place of some silent stars whose vocal limitations had been cruelly exposed. Jack was impressed, however, by the optimism that kept many of the victims going. He recalled meeting one man who had been a popular silent film star but who was now unemployed – hanging round the casting director's office hoping that something might turn up. When Jack asked: 'And if not, I suppose you'll chuck it and try something else?' he received the reply: 'Chuck it? Not me, Sir, no. The film game is the finest in the world. The downs may be pretty bad but the ups are better.'

Jack was acutely aware of the hazards of a long-term film career which was one of the main reasons why he resisted offers of a seven-year contract. He later commented: 'Sooner or later the films do the chucking. Picture acting is not a life job. There are not many who can go on for years as Chaplin, Mary Pickford and Fairbanks have. The stars of today are the shadows of tomorrow.'

Nevertheless, Jack admired the determination of everyone in the Hollywood community to get in on the film scene. He and his mother became very friendly with Marie Dressler who he described as a 'good hearted, hearty woman'. She had begun a second acting career through films just at the point when she was about to retire from the stage.

Sometimes this universal commitment to a successful film career caused problems. One day Jack – seeking a break from the film world – hired a car to take his mother out of town, on a sightseeing expedition. This proved more difficult than he expected for, when they reached the open country and stopped for a picnic, the driver turned round and said 'Mr Buchanan, perhaps you would be interested in this'. He handed over some papers, adding 'I tell you that this is the finest little scenario I have ever written'. This approach was typical for after *Monte Carlo*, Jack was truly an international star. Having conquered Broadway as well as the West End stage, he was now recognised as one of the first of the new talkie film stars in Hollywood. In the February 1930 edition of *Photoplay* magazine Jack was picked out for the monthly feature 'These New Faces' which said: 'He has long been luminary of the London musical comedy stage and a great favourite of the silk hatted song and dance man's school. America saw him in the famous Charlot Revue with Gertrude

Lawrence and Bea Lillie. His spot in the English theatre compares with Clifton Webb in ours.'

In October 1930 the same magazine reviewed *Monte Carlo* thus: 'Lubitsch seems able to imbue actors with his own piquant sense of comedy. You will adore Jeannette Macdonald as the countess – she is beautiful, she is deliciously amusing and she sings gloriously. Jack Buchanan is equally delightful. What a man!'

Jack received countless offers for further work in Hollywood, among them an opportunity to make a film with Constance Bennett at a thousand pounds a week. But he was keen to return home for two reasons. First, he already had an idea and outline for a new stage musical comedy which he had been working on with Duggie Furber. Second, he had decided that, based on his own Hollywood experience, he was now ready to take on the challenge of both starring and directing in British films on terms which he hoped would compete with Hollywood.

As we have seen, his British films were only partially successful internationally, although enormously popular in domestic terms. Nevertheless, in 1930, his stature as both a film and stage star stood at its highest. Typically, Jack took his success lightly and sent a picture to Elsie Randolph of himself in *Monte Carlo* on which he emphasized that the greatest single advantage he had gained from his Hollywood stay was a flashing new look as a result of the star dental treatment he had received.

¶

Impresario

ONE DAY IN THE mid-thirties, Herbert Wilcox, Jack's film direc-
tor/partner was driving through Leicester Square with a friend.
They saw Jack coming out of his theatre office, immaculate as
ever, with a clove carnation in his buttonhole and wearing the
pearl grey trilby which had become his trade mark. Herbert
Wilcox turned to his friend and said: 'There is the most valuable
property in the entertainment world today'.

This assessment of Jack's abilities reflected his extraordinary
range of interests. The independent streak which led him into
management was not restricted to the shows in which he
appeared. When Jack was well over forty, Ivor Brown described
him as 'Still the best juvenile we've got'. But Jack was only too
well aware of the danger of relying totally on his musical comedy
following. He was therefore determined to diversify his range of
acting and to extend his management interests to that of a major
impresario. The success of his musical comedies made it
difficult to find opportunities for straight acting on the stage. As
we have seen, these were first directed to his film appearances.
Soon, however, Jack was fascinated by a new entertainment
medium – the radio.

His interest stemmed from the pioneer work at the very start of
the British Broadcasting Corporation. In 1925, the B.B.C.'s first
year of operation, Jack had broadcast a programme of songs and
sketches from the Charlot Revue on the eve of his departure with
Gertie and Bea for their Broadway opening. Later in the twenties,
he was a regular contributor to *Charlot's Hour* in which 'The
Guv' introduced the stars with songs from his shows.

In the thirties, Jack was among the first actor-managers to

allow parts of his musical-comedies to be broadcast 'live'. In 1932, the *Radio Times* records that 'the entire second act of Mr Buchanan's successful musical comedy *Stand Up and Sing* will be broadcast while it is actually taking place at the Theatre Royal, Birmingham'. At about this time, Jack also became interested in the potentialities of complete radio musical comedies. It was one such, *Goodnight Vienna*, which gave Jack and Herbert Wilcox the idea that led to their first successful British film together.

This process was reversed when Jack came back from making his first Hollywood films. The B.B.C. made a radio version of *Monte Carlo* – the Lubitsch film in which Jack had scored such a big success. Maggie Teyte, the opera singer, took over the Jeannette Macdonald part and the whole production was built up into a prestige affair which was heard in the United States as well as Britain. There were difficulties in reducing a feature film to a one hour radio programme and as one New York critic said: 'There were hitches before the B.B.C. got Paramount clearance and it must be considered whether the programme justified the sweat involved. It is chiefly important for bringing Jack Buchanan back to the air in America'.

Jack was always particularly conscious of his American connections. From 1921 until the outbreak of War, he visited the United States virtually every year – often more than once. When the *New York Times* asked for his list of 'Ten Great Performances' in 1938, he showed his fascination with the legitimate stage as well as his appreciation of performers on both sides of the Atlantic. His list was:

John Barrymore in *Hamlet*
Sir Gerald du Maurier in *Dear Brutus*
Gertrude Lawrence in *Susan and God*
Ray Bolger in *On Your Toes*
Matheson Lang in *Jew Suss*
Alfred Lunt in *Idiot's Delight*
Noël Coward in *The Vortex*
John Gielgud in *Richard of Bordeaux*
Sir Cedric Hardwicke in *Yellow Sands*
Jack Donahue in *Sons o' Guns*

Jack put his American experience and contacts to good use in bringing Broadway productions and artists to London. In 1928, he put on *Topsy and Eva* with the Duncan Sisters and, not long afterwards, John Van Druten's play *The Flowers of the Forest* in which he collaborated with his old friend, the actress turned manager, Auriol Lee. In the thirties, he was involved in a film project for *Sons o' Guns* in which he got Bobby Howes to play the part created on Broadway by Jack Donahue. Just before the War, with Gilbert Miller, he presented in London one of the most controversial American plays of the decade *The Women* in which an all female cast of forty painted an unflattering portrait of the gentle sex.

From his earliest days in management, Jack had shown a deep interest in the business side of the theatre. During the run of *Toni* in 1924, he and his partner, Tommy Dawe, decided that they were up against unfair competition in cabaret shows which paid no entertainment tax. They therefore invited patrons of the Shaftesbury Theatre to buy their admission through purchasing cigarettes or chocolates which carried no tax. The Inland Revenue stopped this move but it was the start of a continuing battle between J.B., the man of the theatre, and what he took to be the natural enemy of live entertainment – the tax man.

Jack's entry into theatre ownership was a logical development in his management activities. In December 1928, he acquired a building site on the south side of Leicester Square and it was announced that Jack, with his partner Walter Gibbons, was to build a new theatre at a cost of half a million pounds. Jack wrote out a cheque for ten thousand pounds for the land and another which substantially underwrote the deposit for building work of a quarter of a million pounds. It left him with shillings but Jack was thrilled with his venture in which he planned a new penthouse home for his mother and himself. The Buchanan Theatre – as it was to be called – would have no pit but would seat 2000 with armchair seating in the balcony. As Jack himself said: 'I want to have as many good medium-priced seats as possible for the people who want to see the show in comfort but cannot afford 14/6d stalls. My idea is for a large capacity house with plenty of good cheap seats. We shall concentrate on musical comedy in the early stages and branch out later. Although I shall not always be appearing in the theatre myself, I intend to be an actor manager in the fullest sense and I want the theatre to be my London home when I am appearing in town.'

Jack's ambitions were not fully realised. His company, Buchanan Estates Limited, overlooked some small but vital details. Among them was the refusal of a milk bar and one or two other small shops at the back of the site to sell their properties. Building went ahead on the assumption that a deal could be made at a later stage. When this failed to materialise, Jack and his fellow investors realised that there would be unsufficient room backstage for proper theatre work. They had to change their plans to convert the half completed theatre into a combined cinema and variety hall.

This was by no means a simple operation and added vastly to

the cost of the project. The problem was aggravated by the difficult financial climate during the world economic recession following the Wall Street crash. When the Leicester Square Theatre (as it was now named) opened in December 1930, Jack had lost a considerable fortune and sold his personal holdings to Warner Brothers. Ironically, they opened the new theatre with a show called *Viennese Nights* which foreshadowed Jack's great film success in *Goodnight Vienna*. Warner Brothers, in turn, sold out to R.K.O. who brought in variety turns such as Jack Hulbert and his *Song and Dance Interlude*, Gracie Fields, Harry Roy and his R.K.O. lions. After a long interlude with non-stop variety, the Leicester Square Theatre became a full-time cinema and Jack was persuaded, in 1933, to resume control as Chairman and Managing Director. This disaster tells us a good deal about Jack Buchanan's character as a businessman and as an employer. His general approach can be summed up simply as 'nothing but the best' and the personal fastidiousness which marked his private life was carried through into all his commercial activities.

Sometimes this 'expense is no object' approach could be difficult for his partners. Guy Bolton has recalled how, before he began work on *This'll Make You Whistle*, he was warned by J.B.'s impresario partner, Jack Waller, of Jack's tendency to let his enthusiasm run away with him in the search for perfection. A typical example of this was at 'Band Call'. In his big shows, this would be the moment – close to dress rehearsal and opening night – when the company would work for the first time with the full orchestra in place of the rehearsal pianist. On such occasions, Jack – carried away with the sheer pleasure of hearing his production's score with its range of tuneful melodies – would begin to improvise new routines for himself and the chorus to the consternation of his colleagues who realised that they were running out of time.

They were also aware that the cost of extensive rehearsals with the full orchestra was prohibitive and, once the musicians were on overtime, costs would soar. This situation would bring out all Jack's entrepreneurial instincts.

Always prepared to work until he dropped in every aspect of the show – performing, lighting, producing and directing – he looked for similar dedication from his company. This brought him squarely up against the increasing trade union organisation of some of his employees. Jack was essentially an enlightened Tory brought up on the virtues of self reliance but with an almost endless capacity for helping the underdog. Although he believed that artists should be apolitical, his own experience in coming up the hard way made it difficult for him to accept the increasing power plays of trade union activities – particularly in the musicians union.

These battles chiefly involved a handful of those who sought to negotiate with Jack on behalf of his other employees. Yet this very attitude ran counter to Jack's general thinking about 'his gang'. The problem was typified by an occasion just before the War when Jack agreed that his company would appear at a charity benefit performance. He asked if everyone would offer their services free but found that the musicians were unwilling to do so due to the activities of their self appointed shop steward.

This so incensed Jack that he offered the individual concerned a one way ticket to Russia. The sequel was revealing. After the benefit performance, each member of the orchestra voluntarily offered to contribute their earnings to the charity on the understanding that the shop steward should not be informed.

If Jack expected much from his employees, he was intensely loyal to those who worked with him. However, he was insufficiently critical of the advice he received and he combined this with a tendency to tackle far too much himself. As a result, there were some business disasters which could have been avoided, and Jack, himself, was often working when almost completely exhausted.

Nevertheless, Jack showed great skill in adapting to changing circumstances. It was typical that his losses on the Leicester Square Theatre were recouped when it became one of London's most go-ahead West End cinemas. He thus concerned himself with film distribution in the widest sense.

This brought him into close and continuing contact with the Yorkshire film magnate, Jack Prendegast. 'Prendy' often acted as Jack's sounding board, for Jack was, above all, an ideas man. He would frequently ring Prendy up in York and ask his advice. When this advocated caution, Jack would say 'I'll think it over, old boy' and Prendy today recalls: 'This usually meant he was going to go ahead. He had lots of good ideas but he left himself wide open to some of the more crackpot schemes. He had a stubborn streak, too, which, combined with his intense loyalty, made it difficult to deter him once he had made up his mind. He had many opportunities to bring in backers like the Scottish shipbuilder, Sir John Brown, who took a great interest in him. But J.B. always wanted to go it alone. He thought that if he had enough irons in the fire, his future was assured. But, sadly, this meant that he got his fingers burned more than he should.'

Nevertheless, Jack from his penthouse office and home on the top of the Leicester Square Theatre began his reign as a major impresario in the early thirties. It was to last for almost a decade – ending only with the War. During this period, Jack's business successes were dazzling for one who was, at the same time, playing virtually without a break in plays and films.

Apart from disappointments with his American shows in the thirties, and the minor hiccup at home with *The Flying Trapeze*, Jack put on three enormous smash hit musicals in the decade. As well as his own extended tours, before and after London, he sent out other companies. Ethel Stewart or Lalla Collins would get the Elsie Randolph part. Eric Forsythe, later to achieve fame as a B.B.C. producer, or his own understudy, Bobbie Gordon – who had adopted almost all Jack's mannerisms including a sniff while talking – would have the opportunity of taking over the J.B. role.

These companies all made money and so did Jack's films which found a ready domestic market. Now that he had his own showplace at the Leicester Square Theatre – to which would soon be added his own studios at Hammersmith – Jack worked closely with Herbert Wilcox to promote the wide range of films in which they had separate or joint interests. Their London showings in 1934 included *Nell Gwynne*, in which Herbert Wilcox gave Anna Neagle one of her first big starring roles, *Brewster's Millions* which was one of Jack's best British films and *The Last Gentleman* described as 'George Arliss's latest and finest portrayal'.

These films were shown under the terms of a distribution contract with United Artists. In September 1934, Jack writing in the Leicester Square Theatre programme described how this partnership marked the first anniversary of 'this theatre's introduction to you as a picture house'.

The anniversary feature *Nell Gwynne* had caused a sensation at its New York première because of the cuts it suffered at the hands of American film censors. Jack said that he was proud to present it in its original form adding, 'I am delighted to announce that we are to present in future several other United Artists features quite as notable.'

In this he was showing his usual commercial acumen, for the publicity over *Nell Gwynne* helped to build up the new cinema's following and it was typical that Jack should bring his film and theatre interests together 'in the Square' when, in 1936, the stage version of *This'll Make You Whistle* was playing at Daly's Theatre while, on the other side of the street, the film version was showing at the Leicester Square Theatre.

While Hollywood had enabled Jack to overcome his financial losses on the Leicester Square Theatre, in the Depression, some of his friends had been less fortunate. Even the great André Charlot had not been immune. When he – who had spent over two million pounds on his revues – was made bankrupt over some trifling debts and when, as he himself described it, 'all I had in the world was on my back', Jack sent him a cheque for six hundred pounds with a note from Gertie Lawrence, Bea Lillie and himself.

This concern for his friends was carried over into Jack's generosity towards those who worked for him. His list of pensioners was enormous. From the earliest days of J.B.'s management, he had protected those who fell on hard times. There was the chorus boy in *Stand Up and Sing* who was badly injured during rehearsals who, for eighteen months during the show's run, had only to appear as 'The Half' to draw full pay although he never went on. There was the fireman who fell from the flies in one of Jack's shows whose hospital and convalescence fees were paid and for whom light permanent employment was found. There were the many others who would come to the box office on Saturdays to collect the envelopes left for them. They included those who had helped Jack in his early days, out of work actors and some who were simply good at a hard luck story.

From his earliest successful days, Jack had been looked on as an impresario to whom others could turn for support in a good cause. At the annual theatrical garden party in Chelsea for the Actors Benevolent Fund he would come with the principals from his current West End hit to man the 'J.B. Cocktail Bar'. When the Glasgow Amateur Operatic Society – with whom he had gained his first experience before the First World War – put on their own version of *Stand Up and Sing* in the thirties, Jack found time to become their honorary president and appear on stage to take a bow with his amateur counterpart Jimmy Urquhart.

Jack's help was equally forthcoming when he was asked to play his part on great society occasions. It was entirely natural, therefore, when Lord Lonsdale approached Jack for help in putting on a cabaret for his golden wedding anniversary.

This party on 28 June 1928 was one of the most glittering social and theatrical occasions of the twenties. A specially constructed garden room was erected on Carlton House Terrace overlooking The Mall and King George V and Queen Mary were the principal guests. For Jack, the principal hazard of the occasion was not so much in working out his routine with Elsie and in fitting in with the other turns (Cicely Courtneidge, Carl Hyson's Ambassador Club Follies, Elizabeth Pollock and George Metaxa) so much as the planning sessions beforehand with Lord Lonsdale.

On these occasions, 'The Yellow Earl' insisted on giving Jack one of his twelve inch cigars. Although a steady cigarette smoker, Jack found the mammoth cigar more than he could manage and, once after turning green trying to please, he surreptitiously tried to dispose of his cigar only to hear Lord Lonsdale's voice booming out 'Quite right, my boy – never smoke them to the end. That's why I have them made specially long for me. Here, you must have another one!'

Smoking was just one of Jack's many activities which was normally used for skilful commercial exploitation. When first going into management with *Battling Butler*, he lent his name to a series of advertisement for Saronys cigarettes. These were couched in high sounding social terms so that Jack was forever encouraging 'The Hon. Bob to smoke the cigarette that soothes'.

In the late twenties, Jack allowed one of his famous publicity photographs to be used by 'Brylcreem'. Soon this was to be followed by other publicity with Jack seen using his Jack Barclay Rolls-Royce, his McMichael Radio and in his many fashion advertisements.

Jack was a walking advertisement for the best in British male fashion. His suits were made by Hawes and Curtis, his dressing gowns by Turnbull and Asser, his shoes by Lobb and his famous pearl grey trilby by Herbert Johnson. Jack did not seek a direct commercial return from these personal connections, although the fact that his 'nothing but the best' approach included dressing the men in his show – even the chorus – by Hawes and Curtis was, no doubt, with the benefit of an attractive rate which reflected his long standing patronage.

Jack showed a similar loyalty in the matter of women's fashions. In his shows he worked almost entirely with Eileen Idare. This was more than just the usual impresario/fashion consultant relationship. For Jack took a detailed interest in approving designs and choice of materials. He also showed himself a loyal employer. Eileen Idare became a great personal friend and she often remarked that J.B. was one of the few impresarios who stuck to his word and did not try to shuffle off responsibility if his leading ladies expressed dissatisfaction with their clothes. Sometimes this called for exceptional tact on Jack's part. On one occasion, he placated one of his leading ladies who said that her dress looked ghastly by saying 'On you it looks perfect – when you dance'.

This broad interest in fashion made Jack unusually sensitive to some of the commercial opportunities it afforded. Among his regular output of freelance journalism was a steady flow of advice for both men and women. In an article 'Clothes and the Man', Jack was seen in illustrations which showed off his wardrobe from plus-fours to morning dress and from city suits to the famous top hat and tails. Similarly, in an article on 'The Modern Woman' which was printed in many provincial papers in the late twenties, Jack summed up his advice to women as follows:

It seems to me that a woman's clothes are indicative of her mood. I do not mean by this that you can tell whether she is in a bad temper or not by the colour of the hat she is wearing – but she will inevitably wear a certain colour on certain occasions because this colour means something particular to her. My main criticism against feminine fashions of today is that they are too much alike. Woman has too little individuality in her dress today.

Jack's main commercial interest in the fashion industry was channelled through the advertisements to which he lent his name. He had learnt from his experience in America where his innovations such as the backless evening dress waistcoat had been linked to his name and widely copied without recompense. (Although he had been startled on one occasion to find a New York men's shop displaying a waistcoat and a sign saying 'Jack Buchanan wears nothing else') Jack took pride in his reputation as 'London's best dressed man' and was now willing to take a hard nosed commercial view. This meant that he was frequently seen in advertisements for scarves, gloves and other accessories which he would not normally have included in his own personal wardrobe. The film historian John Montgomery, who worked with Jack in film publicity in the thirties, recalls an example of Jack's irreverent attitude to these useful money spinners:

> In 1935, it was announced that the 'Jack Buchanan tie' was to go on sale. It was a creaseless tie in a wide range of colours bearing a facsimile of J.B.'s signature repeated many times over. It was priced at two shillings and elevenpence. I bought one, and one day in 1936, I bumped into Jack in Piccadilly. 'Good heavens', he said, 'Are they still turning those things out? Ghastly aren't they?'

Although Jack was able to joke about his range of commercial activities, he did not spare himself in promoting his business and charitable interests. One of his first talking films was entitled *The Silent Enemy* in which, filmed in his penthouse office at the Leicester Square Theatre, Jack was seen appealing for funds on behalf of the London Hospital for Nervous Diseases. As one who suffered from acute nerves himself, it was appropriate that Jack should help a cause in which he clearly had a direct feel for those with similar but more serious afflictions.

A glance at Jack's diaries for 1936 and 1937 – kept with immaculate precision by his White Russian Secretary Rufino Ampinoff – shows how the pattern of charitable, social and business engagements was intermingled and unrelenting. Within one month in 1937, he was with Elsie Randolph, Bill Kendall and Dave Hutcheson for Sophie Tucker's opening of the cabaret season at Grosvenor House; attending the annual dinner of the Stage Golfing Society at the Savoy; serving on the Ball committee of the Variety Artists Benevolent Fund and opening two cinemas in one night. This last activity became an increasing feature of Jack's work as a cinema magnate. In March 1937, for example, he opened a new cinema in Barnsley by telephone while simultaneously appearing and being mobbed by a crowd of 2,000 at the opening of the new Ritz Cinema in Chatham.

As a result of this range of work, Jack built up a knowledge and experience which virtually no other actor/manager of his day could match. He was deeply committed to every facet of the film and theatre world and since he was interested in putting his ideas across in articles and interviews, we can gain a fascinating view of J.B. as an impresario at critical stages in the development of the entertainment world.

Thus, in 1928, when asked about the future of musical-comedy, Jack replied 'There is no reason to fear its decline' adding:

> I do think, however, that the tendency is for shorter runs. Why? Because since the days of long runs, everything that affects the theatre has changed. The mode of living has changed to a very great extent. People travel more nowadays.
>
> There is a restlessness among the general public which has sprung up since the War which did not exist so much a few years ago. I'm not sure that an extended run is the one thing to look forward to in our business. There is always a slight risk in trying to extend a run when business gets near to the danger line. Owing to the clause in theatre contracts whereby one has to give so many weeks notice to quit, one may lose a great deal of money in those last few weeks.
>
> Another point in favour of determining a run while business is still possible is that it gives management time to prepare future plans instead of rushing things for the next production.

Jack went on to argue that musical-comedy was now much more in tune with public moods than had been the case in his early days.

> The romantic element, while it may interest, is usually subservient to the comedy and speed generally of a production. The chorus people of today must be able to do a great deal more than was required of them a few years ago. The old fashioned theory was that a good 'leg show' should fill the stalls with stockbrokers – why stockbrokers should be thought to be so susceptible is not for me to say – and it was no doubt true. But women want to see beautiful and talented girls on the stage just as much as men do.

112

In the same year, Jack was asked for his views about the future of talkies. Only a handful of such pictures had appeared and the battle with silent films was by no means decided. Yet Jack showed his foresight in saying:

If the public want talking films, they will come and it will be a straight fight between the cinema and the theatre. Who can blame the public if they prefer the talking film? Many of the provincial theatres are badly ventilated and uncomfortable whereas the cinemas are the reverse. If talking films do prove a hit, theatrical management will have to look to their laurels with regard to comfort.

It was no doubt this concern for the audience's welfare that prompted Jack's lavish approach to building the Leicester Square Theatre. But in this, as in so many of his activities, he was consistently ahead of his time. Jack Prendegast is undoubtedly right in his conclusion that, in some ways, J.B. was 'a babe in business who often trusted the wrong people'. There is no doubt, too, that he tried to do too much and it would be surprising if so great an artist could also have been an outstanding businessman.

Yet, in the great days of revue and musical comedy before the Second World War, only Noël Coward and Ivor Novello have shown a similar capacity to build up and sustain a successful British theatrical team. While both had composing and writing skills to which Jack did not aspire, neither of them could match his versatility as a performer, nor his success in films in Britain and in Hollywood.

In that sense, his record as an impresario is unlikely to be matched. If he lost money by trying to do too much, he provided more employment and entertainment than any of his rivals. Two current performers recall their impressions of Jack as the complete man of the theatre. For David Niven, 'My first impression of Jack was, as a schoolboy, going backstage and being enchanted with his interest in children despite his many commitments. Then, later, I realised that he was not only a great performer, but a brilliant publicist. In the years before the War, the back page of the London telephone directory carried just two words "Jack Buchanan".'

As Wilfrid Hyde White sees it 'If all the impresarios and managements had been like Jack Buchanan, there would be no need for Equity and no need for musicians unions – for he was a model employer. If only we had some like him today.'

g

Journeys at Home and Abroad

IN THE TWENTIES AND thirties Jack, except when involved in long running shows in the West End, was a compulsive traveller. His journeys fell into three regular categories. First there was the touring necessary during his long running shows. Then there were the holidays in Scotland, in the South of France and in Nassau. Finally, there were the regular trips to America which combined business with pleasure in travelling across the Atlantic in great ocean liners. In many of these travels Jack would often be accompanied by members of The Gang but the most regular of Jack's travelling companions were his mother, his valet Bill Green and his chauffeurs, first Richardson and then MacDonald.

While on tour Jack was especially dependent on Bill Green who had been with him almost from his earliest successful days. A short dapper Londoner, he was the perfect 'Gentleman's Gentleman', totally unobtrusive, discreet and a perfectionist in his work. It was he who, in such large measure, was responsible for ensuring that Jack's reputation for sartorial elegance was maintained. When they travelled from town to town, Green would go on ahead to check on his master's comforts and cater for Jack's intensely supersitious nature.

Thus, it was part of his job to ensure that everything on Jack's dressing table was in precisely the same position no matter where they were playing. He also had to ensure that Jack's lucky golden dressing gown was available to wear on each first night in whatever town he was appearing. On one occasion, this involved Green travelling from Glasgow to London to retrieve the missing dressing gown. It was also part of Green's responsibility to

114

make sure that Jack had his pearl grey trilby to wear during rehearsals or even when he went to the office since he never took it off when he was working. This again, was a superstition which went back to the days when he had been impressed by the great actor/managers who always wore a hat in the office, but which was also part of the 'shy man' side of his nature.

Once these essential details were resolved Jack was free to enjoy his touring and, in particular, to indulge in his twin passions for motoring and golf. His driving had a certain absent-minded quality but he enjoyed fast cars. During the twenties, he ran an 8 litre Bentley sports car of which only six were produced (the racing driver, Babe Barnato, and the theatrical agent, Jack Dunfee, owned two of the other models). In the thirties, however, Jack settled for the comfort of a long line of Rolls-Royce cars.

In whatever town he was playing, Jack would play golf virtually every day. His regular partners were members of The Gang and the local professional. For example, if they were playing Liverpool, as soon as the Company arrived, Jack would say 'Adelphi, nine o'clock tomorrow morning' to a few of his chums. The following morning whoever Jack had invited, Bill Kendall, Richard Murdoch, Dave Hutcheson or another member of the Company would be whisked off to Formby to play a round with the professional Harry Busson.

Jack was an erratic golfer. The litheness which made him such a great dancer was a drawback on the golf course where he frequently swung himself off his feet. But he loved the game and was a generous host. Those invited to play a round with him found that the green fees, lunch, caddies and drinks were all on J.B.

While touring Jack's vitality was much in evidence. In 'working up' his shows, it was often necessary to spend much of the weekend in travelling and rehearsing. Yet Jack never seemed to catch a cold and, when other members of the Company were exhausted in moving from town to town, he would take one of his ten minute cat naps and wake up as though he had had a good night's sleep.

The only time he would totally unwind was at the weekends. While his mother was still alive, he would come back to spend the weekend with her from almost anywhere in England. Then, if he wasn't golfing, he would spend all day in bed on Sunday, just getting up for his meals.

When Jack was on tour in Scotland in the twenties, he took particular pleasure in inviting his mother to stay with him in the best hotels in Glasgow and Edinburgh. Once he took her on a pilgrimage to his old school, Glasgow Academy, where one of his former schoolmasters remarked 'Aarrh, Buchanan, still playing

Above, *Jack's dressing table (note picture of Arran and lucky animal mascots).* Below, *Jack plays golf on his beloved Arran.*

the fool, I see, but there is obviously a good deal more sense to it now than when you were here'. On another occasion, Jack took his mother to meet Sir James Buchanan, who had now become Lord Woolavington. Recalling his unsuccessful attempts at raising finance from his father's cousin, he told her 'Put on your most expensive mink and pearls'.

It was to Scotland too that Jack first turned when he thought of holidays. Although he was regarded as the epitome of 'West End', Jack never forgot his Scottish origins or his love of his home country. Whenever he crossed the border, he would stop the car and get out to celebrate the moment of his return. Often this would be on one of his trips to stay in the family house on the Isle of Arran.

The visits to Brodick were, for many years, an annual event. They became increasingly difficult for Jack, however, as some of the island's visitors started a 'spotting J.B.' game which meant that he had little privacy. Even the locals were not immune and an Arran doctor's two daughters made Jack's holidays into a 'cops and robbers' game by chasing him in their car whenever he appeared.

Partly as a result of this problem and, following the death of his mother, Jack's visits to Brodick became infrequent. He purchased a houseboat which he christened *Iolanthe* and kept on the Norfolk Broads. Apart from these holidays at home, he began to spend more time in the South of France. It was through one of these Riviera visits that Jack made one of his closest friendships. Bill Kendall takes up the story:

> Jack, Duggie Furber and I were having supper one evening in the Palm Beach Casino and Mark Ostrer, the film executive, came over and said there was a charming couple there on their honeymoon and would we like to join them for coffee. They were Peter and Obie Milton. (Lord) Peter Milton was Earl Fitzwilliam's heir and Obie – that was her nickname – was a Plunket. They had just had the 'society wedding of the year' in Dublin since this was a great Anglo-Irish alliance. More to the point, they were a handsome, gay, charming pair and we all got on famously. Little did we realise then that we would all become great travelling companions.

The travelling to which Bill Kendall refers was the Atlantic crossings which, in the thirties, Jack's increasing commitments in Britain, the United States and Nassau required. As an impresario as well as a performer, he was in New York almost every year to discuss the promotion of his films and to catch up on the latest shows on Broadway.

This pattern of combining business with pleasure was a constant feature of the Buchanan travels. To those who criticised The

Gang's leisure activities as frivolous, Jack would point out the need for artists to unwind. He was not unaware of the problems of the world at large; of the depression at home and the menace of Fascism abroad. But he took the view that the best contribution he could make was to entertain as many members of the public as possible and to employ as many of his fellow artists as he could. In doing so, he lived from one crisis to another in the theatre and film world.

Jack's discovery of Nassau was a typical response to this. He had first visited the island after a series of business and professional setbacks. By the mid 1930s, he had purchased land there with the intention of building himself a house. This plan was frustrated by the War but Jack made many visits to the Bahamas where he became friendly with the Governor and his wife, Sir Bede and Lady Alice Clifford.

On one of his first visits (in 1934), Jack was invited to stay at the Governor's beach house. The invitation was virtually a Royal command because the other house guests were the Duke and Duchess of Kent who were on their honeymoon. Jack had known the Duke from his earliest theatre-going days and now became friendly with the Duchess, Princess Marina. They all enjoyed the privacy offered by the Governor's residence although the holiday was somewhat blighted when both the Duke and Jack were badly stung by jelly fish.

It was typical of Jack that on a later visit in 1936 when he had to leave Fred Emney behind, he took not only his musketeers, Bill Kendall and Dave Hutcheson, but also his golf professional, Harry Fernie. They flew down to the islands from New York on one of the earliest Eastern Airlines flights before returning home on the maiden voyage of the Queen Mary where they joined up with Reggie Gardner who had just established himself as Hollywood's newest British discovery.

These crossings on the Cunard White Star ships became a regular feature of Jack's bachelor life. While Jack's two other great British actor/manager contemporaries, Noël Coward and Ivor Novello liked to entertain their circle at their country houses at home or in Jamaica, Jack enjoyed acting as host on the great ocean liners.

His love of the sea was deep rooted in his Scottish upbringing and, through his constant Atlantic crossings with Cunard, he made many friends among the ship's captains, pursers and stewards. His routine on these trips was well established. Lunch for Jack was always the same the first day out. Underdone cold roast beef cut thick, jacket potato, salad and cheese and a bottle of Krug. However, on one crossing on the *Olympic* in April 1935, Jack presented Bill Kendall with a menu inscribed 'To dear old

Bill from his old pal Jack' which as Bill Kendall recalls 'marked the occasion when we persuaded J.B. to leave aside his usual cold beef. Mind you he avoided the twenty-six different hors d'oeuvres, the fourteen meat courses and took the chef's suggestion for the set menu of clams, cockie leekie soup, haddock, chicken and pancakes.'

For Jack, life on board ship meant adventure and excitement and the promise of new things to conquer. It meant five days without 'Five minutes, Mr Buchanan' or telephones, or accountants or over ambitious hostesses.

It also meant a chance to see friends as well as The Gang. On one of Jack's last pre-war crossings, he found it was impossible to book at short notice with the Cunard Line. He, Bill Kendall and Dave Hutcheson had literally bumped into Peter and Obie Milton in Dirty Dick's Bar in Nassau. They all agreed to take the first available sailing on a German Ship, the *Europa*.

Jack found the change from Cunard uncongenial. Although his creature comforts were well attended to, he detected an obvious arrogance in the ship's officers and crew. This was highlighted on the last day on board when many of them appeared in brown shirts and marched up and down the decks celebrating Hitler's birthday.

Jack and The Gang fell in at the end of the column pretending that they assumed this to be some kind of ship's fancy dress parade. He would later joke that 'this gesture and our final pre-war fling may not have ended the War any sooner, but we may have played a small part in lulling the Germans into a false sense of security.'

King of Broadway – In 'Wake Up and Dream' and 'Between the Devil'

ONE OF THE NEW York dramatic critics christened Jack 'King of Broadway' when he first appeared there in the Charlot Revues. His success in subsequent appearances on The Great White Way was mixed.

Jack's work in Hollywood, in British films and in the vastly successful West End musical comedies of the thirties, made his appearances on Broadway infrequent. In 1929, he was able to combine his Hollywood film work with an offer from Charles B. Cochran to appear in the New York edition of his enormously successful London revue *Wake Up and Dream.*

The show was not without its problems, particularly as regards Jack's relationship with his new leading lady, Jessie Matthews. Their big romantic duet in the show was the number which Jack and Elsie Randolph had used the year before, 'Fancy Our Meeting'. Jack and Jessie performed the number not only on the stage but also in after-the-show cabaret performances. As Jessie Matthews has made clear, she and Jack did not exactly hit it off. She has been fair-minded enough to imply that the clash was almost inevitable since she had appeared in the London edition of *Wake Up and Dream* with Sonnie Hale. As she was involved with him in the divorce action brought by his then wife, Evelyn Laye, Cochran decided to bring Jack into the New York edition. In this he was strongly supported by Archie Selwyn who felt that Jack was much better known to American audiences.

Nevertheless, Jessie Matthews was riled over Sonnie's absence and Jack resented some of the criticisms implied by her invidious comparisons, remembering that only three years earlier, she had been in the chorus of the Charlot Revues of which he was the principal star.

With this background, the performance of their romantic duet 'Fancy Our Meeting' was not without its irony. Indeed, Jessie Matthews has implied that it was regularly performed with love on their lips and well nigh hatred in their hearts. Still a remarkable trouper, she said after her one woman show in London in 1976 that her recollection now was of 'The privilege of playing with such a great artist.'

Wake Up and Dream opened at the Selwyn Theatre on 30 December 1929. It was essentially the same production as that which Cochran had put on in London where it was regarded as one of his more spectacular revues. In an American sense, however, this meant that it was inclined to fall between two stools. It did not have the intimacy of the Charlot Revues which had so impressed American audiences and, by Broadway standards, it was not as punchy and spectacular as its American counterparts.

The mixed feeling of the reviewers is well summed up by Robert Garland, who said: 'Mr Cochran's imported London revue is clever as to backgrounds, stunning as to dancing and not so hot where sketches and songs are concerned. In the presence of an orchidaceous audience which paid $22 a seat to be there, Mr Buchanan seemed to be ill at ease and more than a wee bit bit roguish. Kittenish you might be so bold to say. But as lady lobbytalkers insist, he is charming as only an Englishman can be.'

Brooks Atkinson thought that the Buchanan charm was as potent as ever and described him as 'the most gentlemanly comedian on the revue stage. Always clowning in terms of the intellect, he makes his point by slight inflections of the face and fleeting sardonic grimaces.' He singled out Jack's work in a take-off of Sir Thomas Beecham and in the sketch 'Adapted from the French' which succeeded in pointing out how the most pedestrian English domestic drama became full of double meaning when presented in French. In this sketch, Jack as the son of the house, is anxious to marry the family maid Henrietta only to be told by his father that this is impossible since she is his illegitimate daughter. Mother caps this and ensures the happy ending by announcing that he need not worry since 'You are not your father's son'. Jack's big solo number in the show was a typical number called 'She's Such a Comfort to Me' for which Arthur Schwartz wrote the music and in which the Furber and Parsons' lyrics included such immortal lines as:

I love the doughnuts that she bakes,
I love the dough her father makes
His darling daughter
He's bound to support her
She's such a comfort to me

Of this number, Richard Watts, Jr, writing in the *New York Herald Tribune*, said: 'The comedy is best when Mr Buchanan is singing "She's Such a Comfort to Me" or when chatting quietly with his public as bland master of ceremonies. In fact, Mr Buchanan is of considerable help to his show. His material is not always of the best, but he is always easy, assured and likeable, handling himself and his opportunities expertly and attractively.'

Jack's next stage show in the United States *Pardon my English* looked extremely promising. For the first time, Jack was given the opportunity to appear in an all Gershwin show since George and Ira were responsible for both words and music. He sailed on the *Aquitania* on 26 October 1932, timing his arrival so that he could be present at the New York première of *Goodnight Vienna*, which had been renamed *Magic Night* for its opening at the Rivoli Cinema.

A month was allowed for rehearsals before the scheduled opening of *Pardon my English* at the Garrick Theatre, Philadelphia on 2 December. But as rehearsals proceeded, Jack became uneasy about his part. The general uncertainty of all those concerned with the production was reflected in the fact that the opening was postponed until 26 December. Meanwhile, although the show had many good things by the Gershwins (then at the height of their success following 'Of Thee I Sing') including 'My Cousin in Milwaukee' and 'I've Got to Be There', Jack felt increasingly unhappy. His part called on him to play in a banal plot in which he was an Englishman suffering from amnesia, who becomes part of the underworld in Dresden for no apparent reason – where they specialise in the production and sale of banned soft drinks.

Jack's decision to terminate his contract was an expensive proceeding. Ira Gershwin estimated that it cost him $20,000. This was a bold step as Jack himself had good notices after the Philadelphia opening. One critic said: 'Mr Buchanan is debonair and pleasing, a master of airy humour, a natural born dancer, an easy and charming singer in a part that is hardly worthy of him.'

When the show reached Boston, the *New York Times* said of Jack: 'Conscious that he is mis-cast and inspite of much effort to build up his part, Mr Buchanan's position is uncomfortable. Only his sense of theatre obligation keeps him to it.'

This was a well judged observation, for Jack's later assessment of *Pardon my English* shows that his sense of duty affected his health as well as his pocket. Years later he told American reporters:

> I cannot recall that show without a shudder. The whole five weeks I spent in it were appalling. I don't know yet quite what I was doing in it. I'm not exaggerating when I tell you that I was

really ill and came very close to a nervous breakdown. I had to go to Nassau to recuperate. Audiences can be very kind and sympathetic when you're in that kind of predicament, but that isn't right. You appreciate their sympathy, but you don't really want it because you're here to entertain them – not distress them. And then, of course, there's the dreadful feeling that because you can't come on the stage apologising for the play, people may think you're actually enjoying yourself!

Jack returned to England on the *Berengaria* on 15 February 1933. Although there were private visits in between, it was almost five years later when he returned on the *Normandie* for his next Broadway performance. He agreed to work for the toughest impresarios in New York, the Shubert Brothers, in the Arthur Schwartz and Howard Dietz musical *Between the Devil* at the Imperial Theatre. Schwartz and Dietz had had big successes with their revues *The Little Show* and *The Band Wagon* and it was thought that their witty, sophisticated and intimate style would be ideally suited not only to Jack but to his British co-stars.

The Shubert Brothers were so keen to have Jack for their show that they delayed its opening for almost a year while Jack completed film commitments for his own company. *Between the Devil* was mounted as probably the biggest British invasion of the American musical stage in the thirties. Jack was given two leading ladies in Evelyn Laye and Adele Dixon. He was also joined by his old friend, Bill Kendall. The British invaders were supported by a talented American company including the future film director, Chuck Walters, then one of Broadway's most effective dancers, his partner Vilma Ebsen (who had temporarily abandoned her brother Buddy), a close harmony trio, The Tune Twisters, and what was described as 'An assembly of the most beautiful girls on the American stage'.

Pictures of the show reveal that this was no exaggeration and Hassard Short was responsible for the lavish nature of the production which, with its London and Paris sets, was stylish in the extreme. The Schwartz/Dietz score was one of their best and included a number of songs which were to gain fame when used later in films such as 'I'll Go My Way by Myself', 'Triplets' and 'I See Your Face Before Me'.

Jack's co-stars were regarded as the epitome of British glamour. Evelyn Laye, described by the American press as 'brittle and blonde', was then at the height of her success following her appearance on Broadway in *Bitter Sweet* and her many London musical comedy successes. Adele Dixon, whose 'red gold hair and sparkle' were unknown to American audiences, had begun life as a serious actress only a short while before at the Royal Academy of Dramatic Art. She was 'discovered' when she played Suzzie Dean in the musical version of *The Good Companions*. These British glamour girls were involved in a plot in which Jack was Peter in England and Pierre in France maintaining two homes and two wives in a theme which was to be used again on a number of occasions.

The show got off to a somewhat unfortunate start. Jack was detained even longer than expected because of his filming commitments in Britain, where he had just completed four films in six months, starring in three of them. In order to save time, the songs from *Between the Devil* were posted to him in Britain where they failed to arrive before he sailed. Then the *Normandie* lost a propeller on the crossing and Jack's arrival was even further delayed. As a result, rehearsals began in New York without him and the producer actually rang Jack at sea to pass on the score of many of the numbers in the show to his musical coach, Van Phillips. The song 'By Myself', which Fred Astaire was to use to such effect in films later, alone ran up a transatlantic phone bill of $114. Jack did his best to work on the score in this piecemeal fashion and learnt his part with the help of his friend and fellow passenger, Cole Porter, who 'threw' lines at him.

Nevertheless, this approach to a new show was inauspicious. 'Boo' Laye was greatly looking forward to working with Jack. Years before when Jack had lost his first fortune over the building of the Leicester Square Theatre, he had taken her to supper at Ciro's. 'Boo', who was going through a difficult time herself, said it would be nice to be without money worries and Jack had replied 'Well, if you love a show, you'll find that success will follow but you must love your show'.

Recalling *Between the Devil* today, Evelyn Laye is convinced that Jack did not love this particular show. In this she is almost certainly right. For Jack arrived in New York worn out from his immense tasks filming and in launching his own film company. In addition, he had been putting on his own shows with his gang for fifteen years and he had no Elsie Randolph to cover for him while he worked his way into the part on tour.

Evelyn Laye believes that *Between the Devil* could have been successful if the principals had been able to work together from the beginning. As it was, they were compelled to discard much of the business they had already learnt while rapidly running out of time before the out of town opening. 'Boo' Laye recalls with a shudder:

> I was miserable. I felt lost. I felt at sea. I never drank spirits, and nor did Adele, but I must say during those rehearsals we took to Bourbon in a big way. When we got to Philadelphia, I knew Charles B. Cochran was in New York. I rang him up and said 'Will you come and see me? I feel terrible in this show'.

'The King of Broadway' with Evelyn Laye and Adele Dixon in Between
the Devil at the Imperial Theatre in 1938.

Well he came, saw the show, took me to supper afterwards and said 'Well you were quite right ducky. You were terrible. Your make up is awful and I don't like your clothes.' Above all, he thought we weren't married together – we weren't playing together.

Although the out of town critics praised the show and its principals, all concerned felt that there was much in Cochran's criticisms. The New York opening was postponed for several weeks and Arthur Schwartz and Howard Dietz began a major re-writing job. 'Boo' Laye found a wonderful New York make-up specialist and bought a stunning collection from Bergdorf Goodman. Jack worked on building up his comedy work – thinking American audiences might prefer this to the romantic role originally envisaged for him.

The result of all this hectic activity was, as Howard Dietz sees it, 'almost a good show'. The *New York Times* after the opening at the Imperial Theatre on 28 December 1937 said that the show's description 'As an intimate musical was not at all inapt. The actors headed by Jack Buchanan, Evelyn Laye and Adele Dixon are a charming and ingratiating lot. Jack Buchanan carries the principal burden and does it delightfully. He is one of the few comedians from whom an audience could take precisely the kind of role he is called on to perform.'

Brooks Atkinson said: 'Although Mr Buchanan is no bulldog of ferocity on the stage, he does some neat broken field running through the plot, distinguishing himself chiefly in the singing of the "By Myself" solo.'

For Kercey Allen 'Jack Buchanan was the suave Jack with the winning personality. He is "class" and dances cleverly. It is good to have him back with us after so long an absence.'

Not content with these good reviews, the Shubert Brothers announced that *Between the Devil* was to create American theatrical history. On Sunday evening, 23 January 1938, they presented the show as a one night performance at the National Theatre in Washington in response to an invitation from the General Committee for President Roosevelt's birthday celebration with proceeds going to the National Foundation for Infantile Paralysis. In doing so, the show became the first American Command Performance. Arthur Schwartz – who composed a song specially for the occasion entitled 'Command Performance' – thinks that the Shubert Brothers probably undertook this operation not only for the prestige involved but also as a way to bolster up the chances of the show's long run, adding: 'After all, the three principals were great foreign stars and this was a domestic celebration. Then it was a show about bigamy. You wouldn't think they'd want to celebrate that and it isn't entirely surprising that President Roosevelt didn't show up for the performance.'

Nevertheless, the Company was presented to the President at a private reception afterwards and the diplomatic corps turned out in force, led by the British Ambassador, Sir Ronald Lindsay, together with Washington's social and political world. Certainly the Shubert's gesture was not inexpensive. The cost of taking a special train from New York with scenery, 41 actors, 25 stage hands, 18 musicians and a staff of 18 was over six thousand five hundred dollars.

Before the company left New York, Jack, 'Boo' and Adele had marked the Command Performance by implanting their footprints in concrete outside the Imperial Theatre. After his return, Jack was soon to receive an additional honour from an unlikely source when he was made an honorary member of the New York Police Force.

This arose from a robbery when two armed men talked their way into Jack's dressing room at the Imperial Theatre demanding money. Jack, who carried very little cash at the best of times, handed over his wallet and invited the thieves to drink his Scotch whisky. He kept filling up their glasses before sending them off totally drunk. It would be nice to record that they were subsequently arrested, but there is no such evidence. But Jack had put them out of action and was delighted when he was invited down to City Hall to receive his Police badge. Bill Kendall recalls that there was one further hazard to overcome after the robbery: 'The Shubert Brothers put two hefty bodyguards on the stage door and you had to approach them with great caution. I remember one poor, persistent autograph hunter who got flattened and we all gave the muscle men a wide berth.'

For many American theatregoers who had only heard of Jack in the Charlot Revues over a decade earlier, this was also an opportunity to see the work of Britain's leading musical comedy and revue performer. One of them was a young dance student called Gene Kelly. He recalls:

This was the first time I had seen Jack who was already a legendary figure. The thing which impressed me more than anything else was his cool quality. Later, when I got to know him I found he was a delightful man and a real professional. My only regret is that we never had a chance to work together. We talked about it some years later. Our styles of singing and dancing were completely different but I think we might have worked something out. At any rate I regret not having worked with him and I know he felt the same way.

Although *Between the Devil* was not the enormous success that Jack and the authors had hoped for, it was in many ways a fitting swansong to his appearances in the United States before the War. In it, he was seen in an elegantly staged production with two of the leading British beauties of the West End stage.

ℒ

Leading Ladies – 'I Used to Call Her Baby'

ONE OF JACK'S EARLIEST revue successes was in *Bran Pie* with a song called 'I Used to Call Her Baby'. The title was apt. From his earliest touring days with Maidie Andrews in *Tonight's the Night*, Jack used this term of endearment for many of the girls with whom he worked.

His romantic and professional lives were inextricably intertwined. This was not simply a matter of the opportunities open to Jack – surrounded and adored by many of the most attractive women in the theatre and film world. Nor was his following confined to the acting profession. He had many girl friends and female admirers in British and foreign society and gossip between the wars linked him with many great names from Lady Hamilton in London and Madame Dubonnet in New York and with others as far afield as the Ranee of Sarawak and Queen Marie of Rumania. But, perhaps inevitably, it was the girls Jack worked with to whom he was most closely devoted in his thirty years as 'the eternal bachelor'.

A typical example of his care are the letters and cables he sent to one of his leading ladies who was sailing home from New York while Jack travelled by train to Hollywood. Jack wrote to her in April 1930 from the Ambassador Hotel in New York:

Baby Dear,
I have attended to your deck chairs, etc. on the ship, and have arranged that your wine account will be sent to me.
I wanted to surprise you, baby dear, with this but as sometimes things go wrong, I thought I'd tell you, so if by chance they hand you a wine bill, just tell them it is all paid for – and

don't be mean with yourselves. I wish I could sail too.
Love,
Jack

Jack treated all the girls with whom he worked as if they were leading ladies. Therein lay much of his charm. From the earliest Charlot days, he encouraged and 'brought on' his girls so that many rose from the chorus to stardom (including the recipient of the above letter).

The affinity Jack had with his 'babies' was not solely based on a close working relationship. True, he was unselfish and would often show a new partner off to advantage by restraining his own role and, true, he always made his girls feel that he was equally grateful to them for their understanding and co-operation in a successful performance. But his appreciation went much deeper. He genuinely sought women's company and he enjoyed 'women's talk'. Elsie Randolph has recalled: 'When we were on tour and I was going out somewhere, Jack would ring up my understudy and say "Come and have dinner" even when she was planning to wash her hair.' On one such occasion in the early days, the understudy concerned told her friends in the chorus 'I was frightened to death at going out with the great J.B. but you know he seemed even more scared than I was'.

Wyn Clare recalls his shyness as 'terribly attractive' adding to the mystery of 'the elusive Jack'. But the many girls who hoped that working with Jack might lead to marriage had to overcome two great rivals. The first was the theatre itself and the second was Jack's mother.

Elsie Randolph believes that Jack's 'heartbreaker' approach to his girl friends stemmed from his total dedication to the theatre, and one of his first theatrical girl friends, Phyllis Titmuss, who did little to conceal her frustrated love for him, warned his new leading lady, June, in 1924: 'Junie, if you work with J.B., try not to fall in love with him, because he'll only break your heart. He is a darling, he is sweet but all he really cares about is his work. Where a girl is concerned he is like a piece of quicksilver – the minute you try to hold it, it splits into many parts.'

If Jack was totally absorbed in the theatre, there are some who feel that his devotion to his mother amounted to a fixation. She never missed one of his shows and, when they were apart, he telephoned her constantly. For example, before going out to supper after the show, he telephoned every night during the nineteen week tour of *This'll Make You Whistle*. Even in Nassau, he telephoned two or three times a week. He would talk about her constantly and her picture was always at his bedside, in his dressing room and his office.

It would have been surprising if – after the death of his father – Jack as a twelve-year-old boy had not developed an exceptional closeness to the mother who supported him through his early struggles and ran his home for another thirty years. Certainly, Jack's first great partner, Phyl Monkman, felt that his mother was determined to discourage any possible wifely contenders after his divorce in 1919. Yet Phyl was an immense help to Jack at that time. She recalls that, in the final stages of the divorce, life for Jack was difficult since his wife would sometimes arrive at the stage door and demand to see him. On one occasion when she and Jack were about to rehearse for a charity performance at the Comedy Theatre which Queen Alexandra was to attend, they heard sounds of Bulgarian temperament as they came in though the stage door in Orange Street. 'Christ, that's my wife' said Jack and, Phyl Monkman recalled, 'We flew into Ciro's, which was also in Orange Street, until the storm had passed'.

There is little doubt that, at this time, Jack leant heavily on the support and affection of Phyl Monkman. She gave him a gold signet ring for good luck on the opening night of *Bubbly* which he wore on the first finger of his left hand for the rest of his life. Inevitably, gossip began to link their names. Years later, Phyl described how they would lunch every day during the run of *Tails Up*, at the Old Princes Restaurant, adding, with characteristic humour, 'When we went in, I was conscious that every woman in the restaurant was looking at us and envying me. And I remember thinking "If only he wasn't quite so shy!"'

Jack's next British leading lady, June, did not take the advice which Phyllis Titmuss had given her. Indeed, she tells the story today with that marvellous sense of humour that so much endears her to her many friends:

> Oh I fell madly in love with him right away. Boom. That was it. He was so patient, so charming and so hard working. All of us in the two shows I did with him – *Toni* and *Boodle* – were in love with him. Elsie Randolph, Ethel Stewart and me. Even Veronica Brady who played the large tattooed lady was in love with him.
>
> I tried to forget all about Jack but later when I was in America and got engaged to Lord Inverclyde, I thought I'd send a cable. I didn't really want to leave the stage and I was still hoping that Jack would say 'Stop all that nonsense and marry me'. So I cabled him from America 'Have just become engaged to Inverclyde. What do I do now?' He cabled back 'Congratulations and thanks for letting me know'!

Vivian Ellis was fascinated by Jack's relationship with his leading ladies. He believes 'that Jack greatly admired what the Royal Navy allude to as "top hamper". All his leading ladies were similarly endowed, even the elfin June who would willingly have abandoned wealth and rank at Jack's behest.' In fact, Jack said of June 'She began as a child dancer with two assets. One was that her father was an actor: the other was that she was born with perfectly lovely legs.'

If Jack showed a healthy appreciation of his leading ladies' figures, he never lost sight of their professional competence. He had enormous respect for June's dedication who, he said 'was an example of a girl who worked and worked until she forced herself into star parts.'

On the general question of matrimony, however, Jack pitched his sights rather high. In an article in *Ideas* in September 1928 he wrote:

> If I were choosing a wife, the chief virtue I would demand is that an actor's wife must realise his work must always come first. The first demand I would put upon her is a sympathetic and tactful nature. I hate women who say 'I told you so'. The perfect wife is the woman who never wants to know where a man has been if he returns home in the early hours, never questions him when he is tired out after a hard day, is always bright and cheerful, and miraculously succeeds in managing on the money he allows her each week. I should hate to marry a girl who thought me the most wonderful man in the world. I could never live up to her opinion of me. But any wife is preferable to the 'love-me-too-much-wife'; a man hates to be coddled, as much as he hates being neglected. He prefers his wife to be pretty, but not that alone; he wants intelligence and character and he would like her to dress well. A man likes his wife to be admired, for admiration accorded her is a compliment to his taste. And a woman who dresses well is usually equally circumspect in managing a household. Finally, he insists upon her being keen on sports. Exercise is essential to good health, and health makes for a cheerful and optimistic outlook on life which is invaluable to happy and contented marriage.
>
> If this is asking for too much, I can only repeat the advice given in *Punch* many years ago to those about to marry – 'Don't'.

Whatever his reservations about marriage, Jack's romantic life flourished when he was in America with the Charlot Revues. When he first went to New York, he saw a good deal of his old friend, Elsie Janis (and her mother). They entertained him lavishly at their country house on Long Island. Once, after a skating party there, Jack enhanced his reputation for 'sang froid' when he single-handedly put out a fire before the arrival of a fire brigade. Of their personal relationship, Elsie Janis remarked coyly: 'I first got to know Jack, Bea and Gertie when we were all playing in London together. When they all came to New York, I got to know Jack even better – I'm funny that way'.

Gertie Lawrence shared this sentiment. As she said after the first night of Charlot's 1924 Revue on Broadway: 'Jack left the women in the audience with only one thing to desire – Jack himself!' She gave Jack his nickname 'Johnny B'. He, in turn, called her 'Annie' and there is little doubt that they became very close during their partnership with Charlot which lasted over five years.

The American press maintained a close interest in Jack and Gertie's possible romantic attachment. When Gertie was going strong with some of New York's most eligible bachelors, one Society columnist coyly commented 'despite her Wall Street and Park Avenue admirers a little bird tells us that she is happiest with a fellow artist who, so as not to give the game away, we will simply describe with the initials J.B.' Even when they were working on opposite sides of the Atlantic in 1927, they were photographed and extensively reported holding an expensive telephone conversation while Jack was appearing in *Sunny* at the London Hippodrome and Gertie was playing in *Oh Kay* on Broadway.

Those closest to Jack and Gertie at this time in the twenties believe that the interest on her part was somewhat one sided. George Cross who was working at the Prince of Wales Theatre in 1921 remembers Gertie opening the window of her dressing room and addressing a few pungent Cockney witticisms about Jack's fickle nature as she spotted him leaving the theatre with another girl friend. Oscar Hammerstein's widow, Dorothy, also recalls an occasion when they were playing in the Charlot Revue on Broadway and Gertie threw a pot of make-up which narrowly missed 'Johnny B'.

Certainly in the mid-twenties, Jack's affections lay elsewhere. He was captivated by the enchanting Marilyn Miller, then at the height of her Broadway success in *Sunny* and soon to be divorced from her first husband, Mary Pickford's brother, Jack. It was this affection for Marilyn Miller that encouraged Jack to obtain the London production rights for *Sunny* in which he hoped they would co-star. But Marilyn Miller was unable to go to London and Jack faced stiff competition in pressing his romantic claims in New York. His principal rival was an up and coming young American movie star called Ben Lyon who was later to become much loved by British radio and television audiences when, with his wife Bebe Daniels, they put on *Life with the Lyons*.

When Jack returned from his long period of successes on Broadway and in Hollywood in 1930, it was the start of a decade during which his interest in and affection for his chorus girls was reflected in both their success in his shows and, in some cases, in his romantic attachments. Some like Lalla Collins, Anna Neagle and Jean Gillie rose to play leading parts, others like Babbie MacManus and Camille Irwin worked mainly in the chorus. All were united in their devotion to Jack.

As Anna Neagle puts it: 'I was, like numerous other girls, madly in love with Jack. This wasn't as dramatic as it sounds. Every girl who ever worked within fifty feet of Jack Buchanan was madly in love with him. So were the Gallery Girls who waited patiently in queues, often for hours, outside the theatres to see his shows. So were the ladies who clattered their tea cups through his matinées. And so was every other woman who had ever seen him on stage or film, or had heard his voice on records.'

It was with his discovery of Jean Gillie that Jack's professional and private life seemed most likely to merge. Despite their age difference – she was nineteen when Jack gave her a 'bit' part in *Brewster's Millions* and he was forty-five – the press went into raptures when, after *This'll Make You Whistle*, they became inseparable. One reviewer called her 'England's new sweetheart' adding 'No chorus girl has had such a speedy rise to fame as this slim blue eyed brunette'. Susan Kemp, the social columnist of *The Referee*, said that Jack was now seen out dining in public – previously a rare occurrence – and described how difficult it was to keep the attention of her own escort when Jean Gillie 'who people keep saying is the prettiest girl in England' was only two feet away with Jack.

Jack no longer had an obligation to his mother, who died in 1936, and talk of his possible marriage to Jean Gillie grew. Her aunt, Mabel Green, who had been a great lady of the theatre, was one of those who fondly hoped to help in match making. Possibly because of the various family pressures, Jack and Jean Gillie drifted apart. Although they were constant companions for more than five years, she eventually made an unhappy wartime marriage and died at the tragically early age of thirty-nine.

Jack still had not lost his knack of discovering new leading ladies which was now translated to the screen. When Elsie Randolph was unable to appear in *The Gang's All Here* in 1939, Jack had given Googie Withers her first big opportunity in playing opposite him. She recalls that, away from work, Jack still carried a romantic aura which was magic to a young girl: 'One night he drove me home from Elstree where we were making the film and he asked me if I'd like to go out with him. I was thrilled and I said I'd adore to because it was total hero worship – I thought he was super. He said "Well, we'll go to Ciro's." I put on my best evening dress and of course in those days, he had his white tie and tails. We had dinner at Ciro's and the band started. Well, of course, he was *the* famous dancer. But I had started in the theatre as a dancer and we were really able to suddenly dance marvellously together. Everyone else went and sat down and Jack and I danced a solo for half an hour and we were cheered when we came off.'

Apart from those who shared his life on and off the stage, Jack also showed great consideration for those outside the profession who made up his many female fans. These Gallery Girls were his other 'leading ladies'. They showed an exceptional devotion to Jack, part of which was clearly maternal.

Everyone knew that Jack Buchanan was dying of consumption. The fact that this was totally untrue was never fully disclaimed. If anyone mentioned this to Jack, he would cup his chin on his hand and raise his left eyebrow – a sure sign that he was perplexed. If the point was pushed further, Jack would become angry but since he expressed this by relapsing into silence, the legend of his ill health flourished.

Jack's Gallery Girls came to his shows again and again and he kept 'open house' for them. Vivian Ellis was as fascinated by this as he was by Jack's relationship with his leading ladies: 'I would wander into Jack's dressing room where silence reigned. There, while removing his stage make-up, he would be regarded in soundless ecstasy by worshipping Gallery Girls whom he entertained either out of sheer kindness or policy, probably both. Meanwhile, Jack's mind would be miles away – thinking out a new piece of stage business – with an occasional meaningful glance, when he remembered, at his silent audience.'

Many of the Gallery Girls were great characters and some achieved a certain notoriety. One went round London claiming to be Jack's cousin and obtaining goods on credit for which he received the bills. She later widened her activities to include Noël Coward and, as the Master described it, 'was sent briskly off to jail'. There were other ladies who claimed to have nursed Jack through several fatal illnesses and there were the many others who said they had worked with him 'in the early days' implying varying degrees of friendship and gratitude.

To all these ladies, Jack showed remarkable patience when they clustered round him in droves at the stage door. For some he reserved a special place in his affections. These were his professional watchers who were not afraid to criticise and who became unofficial members of Jack's staff. They included Hetty and Sophie Rosen and, perhaps most famous of all, Nan and Dora Morris.

These were the leading lights of the 'Gallery First Nighters'. From *A to Z* on 11 October 1921, Nan and Dora never missed one of Jack's first nights. But they did not confine their attendance to the opening performance. They saw *Sunny* 84 times and went to his shows every week, sometimes twice or three times. Sometimes they saw the show in Manchester or Brighton prior to London and took pride in contributing their suggestions for improvements.

But the first night in London was always their big occasion. They went to immense trouble in finding Jack a first night mascot. Knowing his love of animals, they would usually choose a child's woolly dog or cat. They always knew when Jack was especially nervous (the sure sign was when he kept adjusting his tie) and, at the opening of *Mr Whittington*, they realised his anxieties were not helped by two noisy young men in the gallery so Nan went across and slapped their faces.

There was too a younger contingent which – in the twenties and thirties – represented the equivalent of today's pop fans. To many of them Jack was a 'Flappers' Delight'. They were the ones who sat, as one critic described them, 'in languishing rows'. Occasionally, however, they showed a more frenetic side.

Sometime in the early thirties, Jack agreed to be godfather to an old friend's child. News of this and his attendance at the church service in Suffolk where the christening would take place was published in the press. Half way through the service, Jack and his friend heard the sound of two large motor coaches arriving outside the church and squeaks and squeals which denoted that Jack's younger Gallery Girls were about to invade the church in force. Jack turned to his friend and said: 'I say, ol' boy, I think it's time we beat a retreat. This set is getting too crowded.'

Entracte – Wartime and Early Post War Years

IT'S TIME TO DANCE in 1943 was the last musical comedy in which Jack appeared under his own management. The title of the show typified his response to the wartime situation. Indeed, in the years 1939 to 1945, he probably worked harder than at any time in his life. At 48, he was too old for war service but he threw himself into the business of entertaining both Service and home audiences with renewed vigour.

Jack and Elsie were among the first performers to report to Drury Lane when Basil Dean was forming ENSA companies which would entertain the forces. Towards the end of 1939, when they were rehearsing at the Theatre Royal, they were visited by King George and Queen Elizabeth. The King reminisced about the great days of musical comedy and recalled his backstage visits to see Jack and Elsie. He and the Queen wished them well as they set out on their wartime concerts. One of the first was at the Guards Barracks at Windsor which was arranged through Jack's friendship with (Lord) Peter Milton. This set the pattern for other concerts as the ENSA organisation was somewhat regimented and Jack and his Gang shared their petrol coupons and arranged private performances for Service audiences at the request of many of their friends now in command of units up and down the country.

During the War Jack's career as a radio performer was also established on a regular basis. There was an obvious need to provide entertainment for the Forces – as well as for home audiences – deprived of live shows. Jack was also used to show Britain's friends – particularly those in the United States – that British morale was high. On 6 December 1939, he took part in a

137

Wartime reunions: Above, *With Fred Emney in* It's Time to Dance. Below, *With Elsie Randolph in the same show.*

programme of *Songs from the Shows* produced by John Watt. This programme was given a rave review by *Variety* who said that 'American listeners must be delighted to find their old British pal in such good heart and voice'. However, Jack's big number in the show had somewhat premature sentiments. It was parody of Noel Gay's 'Run Rabbit Run' with lines which suggested 'Run Adolf Run'.

Jack had learnt to take his radio work just as seriously as if it was one of his great pre-war musicals. In 1940, Charles B. Cochran invited him to appear in his radio series 'Cock-a-Doodle-Doo'. The great showman was going through a bad time financially and typically Jack took part without fee, out of friendship. 'Cocky' later recalled how desperately shaky and nervous Jack was before they went on the air. Yet, once the programme began, his totally relaxed manner and unique ability to put over his songs were apparent. With Geraldo and Boys, he sang 'Whose Little Whatsit Are You' and 'All Over the Place' which described the roving sailor's life which Jack envied. Among those on the bill with Jack were Vic Oliver, Jack and Daphne Barker and Sam Browne. Other programmes in the series included every well known West End musical comedy performer but, of them all, Charles B. Cochran later recalled that Jack's had been the outstandingly successful performance.

Jack continued to broadcast at regular intervals throughout the war. In addition to the programmes intended to entertain those at home, he undertook several sessions for the Forces overseas. Some went out live and others were put on gramophone records for use in the field. On one such recorded show, Jack, assisted by 'Pilot Officer Roy Rich and Sergeant Major George Melachrino', presented a potted life story in the form of his favourite songs from his shows.

Meanwhile, Jack's life as an impresario continued. Undeterred by his major setback over the Leicester Square Theatre, he had joined in a business partnership with the monocled comedian, Ralph Lynn, in building a new theatre. This was to be the Imperial Theatre in Brighton and it was typical of Jack's mixed fortunes that construction started just before the War and the need for the subsequent wartime opening could hardly have been more ill timed.

To overcome this problem, Jack decided to put on his own revue which would be called *Top Hat and Tails*. This would be another Gang reunion, for Jack was joined by Elsie Randolph, Fred Emney and Bill Kendall. As resident manager at the Imperial Theatre, Jack put in Walter Williams who had appeared with him in the early Charlot Revues. Jack's personal team was headed by his business manager Gilbert Brown with Wally

Herald and Peter Warren in charge of stage management.

Peter Warren – whose long devotion to Jack was now rewarded with the stage manager's job – recalls the horrendous problems of this production:

> The idea was that we would put on a lot of the old sketches that Jack had used previously with Elsie, Fred and Bill, so as to overcome some of the difficulties of limited rehearsal time. The basic problem was that the building of the Imperial Theatre had been affected by the outbreak of war and we had to get a show on there quickly since Jack and Ralph Lynn were losing a fortune while sitting on a half-completed theatre.
>
> The opening there was the worst evening of our lives. Nobody had been down to Brighton to see what was going on. When Wally Herald and I got there, we found everything in a state of complete chaos. Walter Williams had been a marvellous performer but he was no manager. There was no dressing room space and nothing worked.
>
> Somehow, we managed to patch things up but the dress rehearsal must have been the longest and most agonising of Jack's life. The first night was little short of a disaster. Nothing went right. Jack had been to the dentist and was in agony. Then, he was so exhausted by all the last minute efforts to sort the show out that he literally staggered into his dressing room and some kind person put it about that he'd been drunk on his first night.
>
> Still, we managed to raise a laugh among ourselves. In one sketch, Jack and Elsie were working their guts out. The only other person on stage was Jack's understudy, Bobby Gordon. He only had one line – something dramatic like 'Won't you come in, Sir' – and, otherwise, he just stood there watching Jack and Elsie like someone at Wimbledon. Fred Emney was standing in the wings waiting to go on next. He turned to me and said 'I don't know what Jack would do without Bobby Gordon in this sketch'.

Top Hat and Tails opened in March 1940. Despite the horrors of the opening night, it did good business in a short run but as Alan Melville recalls, 'The Imperial was colossal and fine in a way for the Royal Ballet or Grand Opera but a play or intimate revue with a cast of six or seven and sets got lost in it.' It seemed sensible therefore to take the show on the road. In doing so, Jack was, once again, bouncing back from financial disaster, for the Imperial – which is today a Bingo hall – was clearly a white elephant. This was the second time Jack had lost a fortune.

The making of the next fortune was one of the toughest working spells in Jack's life. Wartime touring was arduous and beset with immense problems. The company lost key members for military service – including Bill Kendall – and there was the constant battle against shortages of costumes and scenery. For

Jack with his 'nothing but the best' approach, the whole idea of rationing was complete anathema. As Elsie Randolph has recalled he was quite liable to try and buy a new top hat with his meat coupons.

Jack's financial fortunes were hit once again when, in August 1940, he put on a comedy thriller called *The Body Was Well Nourished* at the Lyric. The play – one of the first efforts by Frank Launder and Sidney Gilliat, who were to become enormously successful as film directors – opened to good business. It was followed – almost immediately – by the start of the Luftwaffe attack on London and Jack decided that the play must go on tour with himself in the lead.

Before that, however, he was committed to an entirely new venture. By 1940, there was little left in the entertainment world which Jack had not tackled; musical comedy, dramatic acting, variety, revue, writing and composing. But there was one specialised part of light entertainment he had never tried – Pantomime.

When Tom Arnold approached him to play Buttons in *Cinderella*, Jack hesitated for a while. The part is traditionally reserved for small men with a flair for knock-about comedy. But Jack was always tempted by opportunities to play broad comedy and was intrigued by the challenge of giving his own interpretation to the role. He was also tempted by the financial offer of a salary plus percentage of the takings in what was an almost certain success. For *Cinderella* was to be put on in Sheffield with a provincial tour to follow and the cast would be one of the finest ever assembled. Tom Arnold had recruited pantomime specialists like Marjorie Sandford as Dandini, Nuala Barrie as the Fairy, Molly Stoll and Beryl Reid as the Ugly Sisters and Nat Jackley and Jack Clifford as Spottem and Grabbem, the Sheriff's men. In addition, Jack had his Gang members, Jean Gillie as Cinderella, Fred Emney as the Baron and his old friend Adele Dixon as Prince Charming.

He was delighted to be reunited with Adele Dixon after the partial disappointment of their Broadway appearance in *Between the Devil*. When Jack rang her, Adele Dixon recalls: 'I said "But Jack, I've never played in panto before" and he replied "Neither have I, or Jean and Fred, but we'll have fun and there should be some good lolly in it because we're all on a percentage". So what could I say but yes.'

In the event, the 'sure thing' that Jack was counting on was a near disaster. The opening of the show was planned for Christmas Eve but on 23 December, the Luftwaffe struck in the Sheffield Blitz. Throughout the night German bombers attacked not only the steelworks but also the City Centre. Just outside the

Empire Theatre, where Cinderella was due to open next day, a bomb blew a tram onto its side and the theatre was severely shaken. Meanwhile, the Company's principals had to abandon the dress rehearsal and returned to the nearby Grand Hotel.

In the morning, it was decided that the Company should leave for Manchester to continue rehearsals while a decision was made about the Sheffield opening. Not only was the theatre in need of careful examination as to the effects of the bomb blast but also Sheffield's essential services had been badly hit by the massive raid which had wiped out much of the city. There was also the question as to whether this was just the start of a sustained German Blitz. Meanwhile, the tragedy facing many Sheffield families was shared by Jack and his company, for Bobby Gordon, Jack's understudy for over a decade, had been killed by a bomb which hit the digs in which he was staying.

Jack was deeply upset but, when the theatre was pronounced structurally sound, decided that the best tribute to Bobby Gordon and their answer to the Germans was to fulfill the time honoured theatrical cliché by carrying on. It was decided to put on performances at 10.45 a.m. and 2 p.m. each day and the show opened on Boxing Day. Despite all the hazards and difficulties of the Blitz, the theatre was packed. Security restrictions prevented the local press from reporting the true reasons for the delayed opening since no mention could be made of the bombing. The *Sheffield Telegraph* said:

> The time has yet to come for recording the difficulties faced and obstacles surmounted. You can trust the stage people for going to it be the conditions normal or abnormal. Laughter is a good sound to hear in these times and yesterday morning one heard it in full volume. How would Jack Buchanan bear himself in this fantastic environment? Well he bore himself like Jack Buchanan and like a good pantomime artist as well. He took a foremost hand in all the antics and gave and received the knocks; yet one had opportunities of noting his marvellous skill in song technique; his expressiveness in dancing and his special acting style.

Despite wartime constraints Robert Nesbitt, who had worked with Charlot and made his name in producing lavish pre-war musicals, staged the pantomime with gorgeous costumes designed by Doris Zinkeisen. He recalls:

> We had put the show together in the best Tom Arnold pantomime style. It was part of an operation which brought top liners to all the main provincial cities. Although Tom Arnold was laid low with 'flu at his flat in 55 Park Lane during the London Blitz, he realised that Jack like many other big names had closed his show in London and was living hand to mouth

on tour. From this thought came the plan whereby we were able simultaneously to put Lupino Lane into *Aladdin* in Birmingham, Leslie Henson and Stanley Holloway into *Robinson Crusoe* in Manchester and Jack and The Gang into *Cinderella* in Sheffield.

The plan looked like suffering after the Sheffield Blitz. But Moss Empires asked us to try and re-open the Empire Theatre. Tom Arnold, Jack and I took a car over there and met the local Police Chief and the Press. They all said that Sheffield had caught such a packet that it would cheer people up enormously if we could get the show going. So Jack said 'We'll put it on if it's humanly possible'.

After playing in Sheffield for three weeks, *Cinderella* began a hectic tour; two weeks in Edinburgh, Liverpool and Blackpool and a final four weeks at the Alhambra, Glasgow. In Liverpool, one of Jack's greatest admirers, Wilfrid Hyde-White, recalls: 'Buttons! He was the most unlikely man you could have ever envisaged as Buttons. You think of this part as a little man with a red nose. But he didn't sacrifice one ounce of his elegance and he was the greatest god-damned pantomime lead you ever saw.'

There was no break for Jack at the end of the *Cinderella* tour. When he finished in Glasgow on the last Saturday in March 1941, he opened in *The Body Was Well Nourished* on the following Monday. In the play, Jack had the unlikely role of a vacuum-cleaner salesman who finds a dead body in the piano at one of the houses at which he calls.

Jack had taken over the lead from Barry K. Barnes, who had played the part in London. In so doing, he was reunited with Elsie Randolph who, similarly, took over the role originally played by Diana Churchill. Also in the touring company was George Cross who worked both as an actor and stage director and his wife, Eileen Dale, who had a supporting part and understudied Elsie Randolph. She recalls Jack's typical thoughtfulness when she had to take over the lead: 'Elsie broke a bone in her foot on the stairs in a blackout. I went on for her with Jack for eight weeks. He was charming to me. I was given the star dressing room and every Monday morning there were flowers. He even insisted that I had special dresses made for me instead of making do with Elsie's things. This was a tremendous gesture as it was particularly difficult to get hold of more material and so on during the War.'

The tour was long and strenuous. Because of the increasing bomb attacks on the larger cities, it took the company into many of the smaller provincial towns. In the middle of the tour, Jack took several of his Company to work with him at the B.B.C.'s 'hideaway' studios in Bristol and Bangor. This radio series –

Going Places – was escapist fare in which each episode took place in some luxurious and exotic faraway spot which provided a total contrast with their 'make do and mend' approach to wartime touring.

Jack and his touring companies had several close shaves with bombing raids in different parts of Britain during 1941. When he returned to London between tours, the blast of War came even closer to home.

Jack was still living in his penthouse above the Leicester Square Theatre where he also had his office. Bill Kendall had moved in as flatmate soon after Jack's mother had died but he was now serving in the Army. On one of his leaves, the boys went out on the town and Jack later recalled:

> When I got home the next day, Leicester Square had been badly bombed and the first thing I noticed in the heap of rubbish was that all that was left of my home was some bits of a grandfather clock which was lying around the place. There was very little of it, I might say and this really burned me up. I had heard the tick of that clock as long as I could remember and it seemed to me typical of Nazism that it should have so little regard for the best things in our civilisation.
>
> On top of this, this clock was one of the mementoes of my mother and I resented the loss of memories of this kind even more than the loss of my home.

Bill Kendall recalls that one of the reasons why they did not return to the Leicester Square flat that night was because one of their party – a serving officer – had enjoyed himself so much that it was felt he should 'sleep it off' before returning to his unit. Their good turn had an immediate reward since there is little doubt that Jack and Bill could not have survived the direct hit on the flat.

When Jack inspected the damage, he had Elsie Randolph and Bill Kendall with him. They realised how upset he was with the loss of his treasured grandfather clock, the personal mementoes of his mother and his books and papers. Each, however, noted two strange survivors in the bomb blast. Elsie recalls seeing a door which had been blown in under the staircase revealing an enormous pile of unanswered letters and the famous unopened parcels. She comments 'Johnny B obviously felt it was a pity that the bomb hadn't got that lot'. Bill Kendall, on the other hand, noted that the milk bar at the back of the Leicester Square Theatre, which had blocked Jack's theatrical development of the site, had been almost totally demolished, fortunately without any loss of life. 'Would you believe it?' he asks 'There in the middle of the wrecked shop was a picture of Jack's mother which had been blown out of its frame, had come all the way down from the top of the building, and now lay there with a dignified look as if to say "You should have sold out to my son in the first place".'

But Jack had little time for the 'might have beens' of theatrical history. 'Never look back,' he once said 'You're only as good as the show you've just finished or, better still, the one you're in now'. He therefore threw himself into a hectic round of theatre, film and radio work while still finding time for concerts and broadcasts for Service audiences. For his new home, he rented part of Ben Lyon's and Bebe Daniels' house and found an office in the Lyric Theatre where he had taken a management lease. He was soon immersed in his many business interests. There was the future of the Imperial Theatre in Brighton to be decided – although, as Alan Melville points out, Jack having suffered there in *Top Hat and Tails* made sure that his future appearances were at the Brighton Hippodrome; there was the question of future productions at the Lyric; there were other possible tours to consider; there was the future of Jack's Riverside Film Studios and there was Jack's growing interest in working as a producer and stage director.

This was a development to which Jack was giving increasing attention. He recognised the need to shift away from musical comedies which relied heavily on his own performance and, in September 1942, produced *Waltz Without End* at the Cambridge Theatre. This was a musical play by Eric Maschwitz based on the life and music of Chopin which had fair success running until early 1943.

Meanwhile, Jack had once again returned to pantomime as Buttons in *Cinderella*. The cast was virtually unchanged from the previous year's edition but the show was put on for a long run at the Theatre Royal, Birmingham. As there were hotel problems Jack and the Gang took a house in Hagley Road. Adele Dixon recalls that she and Jean Gillie had a lively time: 'Although wartime touring had many drawbacks, we were able to make a reasonable amount of money and – because of the daytime shows – enjoy ourselves in the evenings in our Hagley Road hideout. When Jack suggested the idea, he said "Let's all go into digs, duckie. It ought to be fun" – and it was.'

Jack was back in London in the spring of 1943. With the improved Allied fortunes, he decided that the time was ripe for a personal return to musical comedy on the London Stage. This would be in a show aptly called *It's Time to Dance* with the book by Duggie Furber. Jack would resume his romantic partnership with Elsie Randolph and his comedy teamwork with Fred Emney.

The leading American dance coach, Buddy Bradley – who numbered Fred Astaire as well as Jack among his pupils – was now living in London. He was to arrange the dances in the show as he had in *Top Hat and Tails* and, this time, he would sing and dance with Jack in a number called 'Yankee Doodle Came to Town'. His assistant was Babbie MacManus who had been in the chorus of *This'll Make You Whistle* and who was now understudying Elsie Randolph.

Wilfrid Hyde White describes the audience's reaction on the first night at the Winter Garden on 22 July 1943:

> Because of the War, Jack had been away from the West End for seven years. When he made his entrance, I timed it and the audience stood up and applauded for seven minutes. Seven minutes!
>
> It was almost poetic justice that the applause seemed to provide a minute for each of the years in which he had been away. Certainly it was one of the greatest theatrical ovations I had ever heard.

There were several new features in the show which also aroused great enthusiasm in the audience. Jack and Fred on the track of the jewel thieves disguised themselves as two long-haired musicians. This allowed Fred Emney to display some of his real life talent as a brilliant pianist while Jack, although playing up the visual comedy, also showed his own musical talent with the violin.

The partnership of Jack and Elsie – in what was to be their last show together – ended on a high note. From their first number 'I'm Looking for a Melody' they showed the partnership had lost none of its style and understanding. Moreover, after twenty years of romanticizing by the Gallery Girls, Elsie and Jack were finally married in the finalé, 'An Old Fashioned Wedding'.

Although Elsie Randolph does not regard this show as one of their greatest – there were too many wartime constraints to allow this – this public showed every sign of satisfaction at having Jack and Elsie back. Their enthusiasm was shared by the press. The *Theatre World* described it as 'a triumphant return' and said, 'The whole of the brilliant cast show an irresistibly lighthearted and pre-war touch'. *The Times* was impressed by 'a professionalism which has been missing from our stages' adding, 'Mr Buchanan is the most professional of light entertainers. His effects are slight but they are always made and they never lack the last shade of precision. All the movements of his feet, all the intonations of his voice, indeed all the changes of facial expression appear to be perfectly calculated.'

The show was not without its business problems as Jack's stage manager, Pete Warren, recalls:

> I don't know quite how it happened but Jack got himself badly

caught out with his agreement to put the show on at the Winter Garden. We couldn't get another theatre at the time and we understood people's warnings later on when the show was a big success and we found that – in the small print – we were due to pay substantial increases in rent the longer the show went on. Eventually, Jack managed to transfer it to the Lyric but despite the huge success of the show, he was once again badly affected financially.

These business worries added to the strain on Jack. He had, with difficulty, extricated himself from the Brighton Theatre project and there was the constant drain on his resources from the unutilised Riverside Film Studios at Hammersmith. Jack was determined to hang onto them at all costs as his post-war nest egg. Meanwhile, when told of the shortage of film studios during wartime, he commented wryly to the press 'Anyone can have a couple of floors at my place at almost any price anytime they like'.

When such work was not forthcoming, Jack decided to make his own film musical comedy at the Riverside Studios. In 1943, he joined Tom Arnold in producing a film version of the successful wartime radio series *Happidrome* with Harry Korris, who wrote the script, as Mr Lovejoy, Robbie Vincent as Enoch and Cecil Frederick as Ramsbottom. There were guest appearances by the cabaret artist 'Hutch' and the Carioli Brothers.

The strain of all these activities began to tell. Roy Plomley of *Desert Island Discs* fame was impressed by Jack's strenuous working schedule. He recalls:

> Our first business meeting was something of a sad story. I went to see him at the Winter Garden during the run of his wartime show and I shall always remember the two huge morose elephants holding up the stage boxes at the Winter Garden. I had flogged in all the way from Edgware where I was then living to talk about working with Jack in a radio programme. I was very young and impressionable and very much in awe of this great star. When I arrived to see him after the show, I was handed over to an assistant stage manager who told me I would have to wait at the side of the stage as he already had someone with him. I waited ages and eventually Jack appeared just as he was rushing off to another appointment. He said 'Oh my dear fellow, I'm terribly sorry. Nobody told me you were here'. I didn't argue. He had so much charm and it was obvious that he was trying to do so many things at the same time that I almost felt as though I was intruding in trying to offer him more work.

Despite his heavy workload, Jack's mind was still actively pursuing new projects. In March 1944, he put on the farce writer Vernon Sylvaine's first straight play *A Murder for a Valentine* with Cathleen Nesbitt at the Lyric Theatre. At the same time, he was working on the most important change in his professional career. He was rehearsing the part of the caddish Lord Dilling in *The Last of Mrs Cheyney* which was to mark the start of his long and successful partnership with the Australian actress, Coral Browne.

During the wartime years, she had established herself as the resident leading lady at the Savoy Theatre with enormous success in *The Man Who Came to Dinner* and *My Sister Eileen*. Her professional assessment of Jack's approach to the great challenge of turning from musical comedy to the high style of Frederick Lonsdale's play is interesting:

> There is no doubt that he had a great gift for light comedy. From the first day we rehearsed together, I never – as we say – had to 'bother about him'. He was a completely unselfish performer. He wouldn't try to upstage one by doing things behind one's back while one was speaking one's own lines as even some of the greatest are inclined to do. He gave me the best position on the stage and accepted Tyrone Guthrie's proposals as director without question.
>
> The only thing that worried me in working with Jack was that at no time during our three weeks of rehearsals did he ever take his hat off or take the part from his hand. So I began to wonder if I would ever see his head and if in fact he knew his lines. But on the opening night, the hat came off, the part disappeared as the make-up went on, and he was word perfect.

There was wide professional and public interest in Jack's move to straight acting and he later recalled that of all his intensely nervous first nights, that at the Savoy Theatre on 15 June 1944 was one of the most nerve wracking. The production was one of Firth Shepherd's most glittering efforts. Described as 'A comedy of the day before yesterday' the play was set in the Edwardian era with sumptuous costumes and sets designed by Ernest Stern. Jack was being directed by one of the greatest men in the theatre, Tyrone Guthrie, and was following in the steps of the incomparable Gerald du Maurier who had created the part of the dissolute Lord Dilling only twenty years earlier. He was also working with a brilliant company which, as well as Coral Browne, included Athene Seyler, Austin Trevor and James Dale. Perhaps wisely, therefore, he decided to play his part as *The Times* said 'Not as a good natured cad on the downward grade discovering by degrees that he had more good nature than he had suspected, but as a lover lightly amused by the intricacy of the game.'

This interpretation in which Jack, while unmasking Carole Browne as a jewel thief, falls in love with her despite a lifetime dedicated to bachelor status, lent piquancy to Jack's relationship with his new leading lady. It also pleased the critics. The *Theatre*

World thought the part was 'admirably suited to the good looks and nonchalant manner of Jack Buchanan'. Even the waspish James Agate waxed lyrical, saying: 'In the matter of Jack Buchanan's Lord Dilling criticism just doesn't begin. Jack's Dilling is beloved for his sweetness, good nature and moral pretensions. That's fine by me, and so would Macbeth be, played along the same lines, provided the actor were our Jack.'

Despite this critical and popular success, *The Last of Mrs Cheyney* was not without its problems. These came from an unexpected quarter. Jack had come through the War with narrow escapes from bombing in Sheffield and London but, with the Allied invasion of France only a few days earlier, it was thought that there was little to fear in mounting a lavish production at the Savoy. Once more, the Germans shattered such peacetime thinking.

Immediately after the first night, Jack and Coral joined Firth Shepherd for a celebration supper at the Savoy. Coral Browne recalls: 'We were sitting having dinner when there was an awful crunch. We didn't realise at the time what had happened but it was the arrival of the first doodlebug. We picked up the papers the next day to read – what we expected – would be marvellous notices to find there was nothing at all. Well, there was hardly anything because the papers were full of this thing that arrived from outer space.'

The company refused to be deterred by the nightly bombing attacks. Austin Trevor recalls how the doodlebugs became almost part of the plot. 'One of them was worked into what I must regard as my most famous exit line. Jack had a line to me "Lord Elton, you're not leaving us are you?". One night at the precise moment when he delivered this line, a tremendous explosion shook the entire theatre as a doodlebug landed in the Thames. The entire audience rose, applauded and roared with laughter because they thought I'd left because of the bombing.'

Despite the flying bombs, *The Last of Mrs Cheyney* settled in for a long run. Jack was as active as ever in pursuing his business interests to which, in 1944, he added management of the King's Theatre, Hammersmith. Of this move, Duggie Furber said: 'Why he took it on, I shall never know'. Certainly the Theatre had no apparent policy of attracting long runs and, between November 1944 and October 1945, put on eleven different productions ranging from Ben Jonson to Shaw, Gilbert and Sullivan to Pantomime, together with Ronald Shiner's first London appearance in *Worm's Eye View* (which was almost immediately transferred to the West End).

Jack was still, despite his many commitments, active in entertaining Service audiences. Probably the greatest wartime occasion of this kind was the opening of the Stage Door Canteen on 31 August 1944. Lyons Corner House in Piccadilly had been turned into a Forces Club to entertain the thousands of allied troops *en route* to or from the invasion forces in France.

On the opening night, the place was packed with a predominantly Anglo-American audience. In recognition of this, Dorothy Dickson and Bea Lillie had worked frenziedly to line up some of the greatest British and American stars. They themselves appeared and Anthony Eden came to perform the official opening in a speech in which – thinking of the flying bombs – he said 'They are heading for the last round up'. Meanwhile, the crush grew even greater and there were fears that the balcony might collapse.

At this point, Jack arrived, and as W. MacQueen Pope recalls in *The Footlights Flickered*: 'His mere presence seemed to have a tranquillizing effect on the noisy milling crowd. He went on the little stage, he told stories, he sang and he danced. They cheered and cheered again. He told them what to do to make things easy – to keep the doorways clear, those in front sit down so that all could see. They obeyed at once.'

A little later, Jack was joined by Fred Astaire and, as Fred indicates in his Foreword to this book, after twenty years of just missing each other in the West End, on Broadway and in Hollywood, the two greatest musical comedy stars on each side of the Atlantic finally got together to perform for probably their most appreciative audience ever.

When Fred Astaire left, he was succeeded by Bing Crosby. W. MacQueen Pope continues the story: 'Bing was as good as Jack in his own way. He, too, sang to them, yarned to them, cracked jokes; he signed autographs, he was pushed about as Jack had been and enjoyed it, just as Jack did. Then the two of them went on the stage together and for half an hour they wisecracked at each other, right "off the cuff" and totally unrehearsed – a performance which anywhere else would have cost many pounds. Here were two really great artists working together, each supreme in his own line, each perfectly confident of himself, giving and taking gags, never trying to crab each other, an example of professionalism at its very best. It will live in the memory of all who saw it.'

As the War came to an end, Jack followed up the public's obvious appreciation of *It's Time to Dance* with its return to pre-war style entertainment in both his radio work and in plans for a new revue. He celebrated the renewal of his partnership with Elsie Randolph when they made radio versions of two of their greatest musical comedy successes. In 1944, they recorded *Sunny* and in the following year *Stand Up and Sing*. Both radio versions were adapted by Eric Fawcett, Jack's old understudy and then a leading B.B.C. producer. There were obvious problems in reducing two and a half hour shows to one hour programmes but each was a great success, retaining much of the charm and gaiety of the original shows and, for this reason, they are still retained in the B.B.C. archives today.

Jack's first major radio variety series lasted for over three months in 1945. Entitled simply *The Jack Buchanan Programme*, it was pre-recorded weekly at the Phoenix Theatre. The regulars were producer, Henry Reed, script writers Jack Davies, Jr and Dennis Waldock, together with the orchestra of Stanley Black. Each week Jack worked with a number of well known performers, some of whom stayed on through most of the series. In the first programme, which was broadcast on 23 May 1945, Jack was joined by Moore Marriot, Vera Pearce, Jerry Desmonde, Ilena Sylva and special guest star, Nora Swinburne. The plot envisaged Jack and his companions setting out for Burma 'at the unanimous request of the troops in Europe'. *En route*, they performed the show's signature tune 'Thank your Lucky Stars' and Jack had, as his solo, 'Paddlin-Madeline Home'.

In subsequent shows in the series, Jack invited as his guests Barry K. Barnes, Diana Churchill, Dick Francis, Fred Ewell, Douglas Young, Ellen Keith, Reginald Purdell, Bill Kendall, Ike Hatch, George Cross and Aubrey Mallalieu. The plot involved an extremely slow journey to Burma and in the third programme there was a last-minute technical hitch. The cast were supposed to be at Croydon Airport trying to get seats on a plane which had been reserved for Mr Churchill. This was cut out at the eleventh hour when, in the week between recording the programme and the broadcast on 6 June 1945, Mr Churchill was replaced as Prime Minister by Mr Attlee. Otherwise there were few logical connections to the plot which meandered from London to France and then on to Switzerland, Spain, Turkey, Africa, the United States and home. It was typical of the relaxed construction in the writing that the transition from Switzerland to Spain while *en route* to the Far East was explained by the pilot having turned right instead of left over Sicily.

For Jack, much of the humour came in his playing with Vera Pearce, who was variously described as 'the parachute instructress or the last of the balloon barrages'. The romantic interest was provided by Ilena Sylva who was appearing in *Sweeter and Lower* and who would soon work with Jack in revue. Jack's songs introduced as 'The voice that broke a thousand windows' showed off his versatility. They ranged from some of his best known songs such as 'This'll Make You Whistle', 'Everything Stops for Tea' or to standards like 'What'll I Do' and to the current hit of the day 'Chewing a Piece of Straw'. A feature of his appearances was that in each edition, credit was claimed by some exotic fictitious organisation. Thus one week, he appeared by permission of the East Tooting Tea-Tasters' Society, in another by the Chipping Sodbury Ladies' Cycling Club and in another by the Lewisham Glass Blowers Hand Laundry.

As soon as these radio revues ended, Jack began work on a return to the real thing which would be his first peacetime offering. He joined Robert Nesbitt in rehearsals for a new show at the Prince of Wales which would be called *Fine Feathers*. This had many good things in it but perhaps suffered from too broad an appeal. Jack's West End qualities were combined with the north country comedy of Duggie Wakefield and the vivacious impersonations of Ethel Revnell.

Nevertheless, the show – as in Robert Nesbitt productions at 'The Talk of the Town' today – was superbly staged and its timing was well nigh perfect with the opening night only a month after the surrender of Japan. It found a ready response from London audiences starved of glamour and Jack had some excellent material. He had taken several of his old Charlot sketches and updated them for the occasion. Once again, a dream sequence brought Jack on with the girls as Turkish, Egyptian, Russian and Virginian cigarettes. Once again, he succeeded in reducing 'The old English Glee Quartet' to a shambles in its attempts to tell the world that 'The fox has left its lair'. He had a new sketch by Duggie Furber in which, as an old Etonian, Jack meets an old Harrovian on a desert island and, finding they have a notorious girl friend in common, tells him 'It was she who drove me to drink – and, bless my soul, I have never written to thank her'.

Fine Feathers was Jack's last West End revue. Although this was not apparent at the time, happily almost all the critics combined in their appreciation of the qualities he brought to the London theatre. In many ways, it was in revue that these skills were most apparent. For it brought out not only Jack's ability in song and dance but also his remarkable versatility in comedy, pathos and, above all, in the unique rapport he established with the audience. It was this 'take you into my confidence' style which endeared him to so many, including the critics.

The *Observer* said, 'If such a person as a man about town exists, he is undoubtedly the image of Mr Jack Buchanan, whose lazy charm now serves as a point of rest in this hurtling revue.' *The Times* took up the same theme suggesting that Jack was 'not merely Town, he is a particular quarter of the Town'. J. C. Trewin in *Punch* was even more specific about Jack's 'perpetual suggestion of a June morning haze over the slopes of Piccadilly and the trees of Green Park. Mr Buchanan is at once the most amiable of actors and the most metropolitan. Although, in the Gerald du Maurier manner, he is able to persuade us at times that he is not acting at all – he is acting – like du Maurier – hard at work'.

The principal cause for the critics' enthusiasm was a song which Jack sang and danced in the revue called *When Will They Liberate London* written by Vivian Ellis who had last worked with him in *Stand Up and Sing* in 1930. At that time, Vivian Ellis had been bitterly disappointed in finding that his songs were used by everyone except Jack. He recalls:

Now to our mutual dismay, my song was barred from being broadcast on the grounds that it was too controversial. Here is one of its more 'controversial' refrains:
When will they liberate London?
When will they set her free?
At half past eleven
You might be down in Devon
And the pubs turn you out at three.
When will they run some more buses
And why not send your M.P.
With a string bag, shopping,
To stand there till he's dropping,
And set London free?
 While writing these words the tune comes back to me. Not only the tune but that well remembered voice. True, I've heard better voices but none with that particular *timbre* that could give the most banal words an added meaning. That casual delivery, concealing masterly timing. Those seemingly artless dance routines – and again I've seen better dancers – that were, in fact, the outcome of hours of hard slogging.

Much of this preparation had been done in Brighton where *Fine Feathers* had had its try-out. Jack would carry on working through his meals at the Royal Crescent Hotel although, as Vivian Ellis found, those sessions could sometimes be disconcerting.

Supper was interrupted by the incessant ringing of the telephone. I gathered it was from a certain well known leading lady angrily demanding Jack's whereabouts and that of an attractive redhead from the chorus. Jack went on quietly eating – most of his actions were quiet – while Gilbert Brown, his manager, coped. It was the same story the following morning at breakfast – long silences broken by the crunching of toast. Actually, J.B.'s mind had rambled past the stage door into the theatre he loved and among the artists who loved him – some of them to distraction.

One of those artists was Coral Browne. The romantic relationship which had intrigued audiences in *The Last of Mrs Cheyney* had blossomed off stage. They shared the same down to earth sense of humour and Jack's reserve was offset by Coral Browne's salty tongue and extrovert qualities. There was talk of their marriage and many in the theatre world thought this could lead to a partnership which might rival that of Alfred Lunt and Lynn Fontanne.

From the end of the War, Jack and Coral spent much of their free time together. Coral Browne was still committed to appear for Firth Shepherd in plays at the Savoy but she and Jack were constantly looking for a suitable vehicle in which to resume their stage partnership.

For the moment, however, Jack needed a long break from acting to sort out his increasingly complex and financially strained affairs. There was the King's Theatre, Hammersmith and his film studios which were a continuing drain on his resources and he now had the major television finance commitments which require a detailed later account. Meanwhile, with Bernard Delfont, Jack had acquired a lease at the Garrick Theatre.

This partnership was one which Lord Delfont – as he now is – recalls as 'One of the happiest'. When Jack sought to take over the whole of the Garrick lease – to return to full actor/manager status – the partnership was ended in mutual agreement and goodwill.

The Garrick was now to become Jack's permanent working base. He installed himself there in the tiny management office under the roof and sought new projects which would ease his financial difficulties. One of the first saw yet another extension of Jack's professional activities. As his first production at the Garrick, he put on *Treble Trouble* in which he directed Richard Goolden (who recalls that Jack 'was much too nice and well mannered to crack the whip').

For his next production at the Garrick, Jack saw his opportunity to resume the partnership with Coral Browne. Hoping to repeat their earlier success with a Frederick Lonsdale revival, they joined with Austin Trevor and Heather Thatcher in *Canaries Sometimes Sing* which opened in November, 1947.

The choice of vehicle was unfortunate. The critics were virtually unanimous in complaining about the waste of talent in this nineteen twenties story of a *menage à quatre*. The four players were all praised; Coral Browne 'as one canary who pecks beautifully'; Heather Thatcher for 'making do admirably with shoddy material'; Austin Trevor as 'a delight playing a cloth headed conventional ex-soldier' and Jack, as his rival with 'the perfect

brandyside manner'. But as *The Times* summed up their problem: 'The weakness of the whole thing is that since none of the
characters can be supposed to care twopence for any of the others,
or indeed for anything, it soon ceases to matter what they do or
say.'

The public apparently shared the critics' views about the
worthless nature of the characters in the play. Austin Trevor has
recalled, however, that there was one totally dedicated admirer
who could be counted on to attend every performance. This was a
rat which on one particular night came and sat just under the
footlights out of view of the audience, but close enough to drive
Coral Browne and Heather Thatcher mad while it watched the
entire Third Act.

The rat was not the only animal to divert the cast and the
audience's attention. In the play, a live caged canary was used on
the set to symbolise the confined, narrow and selfish lives of the
four players. Coral Browne recalls: 'That canary did not utter a
cheep all through rehearsals. On the opening night, it took one
look at Jack and sang its guts out everytime he tried to say a line'.

Despite the setback in London, Jack and Coral took *Canaries
Sometimes Sing* out on a month's provincial tour and began
making plans for their future work together. Their debates on the
subject demonstrated a certain sharp edged humour which was
the solid basis of their mutual affection. Thus, when Coral was
invited to make a film called *Piccadilly Incident* Jack said, 'Ah,
ah, old girl, just wait till you get to Hollywood'. To which Coral
replied 'What – with a face this size?' Jack, in a true spirit of
encouragement ended the conversation by saying: 'The screen
was big enough to take Marie Dressler's face and she, too, went
into movies late in life!'

Coral was soon able to reply in kind. Alan Melville, Jack's
fellow Scot and life-long admirer, was now well established
following his success as the author of *Sweet and Low* and a
string of other successful revues. However, he had a yen to write a
straight comedy and was determined to produce something
which would be Jack's and Coral's next play together. He recalls:

I wrote the play so tailor-made for Jack that obviously no one
else could have ever played it. I spoke each of his lines aloud
after I'd written them – using my J.B. impersonation – and I
really knew I'd got him. I sent the script to his office at the
Garrick – managements were different in those days – quite a
lot of them could actually read and they were with certain
exceptions polite to authors. They certainly didn't keep a script
for months on end, and then send it back with a lot of coffee
stains or worse all over it, saying they felt it had dated. I got a
summons to see J.B. the very next day – there he was sitting at

the desk, having his boiled egg and wearing the trilby – and with my script right in front of him. He said 'I like it, old boy. Damn funny. But, of course, it isn't me. I'll put it on, but I could never play that part'.

Alan Melville and Coral Browne were devastated. Both felt that the play was perfect for the Buchanan/Browne partnership. It was Coral who finally convinced Jack in typical fashion when she said 'Of course it's you – you bloody fool. He's selfish, he knows he's only got to lift his little finger to have everyone swooning, he's got all the charm in the world and he's a very lovable high class shit. It's *you* dear!'

This loving compliment so impressed Jack that he agreed to play the lead in Alan's play. However, this would have to wait until the following year, for Jack was now committed to a series of American visits. These were concerned with three major objectives. First, Jack was deeply involved in his television business negotiations in America. Second, he planned a return appearance on Broadway. Finally, he had – unknown to Coral Browne – a new romantic interest in America which was totally to change his way of life.

Act 2~
Man and Wife

𝕸

Marriage in America

'SUE DARLING, COME AND meet an old friend of mine just arrived from England. Jack Buchanan, this is Suzzie Bassett.' This was how Jack and Suzzie were introduced to each other at a cocktail party in Nassau in January 1947.

Susan Bassett – an exquisitely beautiful tall, slim brunette – was the wife of Theodore (Ted) Bassett, one of America's leading amateur golfers. She came from Maryland – that lovely State lying on either side of Chesapeake Bay on the Atlantic shore which has always had a close affinity with England, stemming from its foundation in honour of Maria, wife of King Charles the First. The State flower of Maryland is the black eyed Susan and Suzzie Bassett – of the sparkling blue eyes – is a true daughter of the state.

She lives in Maryland today and it is her account from the journal she kept, from her diaries and, above all, from a lively and retentive memory that provides the basis for much of the material in Act II of my account.

Suzzie takes up the story of their first meeting:

The setting was worthy of one of Jack's Hippodrome productions – it was Nassau, the patio of a lovely house on Emerald Beach in early January 1947. It was a perfect night, warm and soft and the sea still alight with mauve and emerald tints, and we even had background music. The omnipresent Nassau guitar players were crooning in their 'conkey Joe' voices an old Nassau tune called 'Mah Lima Bean'. Perhaps not the most romantic tune for a first meeting, certainly not up to 'Fancy Our Meeting'. Anyway there wasn't anything very remarkable or memorable about the meeting, we were both guests at an early season cocktail party, most of us refugees from New York's icy blasts, or from England's damp cold.

Neither Jack nor I knew it then, or indeed for many months, but this was the beginning of a new world for both of us. For Jack the unfamiliar world that lies in a home with a wife and little step-daughter – for me the magical world of the theatre and limelight. We fell in love and we never fell out of it. Our new life together was to call for tremendous mutual adjustments, but it was always an adventure, and as the fairy tales go, we really lived happily ever after. Always love, and always fun. That is how it all began for Jack and me. We married two years and twelve days later.

'As Suzzie indicates, there was no instant recognition of their romance and, indeed, she had little idea of his interests and profession. For Suzzie had reached college age during the war and made an early marriage in America when there was virtually no opportunity to appreciate British films or theatre.

This led to a charming little scene which Jack and Dave Hutcheson were fond of recalling. Jack had brought Dave with him to Nassau, where his extrovert qualities quickly made him the centre of attention at parties. Jack, on the other hand, was there to rest and relax and that is precisely what he did. He had his swims, his golf and many evenings dined quietly alone and went to the movies. When he was at parties – as on this occasion – he was so shy that he seemed to stand in the corner or on the fringe of the crowd.

After the cocktail party, Suzzie was asked what she thought of the famous English actor and she replied that David Hutcheson was terribly attractive and immense fun. 'But he isn't the one I mean' said her host, 'the other one, Jack Buchanan, is the great star'.

Suzzie found that no one appreciated this story more than Jack. 'Lowered dignity, Suzzie,' he said 'it never fails, it's the basis of all comedy, and I've not suffered it myself for a long time.' If Jack and Suzzie found that they had a sense of humour in common, for Suzzie this was a difficult time:

> I was in Nassau with my husband, Ted Bassett, and our little daughter, Theo. We had taken a house called *Four Winds* out on Cable Beach, and had come down with our Nanny and Housekeeper to spend the season, as was our habit, from January until May. As wonderful as it was to be in the sun and away from the long cold New York winter, I was unhappy and confused. Our marriage wasn't working, and like many, seemed to have lost its meaning during the long separations of the War years. My husband and I were strangers to each other, and we shared so few interests that we grew further and further apart, and try as we might, we were unable to regain our early happiness together.

As extra men are always at a premium at any resort, particularly when they were as attractive and unattached as Jack, we began meeting over and over again. We seemed to gravitate naturally to each other at parties, often because in Nassau the usual after-dinner occupation is bridge, backgammon or gin rummy for high stakes. Jack seldom played cards, certainly couldn't play them well, and explained to me that his work in the theatre was entirely dependent on chance, he didn't find it relaxing to gamble for fun or excitement. I am a complete dunce at most card games, and a confirmed non-gambler. So as the tables were made up of the expert players, Jack and I were carefully avoided – no one wanted to lose with either of us. So we would find a quiet corner and indulge in the gentle art of conversation. I heard of his early childhood in Scotland, his boyhood vacations on the Isle of Arran, his early dreams of going in the Navy, and of his life in the theatre. He called himself 'The Buchanan Taxi Service' and frequently would drive me home from the Bahamian Club when I tired of waiting for Ted to finish at the 'Chemin de fer' table, coming in for a late swim with me and my current house guests, and fixing bacon and eggs as the dawn came up. This was what he loved best, being with a few cosy people talking 'pro' talk, new and fascinating to me.

This was the real Jack Buchanan, difficult, I suppose for his many fans to visualize. A quiet, humble man, with tremendous humour and a rare sense of the ridiculous. But never the centre of the stage at any party. He acted and performed on the stage, never off.

Jack and Suzzie met again in New York in the summer of 1947, but it was not until their long separation from September 1947 to March 1948 that their marriage plans began to take shape. During this period, Suzzie and Ted Bassett had separated and she was living in a flat at 400 Park Avenue in New York with her daughter, Theo.

It was a difficult time for both Jack and Suzzie. He was tied to his desk at the Garrick Theatre trying to recoup – through the sale of his film studios – substantial losses on the King's Theatre, Hammersmith and his television business. Suzzie had all the problems of making separation and divorce arrangements which she hoped to complete at Reno in the autumn.

Meanwhile, she and Jack were constantly in touch by transatlantic telephone calls. When Jack sailed for New York on 19 March, 1948, it was clear that 'the eternal bachelor' was unlikely to remain single for much longer. As Suzzie's journal records:

From the time that we met in January 1947, until we married in January 1949, Jack made six round trips across the Atlantic, always on either the *Queen Elizabeth I* or the *Queen Mary*.

It became a running gag with the crews of the ship. Between the expense of the trips, and the expense of the transatlantic telephone calls, I think he figured that in the long run it was a much better, and more economical idea, to marry me and take me back to England.

The only immediate threat to this plan was Suzzie's eight-year-old daughter. Theo was a solemn little girl, obviously – in Suzzie's words – 'feeling the effects of the last confusing year, her home changed, her parents separated and so much strangeness for a child to assimilate. She had become possessive of me, she no longer had her nanny, and the more we were together, the more she liked it. She told me when we moved to our new apartment that she didn't really miss Daddy as he was always at the golf club, she saw more of me, and that she didn't know why ladies bothered with husbands.'

Jack had to postpone his efforts in winning over Theo. While in America, his energies were fully diverted to his television business, his help with the divorce arrangements – in which he used his good relationship with Ted Bassett to smooth over many of the obstacles – and the new challenge which faced him in returning to the Broadway stage after an absence of ten years.

Jack was to appear in *Harvey* the whimsical Brock Pemberton play about a man and the imaginary rabbit with whom he converses. The play was one of Broadway's biggest hits and Jack had to follow his friend, Jimmy Stewart, who had made the part virtually his own. Jack's appearance was for a short season at the 48th Street Theatre. Suzzie recalls:

He had to work up the part in the most difficult circumstances. Because the play was already established, union rules prevented the management from altering the set between performances. There were two different sets in *Harvey*, the family sitting room and the doctor's waiting room. Jack had to rehearse in the sitting room set with a single work light and without the help of any of the other actors.

On his first night, I went with Bob Nesbitt who had come over to New York on business with Jack. It was a good house but it was not a gala occasion. Jack was simply one of the guest stars taking over the lead for a short run. The first entrance for Jack as Elwood P. Dowd is when he comes on with a picture under his arm of himself and the rabbit.

When he made the entrance, Bob Nesbitt whispered to me 'My God, he's on roller skates' and he certainly seemed to be rushing things. I had never seen him work on the stage before and I was worried about the American audience's reaction. But he slowed the part down and won them over in the way he always did. It became one of his favourite plays. He loved its philosophy which suited the fey Scottish side of his nature and he always said that Edward P. Dowd was 'the loveliest part made for man'.

The American Press were intrigued by Jack's appearance in *Harvey* and gave him rave reviews. The *Brooklyn Eagle* said:

Something akin to a tingle of exhilaration came to the audience of the 48th Street Theatre last night, with the appearance of Jack Buchanan. He performed with alcoholic suavity and a wistful handling of the part brought out the laughs as early as the first scene in the first act.'

The *New York World Telegram* said:

The most obvious challenge to anyone taking over the lead in *Harvey* is how the newcomer will compare with Frank Fay who created the part. It must be stated that Mr Buchanan acquitted himself with honour at his opening performance. As might be expected from so experienced a theatre man, his best scene is also the most difficult. Half way through the play, there is a long monologue when Dowd explains to his invisible long-eared friend just what his friendship with the rabbit means to him.
Here Mr Buchanan was splendid, demonstrating all the pathos of a man who chooses to be simple in a childlike way, realising that the sophisticated world would have little patience with him. Hard-boiled Broadway characters were admitting last night that Buchanan had them choked up.

Immediately after *Harvey*, Jack and Robert Nesbitt began negotiations with Vincent Freedly to put a British revue on Broadway. This was a project which was close to Jack's heart and he hoped there might even be an opportunity of a reunion with Gertie and Bea so that a new American generation could see the Charlot triumvirate that had triumphed on Broadway soon after the First World War.

Nothing came of these negotiations and Jack had to content himself with an offer to appear in a straight play on Broadway during the coming winter season. His reasons for seeking a prompt and lengthy return to New York were now personal rather than business, for he and Suzzie had agreed to marry after her divorce.

Meanwhile, Jack began a period of hectic Atlantic commuting. His diaries show that he returned to London at the beginning of June in time to put on *The Lady Asks for Help* at the Garrick in which Bill Kendall appeared. A few weeks later, his sale of the Riverside Film Studios was completed and Bill was with Jack when he received his cheque for a quarter of a million pounds. This was an enormous sum in 1948 and Bill said 'All you need to do, old boy, is to put it on deposit, perhaps put on one show a year and you need have no more money problems'. But Jack had substantial debts to clear and major investment commitments.

On 23 July he sailed for New York on virtually a round trip. He saw Suzzie off to Reno where she was to get her divorce. There were business meetings with his old music publisher friend, Louis Dreyfus and his American impresario collaborator, Gilbert Miller. He was back in London by 12 August. Jack had now rented a house at 8 Hay's Mews where he returned hospitality to many old friends, who, he thought, he might not see for a long period if his private and professional plans materialised in America.

There were drinks and dinner parties with The Gang and their partners for, strangely, they too showed every sign of becoming domesticated. Bill Kendall was Obie Fitzwilliam's constant escort, Elsie Randolph was now Mrs Vernon Handley-Page and Dave Hutcheson was soon to marry the Countess of Warwick. On nights out with the boys, Jack saw 'Prendy', Fred Emney and Duggie Furber.

On 16 September, he sailed for New York on the *Queen Elizabeth* for yet another round trip. He arrived in time to greet Suzzie on her return from Reno and California where she had regained single status. The American press were, by this time, curious about Jack's constant to-ings and fro-ings but they were happily misled by Jack, who took the opportunity of announcing that he was bringing an all British company to open on Broadway in Sacha Guitry's *Don't Listen Ladies* which was then playing to capacity audiences in London.

On his return to London, Jack began rehearsals for the play which was to have a short try-out in Brighton at the end of November before the company sailed to New York on 15 December. There was a hectic round of chores, fittings at Hawes and Curtis for a new suit and shirts, and meetings with lawyers and accountants to resolve Suzzie's future citizenship and taxation status after she was married to Jack. These were complex matters particularly as both Jack and Suzzie felt it was right that Theo should retain her American nationality.

All this left Jack – never a quick study – with little time to learn his part in *Don't Listen Ladies*. This would have been an exceptional challenge at the best of times since the play was to open with Jack speaking a long soliloquy. Alan Melville came to see the play at the Theatre Royal, Brighton and recalls:

> Jack dried up at least half a dozen times quite early in the proceedings. There was one of those terrifying wraiths in the prompt corner who mumbled instead of giving the prompt loudly and clearly. At about the fifth or sixth dry, Jack couldn't hear what the missing line was: he strolled across in his usual

nonchalant fashion to the prompt corner and said 'What was that?' Mumble, mumble, mumble said the wraith. When at last he got the gist of the line, he said all too audibly for the audience 'Good God . . . only the top of page *two?*'

Only Jack could have got away with this and he even managed to raise a cheer from the audience. His relaxed attitude revealed his inner contentment. He was soon to be married and he looked forward to a long run in a play which *Variety's* London correspondent described as 'a frothy typically Gallic comedy which brings a breath of Paris to jaded London . . . its scintillating nonsense should sparkle for many months to come and it will soon delight New Yorkers.'

Jack and his Company therefore sailed for New York in confident and happy mood. He was delighted to have playing with him old friends in Adele Dixon, Ivy St Helier and Austin Trevor. For his leading lady, Jack had chosen the glamorous South African Moira Lister who had just had a great success in Noël Coward's *Present Laughter* and who was making her début on Broadway.

She recalls her excitement at the marvellous reaction the company received on its arrival: 'It was incredible. Being who he was, there were parties thrown for us every night. My room was filled with whisky, paper tissues and even baby's diapers (I don't quite know what they thought I was going to use them for). Anyway, it was all part of the big American hullo. Whenever we went to Sardi's or the Twenty One, Jack would be greeted by everyone and we were all included in a feeling of tremendous welcome.'

Jack, however, had some worries about the play. As he told one reporter: 'First there was the seamen's strike; then there was the great fog over England, and when we finally did get to sea it was simply one gale after another all the way across the Atlantic. We had planned to play a fortnight in Boston before bringing the show to the Booth, but now that's been cut to a weekend at Montclair. I guess it's nothing we can't rise above' he ended optimistically.

After the weekend opening in Montclair, New Jersey on Christmas Eve, Jack's cheerfulness seemed justified. The local press enthused over 'This sprightly and personable British cast . . . Jack Buchanan, looking for all the world like Clifton Webb and minus the songs and dances he used to do, does the Guitry role to perfection.' But the New York critics generally took a harsher view after the opening night at the Booth Theatre on 28 December. *Time* Magazine said 'Suave Jack Buchanan of Charlot Revue fame behaves towards the script as a man of gallantry pretends that an aged flirt is still a lustrous belle'. For *Cue* Jack gave his lines 'the maximum of eloquence,' Moira Lister was

'appropriately succulent' as the wife and Adele Dixon 'equally
attractive' as her predecessor. But the play depended 'almost
entirely on the eternal Gallic preoccupation with the epigram
and the horizontal.' The key to the critics' displeasure almost
certainly lay in the author. New York newspapermen believed
that Sacha Guitry had been anti-Semitic during the occupation
of France and the all powerful Walter Winchell went so far as to
hope that he choked on his royalties.

But the players did not need the critics' reaction to tell them
about the play's prospects. As Adele Dixon recalls: 'The audience greeted us in complete silence. American audiences are
very strange. They don't boo or hiss. They were just completely
silent and walked out. The curtain came down and we had one
call but it is nerve-wracking to take a call in virtually dead
silence.'

For Moira Lister, the failure of the play was a devastating
experience:

> Having had this extraordinary reception when we first arrived –
> the great Jack Buchanan bringing a British company over
> made the contrast of people's reaction after the play all the
> more poignant. The moment we opened and the play was a
> disaster, those same people who had entertained us earlier – if
> you saw them in a room – they turned their backs. It was really
> a horrifying experience. For example, when we went to Sardi's
> only a few nights after we had been fêted there, some of the
> same people buried their heads in their food and pretended
> they hadn't seen us.
>
> The American management posted the closure notice on
> our first night, something which, thank God, has never hap-
> pened to me before or since. However, very foolishly, Jack kept
> the play on at his own expense for six weeks. He didn't want an
> outright failure, wanted to be with Suzzie and he was very
> generous to all of us like myself for whom this was a first great
> opportunity on Broadway.

But for Suzzie, the disappointment over the play's failure was
even more personal as the plans for the wedding in April now
looked forlorn. Under Equity rules Jack, as a foreign performer,
would not be allowed to open another show for six months.
Meanwhile, the meagre allowance of dollars allowed to him by
the Bank of England would soon be exhausted.

Suzzie's journal records subsequent events:

> The first few days after the show closed we were faced by
> several dilemmas, lack of dollars, the heartbreaking prospect of
> being separated again and my responsibilities towards Theo.
> One day, lunching in his sitting room at the Ritz-Carlton,
> while we were trying to find a solution, a cable was delivered,

which Jack – with his usual exquisite manners – put on his chair arm, unopened, as we chatted. I was curious and insisted he read it and he said 'It will probably be just my accountant asking for 'another thousand pounds, ol' boy.' Anyway, he eventually opened the cable. It was from London asking if Jack would return immediately to replace Francis Lister in the London production of *Don't Listen Ladies* with Constance Cummings, as Lister was too ill to continue.

We were stunned, it seemed the obvious choice, and I said as much. Jack said 'I'll only go on one condition. That is – you must marry me at once so that we can sail on the return Maiden voyage of the *Caronia* on Saturday.' I said 'But darling today is Tuesday' and Jack replied 'I know but we can do it if we get our skates on.' Thanks to the help of friends that's precisely what we did.

On 14 January 1949, Jack and Suzzie were married at a friend's house in Lakeville, Connecticut by their host, Cambell Becket, who was a local judge. Jack's chauffeur, MacDonald was one of their witnesses. Even he was taken completely by surprise. Acting as Jack's valet on the trip to America, he asked why Jack needed his new Hawes and Curtis formal grey suit for what he assumed would be a weekend in the country. 'Because I'm getting married in it' Jack replied.

In England, the British Press had a field day as 'Eternal Bachelor Jack Weds American Society Girl'. For some of Jack's friends in the theatre the news came as a distinct shock. Alan Melville has told how he was lunching with Coral Browne when the news came through. He was worried in case Jack would not now be able to appear in his new play and Coral, who took the news much more personally 'went right off her lunch'.

When the *Caronia* docked in Southampton the press were there in force to greet the newly-weds. As Suzzie's journal records:

My first experience with the press was a terrifying one but I had on one of the first 'New Look' outfits, which caused quite a sensation. Jack carefully coached me, trying to avoid the obvious pitfalls – particularly about what I thought of England, and what I intended to eat. A few weeks before Lana Turner had got a very bad press. When asked about food, she had said that as there was nothing to eat, she had brought masses of steaks to eat while in England. When they asked me that one, I said I expected to eat exactly what everyone else did.

We had left Theo behind with my devoted housekeeper. We planned to go back and collect her, then on to a delayed honeymoon in Nassau and bring her back with us to London. During the press conference, one of the reporters looked around the stateroom and asked 'Where's the little girl?' Before

I could answer, a familiar voice purred 'Here I am' and Elsie Randolph made a star entrance, in mink and a hat covered with egret feathers. She had driven down with her chauffeur-driven Rolls to fetch us and drive us to London.

A few nights later, Jack and Suzzie made their first public appearance together when he went on for his first performance at the St James Theatre in *Don't Listen Ladies*. At the start of the long soliloquy, Jack reflects on the problems of a man who is married to a wife twenty-five years younger than himself. As this was almost the same age difference as that between Jack and Suzzie – and since Jack had been so long a bachelor – the audience listened to his opening speech with particular care. When he came on and spoke the opening words 'Never marry' the entire audience rose and gave both Buchanans a standing ovation.

Left, *Jack and Suzzie's wedding picture presented to their cook, Minnie Harris, after arriving on the* Caronia *in 1949. Above, Suzzie and Theo. Below, 'Life with J.B. at 44, Mount Street' – J.B., Suzzie, George Macdonald and the Rolls with the Bonzo mascot.*

New Life

As HE HAD GONE straight into the London production of *Don't Listen Ladies*, Jack had little time to see much of his new family. Unlike his New York experience he was now involved with a solid hit at the St James Theatre. The part of the middle-aged French antique dealer with a young second wife caught the imagination of London theatregoers. They particularly enjoyed Jack's confidential asides to the audience when – immaculate as ever in his Anderson and Sheppard suits – he would come to the footlights and preface his remarks with the phrase that gave the play its title 'Ladies, I implore you – please don't listen'. He would then deliver himself of a few cynical observations about women.

Jack was in no way embarrassed when the Press called him 'Evergreen' and made the obvious connection between his public role in *Don't Listen Ladies* and his private life with a young wife. He had never been fitter, his energy was boundless and he took the greatest pride in the stir that Suzzie made. Soon after their arrival in England, Jack took her for supper at the Savoy Grill. By then the newsreel and press coverage had made all London aware that Jack was married. During dinner, Suzzie was conscious of the keen interest which every woman in the room was taking in her. Eventually, she recalls: 'I got up and went to the powder room. As I did so, at least half a dozen other ladies followed me. One of them – rather more bejewelled and perhaps a bit tighter than the rest – came straight up to me and said "How did you get him to propose?" At that stage in our lives, I wasn't fully aware of Jack's "elusive" history but, in any event, I said "He just asked me".'

But Jack and Suzzie could not avoid some of the inevitable problems in the marriage between a 'pro' and a 'non-pro'. While *Don't Listen Ladies* was still running, Jack was already thinking of his next play. This would honour his commitment to appear as an impoverished Scottish Earl in Alan Melville's play *Castle in the Air* with Coral Browne as his leading lady. Planning of the production was complex as Jack had promised to take Suzzie off on their delayed honeymoon in Nassau before starting an eleven week tour of the new play. Consequently, he was involved in several working lunches with his author and leading lady. This led to Jack's and Suzzie's first 'tiff'.

Suzzie, like every other newly-wed, was not over enthusiastic about being excluded from these meetings between Jack and his old girl friend. When she expressed her disappointment, Jack just said, very quietly, 'Darling, you really must understand that these are working sessions. If you come along, we would not be able to confine ourselves strictly to "shop". In this business one has to get together with one's leading lady and there's no point in feeling jealous. We have to trust each other or we'll simply be burned up in no time at all.'

Suzzie accepted Jack's advice but her suspicions about his reluctance for her to meet Coral Browne were well founded. Jack – who loathed rows – was worried lest any lingering resentment on either side might lead to an explosion on sight. In this he did the two ladies less than justice. Coral Browne's theatrical friends all agree that her somewhat basic conversation hides one of the softest, most generous spirits in the business. Suzzie, who would not have been slow to recognise this, already had enormous respect for Coral's superb acting talent.

Nevertheless Jack – who all through his life would go to enormous trouble to avoid off stage drama – decided to enlist Alan Melville's assistance. He takes up the story: 'We opened the tour in Bournemouth and I was detailed off by J.B. as a sort of bodyguard and keeper-aparter. After a few days of this, Suzzie and I decided it was crazy and I took her round to Coral's dressing room. The two ladies looked at each other and both said "Well!" and became bosom chums there and then, as they still are to this day.'

Castle in the Air opened at the Adelphi Theatre on 10 December, 1949. This theatre had not been Jack's first choice. It is huge and usually reserved for large scale musicals rather than plays with a cast of five. However, the National Coal Board decided to give a helping hand.

While the play was still touring, they let it be known that they were not happy with the plot. This concerned Jack as an impoverished Scottish Peer whose Castle is threatened by a compulsory purchase order under which it would be converted to a miners' hostel. It was announced that two Coal Board officials had purchased seats in the back stalls for the opening night and, in a press statement, the N.C.B. said:

> The Board has had several reports from people who have seen the play while it was on its pre-London tour, that there were lines to which offence might be taken and our attention was drawn to the fact that it is opening in London. It was suggested that we ought to see for ourselves whether there were passages which might cause complaints. We asked to attend a rehearsal, we also asked to see the script. The answer given was that it had been passed by the Lord Chamberlain's Department which was the only form of censorship recognised by the theatre.

Jack and Eric Braun (who was handling the show's publicity) were delighted with this manna from heaven and invited every newspaper in London to be present in strength for the opening. Sure enough, the two officials appeared and, after the show, approached Stanley French – who was presenting the show with Jack – saying that there were offensive references to the Board in the play and that they wanted an assurance all references to it would be removed before the next performance. Otherwise, they would report the matter to the Coal Board who would consider bringing the matter before the courts with a view to having the show closed.

This pompous announcement was precisely in keeping with the stuffy image of the N.C.B. conveyed by Bill Kendall who played the official who tells Jack 'We have powers to requisition'.

The purists pointed out that, in real life, the N.C.B. could not obtain requisitioning powers, the Board's legal threats looked extremely flimsy and their attitude left them wide open to ridicule. The newspapers' response was well summed up in a *Daily Mirror* editorial headed 'National Board Of Comedians' which said in part:

> It is a cherished convention that officialdom is pompous, self-important and continually making itself absurd for the delight of the population. To the happiness of every breakfast table, here is the National Coal Board fitting these conditions to the letter and making a fool of itself because somebody has made a joke about it on the stage. We say to the N.C.B. 'We don't mind your entertaining us, but clowns should not seek to be censors. Is your coal face red? It ought to be.'

Next day, the Coal Board – having made a laughing stock of themselves – climbed down and said no further action was envisaged. But as Jack said to Alan Melville 'They've given us £10,000 worth of free publicity and the advance bookings are just like musical business, old boy'. To those who asked whether he had encouraged the Coal Board's intervention, Jack would reply with a twinkle in his eye 'Don't ask me, old boy; if people are determined to make bloody fools of themselves, let 'em'.

Amid all this furore, there was a danger that the intrinsic merits of the show and its performers might be lost. But as the *Evening Standard* said: 'Even without the intervention of the Coal Board, *Castle in the Air* would have won its own public.' All the players were praised and of Jack's performance the report said 'As a light comedian he has a sense of timing that is a joy to watch'.

This was not lightly acquired. Alan Melville in his first play for Jack was deeply impressed by his thoroughness of approach to all aspects of the production:

> The care with which Jack put on *Castle in the Air* – as well as playing the leading part so superbly – was typical of the man. He engaged the then unknown Malcolm Mitchell Trio to play in the interval. Usually there was that tired old pianist or maybe a scratchy record or two on the public address system. But Jack had seen the Mitchell Boys somewhere and thought they were great and deserved a break which they certainly got.
>
> Then there was a line in the play spoken by Jack to Bill Kendall who was supposed to be looking over his country house.
>
> Jack: 'It seems to be the ideal place for you, it's got forty-eight bedrooms'
> Bill: 'Running water in all?'
> Jack: 'In some cases, only down the wall'
>
> God knows it wasn't hysterical but it never raised a titter all week in Bournemouth and this really got Jack down. We played Edinburgh the following week, and on the Monday afternoon, I went to the theatre to collect some tickets and for some reason went into the back of the stalls. There on stage was Johnny B. alone with a single working light. He had no idea I was in the theatre but I sat down and watched him fascinated for over half an hour in which he said that one single line about 'Only down the wall' over and over again in every possible different way. And then suddenly, he knew he'd got it: he snapped his fingers triumphantly and marched off the stage. That night and for every performance during the next two years, he never got to the end of the line because of the laugh.

In so small a cast, such dedication helped to promote the happy feeling of truly playing together. The company of five and their small band of support staff and relations were soon knit together into a family. When Euan Roberts – who so effectively played Jack's 'man of all work and no pay' – was about to become a father, 'You would,' Suzzie remarks, 'have thought that the company was having the child'. His wife, Marjorie Vosper, had a long and difficult labour and, in the final stages, there were bulletins given out as each member of the cast came offstage. At the christening party, the entire company appeared.

They were almost all present soon afterwards in Hertfordshire when Coral Browne married Jack's understudy, Philip Pearman. Suzzie had a new Lachasse dress for the occasion of which Jack said 'You're not supposed to outdo the bride, baby. You've had your great day', quickly amending this with an apologetic smile, 'Or rather, I should say you've had your two days to shine'.

At the wedding reception, the champagne flowed freely and Coral Browne recalls how Jack's dry sense of humour was in evidence: 'When we were all very nicely thank you, Johnny B came up to Philip just as we were about to leave on our honeymoon and said "Well ol' boy, you've got the girl and *now* you've got the part. You can go on for me tonight!"

O

Old Friends

WHEN ON TOUR WITH *Castle in the Air*, Jack and Suzzie had an opportunity of seeing many of Jack's old friends. The tour began in Brighton where, one evening after supper, Ivor Novello played the score of his new musical *Gay's the Word* and Suzzie played canasta with Bill, Ivor's dresser and Juliette Duff. The following week, the Buchanans were in Yorkshire staying at the industrialist, Bob Asquith's, house. Jack – with his insatiable curiosity – went on visits to local industry and played golf with Bill Kendall. Suzzie explored the delights of the Brontë country and good Yorkshire cooking.

This opportunity for culinary appreciation was one of the great advantages in early post-war touring. For austerity Britain in 1950 still had food rationing except for those staying at hotels. Jack with his long standing friendship and patronage was given the hero's treatment wherever he went. Nowhere was this more evident that in his birthplace. When the tour reached Scotland, Jack was greeted as a long lost member of the family by Luigi, the *maitre d'hôtel* in the Malmaison Restaurant at the Central Hotel in Glasgow.

When the tour went on to Aberdeen, Suzzie was introduced to Arbroath smokies and haggis. She also came face to face with the stern Scottish sex discrimination which kept her waiting in the Steward's Room of the Royal Aberdeen Golf Club – rather than the clubhouse – while Jack and Bill finished their round. Before the provincial tour ended, Suzzie also came literally face to face with some of the demands imposed on celebrities. When they were checking out of the Central Hotel in Glasgow, she saw a woman come up to Jack. There was a brief moment of conversation before Jack raised his hat and – with heightened colour – rejoined her. 'What was all that about?' asked Suzzie. 'Would you believe it?' said Jack, 'That woman came up to me and said how much she'd enjoyed my performance last night but would I mind if she asked one question that had been running through her mind all evening. I said, "Of course not", thinking it would be something to do with the play. "Well", she said "do tell me. Are your teeth your own?" and I said "They certainly are. Here, do you want to feel them to make sure?".'

After some of the hazards of touring, it was almost a settled domestic life again when the tour moved on to Golders Green and Croydon and the Buchanans could live at home. Home was now 44 Mount Street in Mayfair. Jack and Suzzie had found the bachelor flat at Aldford House too small – although they managed to do a good deal of entertaining before they left. They often saw the other Gang newly-weds, David and Mary Hutcheson. There was also a constant stream of friends travelling to and from America. Jack's Hollywood co-star Jeannette Macdonald arrived with her husband Gene Raymond who talked about a possible appearance in a new play *Detective Story* which Jack had bought in America. Michael Rennie – then one of Britain's most successful film stars – came to dinner just before leaving with his wife Maggie McGrath (who had been one of Jack's glamour girls in *Fine Feathers*) to work in Hollywood for the first time. There were charity functions to attend and Jack and Suzzie would often go on to Ciro's for supper on the balcony. On one such occasion, shortly before they left Aldford House, the Press insisted on taking a picture of 'The Buchanans at Home'. This maintained the elegant standard expected by the public with Suzzie in her Michael ball gown made from Nassau material and Jack in his familiar top hat and tails.

At weekends, the Buchanans sought escape from the hectic work and play commitments of town. At the end of the War, Jack had become friendly with Lord and Lady Selsdon who had a charming country house at Hollycombe. Peter and Betty Selsdon were a dashing pair. He was a racing driver who had won the Le Mans Twenty-Four Hours Motor Race. Betty as a glamorous débutante had met and danced with Jack at the Four Hundred Club. Their friendship grew despite Jack's impatience when he found that Betty Selsdon had swallowed all the stories about his imminent demise from T.B. which she recalls 'made me dance with him at arm's length as though he was made of glass'.

For step-daughter Theo, these were happy times. Now married with children of her own, she recalls:

He *was* my father. Of course, I had my own father of whom I was and still am very fond. But Johnnie B. was a *real* person. There was nothing false about him. Looking back on those childhood years, I realise that he gave me so much. He always had time for me. Especially if one had a problem, he would always help anyone out in any way he could.

I suppose that was his charm. It wasn't just charm for women. He had it for men too and especially for children. I think children instinctively spot a phoney but, with him, his charm was as natural as breathing.

Jack showed his devotion to Theo in many ways. He took the keenest interest in her progress at Lady Eden's day school in Kensington. When in London, he would visit her arousing squeals from the little ones and blushes from the matron, with even Lady Eden peeping through the curtain to see the arrival of her hero.

When Theo was appearing in her first school play, Jack gave her the full professional treatment. He booked an appointment with Nathan's, the theatrical costumiers, and made her up himself. When she went on, Jack was as nervous as if this was his own first night. He stayed to the end and almost missed his own performance.

When Jack was touring, there would be little notes and poetic messages from the actor manager to his new pupil. On one occasion, he wrote an end of term poem:

You are the girl I always misses
When you're away with all those cisses
So welcome home to chips and fisses
And lots and lots of love and kisses.

When Theo had her tonsils out, Jack sent her a special 'get well' poem looking forward to their next weekend at Hollycombe:

Now your tonsils are no more
And King Farouk has gone home sore
We shall go and have some fun
Down at good old Hollycum
Oh me, oh my, oh mercy me
How clever can that Johnnie B?

Back in town, Jack and Suzzie were soon entertaining as often as ever in their new home in Mount Street. At their house warming party, Alan Melville sent a telegram with a quotation from Jack's favourite poet, Robbie Burns: 'Lang may your lum reek'. Sylvia and Danny Kaye came for supper. So, too, did Laurence Olivier and 'Prendy' whenever he was in London. Then there were the 'outside events'. Jack was able to arrange for Suzzie and Theo to see the Trooping of the Colour with the

Duke of Gloucester. They came on to join him for one of the last of the theatrical garden parties where he was auctioning ladies' hats, keeping up a flow of patter which, eventually, compelled him to buy his own wares ('Do you want it, baby? Well no one else does so its yours – and very pretty you'll look!'). There were the lunches and dinners at their favourite dining club, 14 Duke Street. When the British Tourist Chief, Sandy Maxwell, spotted them there one day, Jack was at one table with Suzzie and her ex-husband Ted Bassett. At the next sat Lord Warwick and his ex-wife Rosie who was about to marry Ted Bassett. They all joined up for coffee and, in the process, so confused Sandy Maxwell that he left in disarray.

Towards the end of the year, more friends arrived from America. Beatrice Lillie opened in cabaret at the Café de Paris and, on the first night, Jack was terribly nervous for his old friend. Gloria Stewart, Jimmy's wife, arrived in town and the Buchanans took her to see *His Excellency* in a private box. Clifton Webb took them to the première of his new film and then on to Noël Coward's birthday party. This was a grand affair at Noël's studio in Gerald Road. Suzzie recalls:

> When we got there, we seemed to be stuck with some of Noël's more sycophantic fans. In any event, Jack and Clifton had always been great chums and were dying to catch up on each other's news. So we found a quiet corner and a table for the three of us where there was lots of Champagne. We were immersed in deep conversation and the time simply flew. Suddenly we were aware that there was hardly anyone around us except The Master himself who said 'It's terribly late and you really must go home'. At this, Clifton who was always a great one for putting on his outraged dignity act, said 'Jackson (he always called Jack that), I have never been so insulted in my life; would you be good enough to escort me from this sordid scene?'

New Year's Eve and New Year's Day 1951 were spent quietly at Mount Street with David and Mary Hutcheson. This was a true Scottish Hogmanay celebration marred only by Dave's attempt to cure Mary's hangover by dispensing Jack's finest liqueur brandy with ginger ale as a cure. Jack was not amused.

He had now finished his long run in *Castle in the Air*. There were plans for a new play by Alan Melville for Jack and Coral Browne. For Jack, however, the classic actor's term 'resting' was singularly inappropriate. He was busy with television and radio work and there were lunches and dinners at Duke Street after the ballet in Covent Garden with Sir Malcolm Sargent and Alicia Markova. This was part of their collaboration for a documentary film on *Giselle* which was released in the following year with a narration spoken by Jack. He was also busy reading plays both as possible vehicles for himself and for the Garrick where, soon afterwards, he put on *The Gay Invalid* with A. E. Matthews and the longtime Hollywood star, Elizabeth Bergner. For business reasons – because he hated anyone else's first night as much as his own – he took Suzzie to the opening of *Kiss Me Kate*, to Laurence Olivier's production of the Menotti opera *The Consul* (which Jack found impressive and moving) and, with Bob and Iris Nesbitt, to *The Latin Quarter*.

There were, however, some private moments. On Sunday nights in London, the Buchanans would often go to see films at the Plaza (which Suzzie found 'the most comfortable cinema in the world') and then home for Martini sessions with 'Mah Baby'. There were weekends in Brighton where Jack and Suzzie began to spend more and more time with new friends like the theatrical impresario, Al Parker, and his actress wife, Maggie Johnstone and old friends such as Anna Neagle and Herbert Wilcox. On one such weekend, Jack was persuaded to play golf in a 'Pro-Am' tournament at East Brighton where he put two tee shots in the hedge at the first tee to the delight of a large gallery.

On backstage visits, Jack and Suzzie took Theo to see Fred Emney in *Blue for a Boy*. There had been terrible jokes and asides from Fred during the show and, afterwards, he slipped Theo a pound while Jack gave him the usual treatment by patting his tummy and saying, in a terrible voice, 'How's everything old darling?'

On another visit 'behind', Jack and Suzzie went to see Ivor Novello at the Palace Theatre early in the run of *King's Rhapsody*. In his dressing room after the show – with the hefty financial takings written in lipstick on the mirror – Jack said to Ivor 'You *are* a clever son of a bitch. You hardly ever appear, and when you do it's in the best scene and while you're off they do nothing but talk about *you*.' Jack went on to say how he wished Ivor would write a play like this for him with perhaps a shade more comedy. Ivor replied, 'Yes, you should be playing this, Jack. I don't know what to do in the drunk scene with Vanessa.' 'Fair do ol' boy,' said Jack, 'and I would never have the nerve to do your ending.'

This conversation came back to Jack and Suzzie with cruel irony in the first week of March when Coral Browne rang to say that, immediately after one of his nightly performances at the Palace Theatre, Ivor had died. At the funeral the following week in Golders Green, sitting with Anna Neagle and Herbert Wilcox, they reflected sadly on the loss of Charles Cochran only a few days earlier and now one of Jack's first friends in the theatre, who had done so much in helping with his early success.

Bobby Andrews – who had always been the court jester in

Ivor's close knit circle – tried to cheer everyone up by saying 'Ivor wouldn't be here himself if he could help it'. For Suzzie this was one of her first experiences of the horror of celebrity funerals with fans waiting for autographs outside the church and running after the departing cars to see who was inside. Jack hated all this and felt – with Suzzie – that the massive crowds were not only frightening, but destroyed any sense of dignity.

Suzzie's journal takes up the story:

The day after the funeral, 13 March, Jack came home from the office for lunch, sat in his chair opposite me in the drawing room, looked long and hard at me and said 'Baby, they want me to take over Ivor's part in *King's Rhapsody.*' We both stared at each other frozen and goosebumped all over. 'Tom Arnold came to see me this morning. It seems they feel I am the only one to follow Ivor in this role; the company would be happy with me and no-one else. Do you remember how Ivor and I joked about it the night we went backstage? It is almost as if it were meant to be. Tom remembered what Ivor said to me that night, and Ivor had said to Zena and Olive and Bobby, how well he thought I would play the part, that it suited me better than it did him. What do you think, baby? Alan's play isn't ready, I'm restless and want to go back to work, nothing else on the horizon, I think I can play the part, the question is will they accept me, the audience, I mean, in Ivor's place.' 'For a start,' I said, 'let's have a monster gin and tonic, because, of course you'll do it. There are several perfectly good and emotional reasons why you should, and also you've already been thinking of what you could do with the drunk scene, haven't you?' Jack looked at me with his quizzical sideways look and said 'My God, the little women, you can't beat them. But is it all right with you, darling? We missed our American trip because of Theo's measles and if I take this and open in two weeks, which is what Tom wants, it means no trip home for you for some time, that is unless I'm an almighty flop in the part.'

Two weeks feverish rehearsals followed, Jack learnt the part very quickly and I worked with him every evening for hours on the script. There was a frantic rush for his costume fittings. He wouldn't wear the same kind of dressing gown and went off to his beloved Hawes and Curtis to get something special for the occasion. As the time went on he became more and more nervous and on the 1 April, the Sunday dress rehearsal, he was in a panic. He had his usual tummy trouble coming back again and I gave him milk and soda and poached eggs and hoped for the best.

Palace Theatre – 'King's Rhapsody'

JACK'S FIRST APPEARANCE IN *King's Rhapsody* was at the Palace Theatre at the top of Shaftesbury Avenue on Monday evening, 2 April 1951, his sixty-first birthday. Suzzie's journal reflects the nervousness they both felt:

> I sat in my box, as far back in the corner as I could get, praying with my eyes tightly shut. He got a tremendous welcome and there was ease and warmth in his voice in the first scene with Zena. As he went on, so his confidence seemed to grow and his voice was deep, fruity and caressing. I opened my eyes, I knew Ivor was with him, and with me in the box and that all would go well. This was the first and last first night I actually enjoyed. As Jack got into the part, the tension left me and, as the evening wore on, I felt relieved and warm and thankful. We went quietly home for dinner together – which is what he enjoyed best – and went to sleep in each other's arms. He was content that he had done his best and that it seemed to go down well.

The Press shared this view. Stephen Williams' review in the *Evening News* was typical of the many rave reviews:

> With consummate art, with perfect tact, and devoting all his sparkling talents to the general success of the play, Jack Buchanan last night took over Ivor Novello's part in *King's Rhapsody* at the Palace Theatre.
> His curtain speech was a model of good sense. He did not refer to his predecessor: he merely said that he had done his best to fulfil an unenviable assignment and hoped he had not disappointed us.
> He had not. I doubt indeed if Mr Buchanan could disappoint us in any part he undertook. I doubt if the English stage has

181

often seen such a well-graced actor, whose every sentence is so beautifully timed, whose every gesture so beautifully measured.

Jack's fellow performers rejoiced in his success. They knew it was an enormous challenge for Jack to follow Ivor Novello – perhaps the last of the great matinée idols. They also knew that his success would guarantee the show's long run.

Soon after Jack's first appearance in *King's Rhapsody*, the Buchanans entertained most of the company, together with old friends like Phyl Monkman, at Mount Street. During the evening, Zena Dare, the regal leading lady who played the part of Jack's mother, told him, with a twinkle in her eye, that she would walk off the stage if he tried any ad libs or jokes with her. Jack said that this was fair enough as long as she, too, behaved herself.

This exchange arose from an incident early in the run which Vanessa Lee observed at first hand:

Zena Dare was a highly nervous lady. When she was playing a scene with you, she would often grab your arm and hold it tight until you were black and blue. One night, soon after Jack joined us, she said to me in the wings, 'I must ask Jack a most important question'. She went up to him literally a few seconds before he was about to go on and said 'Jack, how long do you boil a haggis?'. He took one horrified look at me and shot through the door and got through the scene. When he came off, he said 'Can you imagine. Zena who is so nervous and knows how nervous I get. How could she do that to me? You wait, I'll tell her what to do with her haggis'.

The next night, in the same scene, Jack made a splendid entrance in his magnificent uniform and went straight up to Zena Dare, bowed to her as the Queen Mother, and said 'Good morning, Mama'. Then, in a whisper 'You boil the bloody thing for two hours'.

King's Rhapsody continued its long run and allowed the Buchanans to follow a more settled life. In town, they saw more of their old friends. Jack would get a 'pink ticket' every so often for a night on the balcony of the Café de Paris with Duggie Furber. Suzzie saw more of Coral Browne and established a mutual interest in needlepoint.

Weekends out of London were usually divided between Brighton and Hollycombe. The Buchanans had now rented a flat in Brighton where they saw their chums the agent Bill O'Bryen and his actress wife, Elizabeth Allen. At Hollycombe, the mixture was the same as ever with Jack and Pete Selsdon getting their golf highly organised and Suzzie being roped in for 'good works' locally.

Jack presented a Hollycombe Challenge Golf Trophy – a somewhat hideous figure in a kilt. Pete devised an extremely complex set of local rules in which alcoholic intake and golf handicapping were inextricably intertwined. Bob Hope came down for a weekend with the boys while he was appearing at the Palladium. As Suzzie recalls: 'We had an enormous Sunday lunch but all Bob wanted to do was get out on the golf course.' He soon pronounced Eno's as 'great stuff' in overcoming the alcoholic handicapping and dubbed Jack and Pete as 'tigers of the gorse'.

On Monday, 8 October 1951 *King's Rhapsody* began its long provincial tour in Ivor's home town Cardiff. Jack had some worries about following so obviously in the Welshman's footsteps but the audiences received him warmly. On the train travelling to Cardiff, he told Suzzie how strange it felt to play, in Ivor's place, in the town where – 39 years earlier – Ivor had discovered him.

Olive Gilbert – who had been one of Ivor's closest friends and who had appeared in virtually all his big musical successes – was one of those in the *King's Rhapsody* company who became devoted to Jack. She recalls how Jack showed how he could have danced in the show:

> We were in Glasgow and I had supper with him at the Malmaison. Someone – rather the worse for drink – came over and said 'You didna dance, Jack . . . we wanted to see ye dance!', and when everyone had gone – when there was just Luigi and one or two waiters left in the restaurant – Jack said to me 'I *could* have danced in the show, you know. I could have danced to your big number. And he got up from the table and danced as wonderfully as ever – up and down the stairs leading to the restaurant, in between the tables, and across the restaurant floor while I sang 'Take your Girl' from the show.

In Bristol, Jack was carried away by the conviviality of the bottles in Harvey's cellars and put down a pipe of port for Theo. He loved Bristol because of the ships and was given lunch aboard one of them. Then it was time to return to town for a short break and to play two weeks at the Davis Theatre, Croydon.

This meant that Minnie the cook would have ample scope for the 'good plain cooking' that Jack so much enjoyed and there were parties at home both for Christmas and New Year. At their Christmas dinner, the Buchanans had Elsie Randolph and her husband, Vernon Handley Page, Vanessa Lee and her husband Lord Peter Graves, Robert and Iris Nesbitt, Coral Browne and Philip Pearman and John Palmer who had been Ivor Novello's understudy. At their big New Year party before setting out on tour again, Suzzie recalls: 'Jack was the perfect host. We had our special drink together before the first arrival. The flat was looking lovely with masses of white lilacs and Minnie had excelled herself.' The guests included the Val Parnells, Lyons, Nesbitts, Arnolds, Selsdons, O'Bryens, Wilcox's, Duggie Furber and Alan Melville.

The contrast next day in Birmingham was stark. Suzzie's journal takes up the account:

There really didn't seem to be much to do or see in Birmingham at this time. I kept myself busy in dealing with Jack's mail and started a needlepoint and felt skirt class for the company. Soon almost everyone had the craze. Jack pretended to be peeved. 'For heavens sake, when I come in the stage door, all I hear is "Where's Suzzie? I've made a mistake in my needlepoint" or "Is Suzzie here yet? Ask her to come along and measure my hem". It used to be "Hello Jack darling, how are you? Did you have a nice day and play golf?" I don't get that anymore thanks to all those bloody needles and threads.'

On Wednesday, 6 February 1951, King George VI died. The Company's general manager, Wyn Newman, phoned us first thing in the morning and said to Jack, 'You realise there will be no show tonight.' Jack, who hadn't heard the news, said, 'Any other jokes?'. But he was terribly sad and talked about him in his early days when he never expected to come to the Throne. Jack said that the King's friendship with Louis Greig was a great help to him when he was literally thrown in at the deep end. He also said that he had known the King about as well as anyone could do in the theatre world and had always had respect and admiration for him.

We met for an awkward rehearsal as we had to cut out a lot of dialogue. This is extremely difficult as the play never stops referring to Kings and Queens and to the possibility of death. It was all thoroughly depressing with wintery cold rainy weather outside. We were all in the deepest gloom and I had never seen pros quite like that before. When we returned to our gloomy brown hotel sitting room, Jack said, 'Let's get out of here, baby. I must get some air and take a long walk. I think I'll go mad if I just sit here and think.'

So out we went into the dusky streets of Birmingham just as everyone was coming home from work. Jack had tears in his eyes and a lump in his throat and walked with his grey trilby pulled well down. I can shut my eyes and see that walk but I can't describe it. As Fred Astaire said, 'It was a lovely walk'. Jack himself said that he and Danny Kaye walked in exactly the same way with feet turned out almost in the ten to two position. Anyway, we walked rapidly and quietly through the misty streets without attracting any particular attention. Suddenly, from out of nowhere, appeared a chubby little bundled up char-lady type. She had an imitation leather shopping bag stuffed with cabbages, a muffin hat and a wonderful W.C.

Fields' nose. 'That's Jock Buchanan' she cried in a terrifying voice, which seemed to carry for miles. She repeated this announcement to a bus queue who couldn't have been less interested, buried as they were in the evening papers, reading about the new Queen flying back from Kenya. We bolted down an arcade, and emerged to find the same determined figure in front of us. There she was, peering up at Jack, under his hat brim and in the same terrible voice, stopping people as they rushed to catch their bus, by saying 'That's Jock Buchanan'. Jack, scarlet in the face, tipped his hat, smiled and grabbed me by the arm as we set off down yet another turning. This went on for at least quarter of an hour. By then, I was breathless and giggling. It had become a game. Heaven knows how the lady did it, but she must have known every short cut and turning in the centre of Birmingham. She didn't seem to want an autograph, for she only repeated the same cry when she caught up with us. She seemed only to want to point us out and gloat in some extraordinary way at her new found prey.

Strangely, that broke the gloom for us and we came back to the hotel, had dinner in our sitting room and talked happily and quietly about the memory of the King and of the new Queen. Jack said that having this lovely young girl on the Throne could begin a new era for Britain's greatness. He thought she could inspire and revive the great achievements of her subjects in a new Elizabethan Age. He told me how he had met the young princess as she then was, at a Royal Garden Party. Apparently the King had introduced them and referred to the fact that the Royal Family's favourite joke was one which he had first heard in one of Jack's shows.

After Birmingham, we went on to Liverpool. Jack always enjoyed playing there because he was well looked after at the Adelphi Hotel and he could play his golf at Formby. This meant that I had to face up to another of those little marital adjustments. Formby was under snow but Jack insisted on playing a round despite the gale that was blowing off the Irish Sea which soon turned to sleet. I was in tears thinking we would never get to the end of the damn course – blue with cold, feet past feeling and soaked to the skin. When the Clubhouse finally came in sight, I plunged blindly on, crying with relief, through bunkers, across greens, into casual water in a direct line for the bar and a great big hot buttered rum to revive me. Jack always wanted me to be with him and walk around, but his idea of fresh air and mine were two different things. The round at Formby was probably perfect for a man who spent the first twelve years of his life in a kilt and who had wonderful circulation; who didn't care for and didn't use central heating; who wore the thinnest tropical weight suits all the year round; who seldom wore an overcoat and hardly any underclothes. This was fine for him, but not for a hot house plant like myself – the product of central heating and golf in Nassau. Fortunately, by the time we reached Leeds and Coventry, the weather had improved. We had a lovely weekend at Tibbs Farm where Eileen Idare lived. She had always described Jack as 'The man with the navy blue eyes' from the early days when she did the girls clothes in his shows. While we were at Coventry, we stayed at the Falcon in Stratford again. John and Bonnie Green were over from Beverly Hills and spent a weekend with us. We introduced them to Pimms and took them to the Races at Warwick. Jack and I had a big winner. All the bookies gave him tips but he chose the horse that winked and it came home for us at a good price.

The last night of *King's Rhapsody* was in Coventry on Saturday, 14 June. Everyone was depressed at the Company breaking up after more than a year together. Jack had become particularly close to his harem of Zena, Olive, Venessa, Wyn Newman (and me!). I bought coffee spoons for all the members of the Company at Stratford and wrote a little poem. When I told Jack about this, he said 'Fine, it will cheer them up.' But when I read it, they all began to cry. I did too, saying, between my tears 'It's supposed to be funny'. As a surprise for Jack, at the Saturday matinée, I went on in the ballroom scene. I wanted to faint at my first experience of the lights and the open gaping maw of an audience. All the dressers and stagehands were in the wings watching me to see if Jack would notice. He saw me as he came on and made a detour and ad libbed 'You're looking lovely tonight, my dear'.

The Queens

IN THE LATE FORTIES, the New York social and theatrical columnist, Lucius Beebe rhapsodised over Jack's role as one of the last great transatlantic actor/managers. Under the heading 'Fourth Crossing in One Year Brings Buchanan to Broadway', he wrote:

> There is something compelling about the legend of the spacious years when Broadway and the Strand were but continuations of the same street. Those were the brave times when the sailing lists of the *Mauretania* and the *Kaiser Wilhelm der Grosse* were awash with the names of actor/managers, actor/producers and playwrights whose interests were evenly divided between the two shores of the Atlantic; Winthrop Ames, Charles and Daniel Frohman, Henry Miller and a score of other transatlantic commuters who made the transition from the Savoy Grill to the Astor as easily as that from home to office and almost as frequently.
>
> Since the most recent of wars the traffic in notables from the shores of Albion may have been abated and the glory of their passage and their hold on the public imagining diminished, but there is no need to mourn the passing of the transatlantic actor/manager while Jack Buchanan is still available as one of the Cunard White Star Company's most profitable patrons. When Buchanan arrived last week aboard the *Queen Elizabeth*, it made his fourth crossing for the current year and pretty well established him in the class of the Frohmans who, like the Morgan partners, had space reserved on every sailing of importance against their sudden whim and convenience.

Jack's first post-war crossing had been with Dave Hutcheson on the *Queen Elizabeth* in 1946 on the trip that brought them on to Nassau and the meeting with Suzzie. She recalls:

Jack told me they felt like schoolboys at the end of term. They had drinks with the press, drinks with Lionel Careen, the ship's purser, drinks with the Cunard officials and drinks with completely strange fellow passengers. They ran around the great ship like maniacs, down to the pool to arrange for massage and steamroom time, up to the smoke room to see Mac-Queen, the head steward, on to the Verandah Grill to order the special table in the corner, to the Observation Bar to shake hands with the barman, and then to Murphy, the starboard Garden Lounge steward. Whooping along the decks, peering over the great bows, tearing two steps at a time down to Lionel's cabin in time to hang from the portholes waving goodbye as the ship slowly pulled away from the pier. And then, as the tugs nudged the 87,000 tons of beauty and steel and spirit out into the stream, they heard the three throaty blasts which say that the great lady is really on her way. Quieted, and very Scottish for the moment with tightening throats and moist eyes, Jack and David went up to the Verandah Grill.

Jack came back that late December in 1946 to the New York that he had first won with Bea Lillie and Gertrude Lawrence in Charlot's Revue in January 1924. Home again to the city he loved next best to London, to the hotel where he always stayed, the very British Ritz-Carlton. The dear familiar Ritz. Scotty, the floor waiter, the same elevator boys, the dear old ladies behind the theatre ticket desk and the same staff at reception. All old friends and genuinely delighted to see him. The Men's Bar, and the little 'mixed' Bar behind the reception desk where Jack and I were to spend many happy hours just being in love and hoping and planning. The patient and trusting Ritz where Jack would let his bill run for months, not I hasten to add from any shortage of funds, or Scottish proclivity of watching the pennies, but to a decided aversion to opening any letter or bill. I found, some years later, a receipted bill for $5,780, which is a lot of trust from any hotel.

Just as roast beef and jacket potato and champagne was the traditional lunch on the ship, the first lunch in New York was always a Hamburger Maison at '21'. Somehow the ship always seemed to land in the morning, with just time to taxi to the Ritz, drop the luggage and get to '21' for the lunchtime session. The first drink was always a 'demi-tasse' (gin and ginger ale on the rocks) with Emil, the head bartender. Of course, the first day back the greetings were prolonged and numerous, and part of it, the usual matching of coins with Emil for a dollar bill. I think Jack's return after the long war years called for a longer handclasp, and knowing my boy, a certain telltale shine in the eyes.

After that first post-war Atlantic crossing in 1946, Jack had resumed his pre-war habit of sailing to America every year – sometimes more than once. These were still the great days of sea travel when the 'Blue Riband' for the fastest Atlantic crossing was passed from one new great liner to another – the *Queen Mary*, the *Normandie*, the *Queen Elizabeth*, the *United States* and the *France*.

Jack remained faithful to the Cunard White Star Line, He alternated between the *Queen Mary* and the *Queen Elizabeth* and he found on his many crossings that in the full complement of first class passengers were many of his fellow artists and old friends. In this way, he was able to enjoy relaxed reunions with Ivor Novello, Dorothy Dickson, Bobby Andrews and the other members of The Big Three, Bea Lillie and Gertie Lawrence. On one trip soon after the War, 'The Triumvirate' were with New York's leading theatrical lawyer, Arnold Weissburger – the friend and confidante of almost every great star. He recalls that the conversation turned to a serious consideration of re-creating a Charlot Revue on Broadway. Gertie was turning over ideas for her material; should she use some of her first great successes such as 'Limehouse Blues'? How much new material would she need? Bea was similarly preoccupied. How would a new generation take to 'March with Me' and who would write the new comedy material? Jack, all the while, remained silent. 'What are you going to do, Johnnie B,' Gertie asked him. Silently, the elegant figure stood up and touched his toes. 'What on earth is that supposed to mean?' asked Bea. 'It's my new act,' said Jack 'Keeping my end up!'

Jack continued to travel in style. When he arrived on the *Queen Elizabeth* in December 1948 for what was to be his last bachelor trip, MacDonald and the Rolls were in attendance, Suzzie's journal recalls:

My unforgetable memory of MacDonald was when he came with Jack (impeccably dressed as the gentleman's gentleman in dark overcoat, starched collar, neat dark tie and bowler hat) to get me while they fetched the Rolls from Pier 90. It was waiting in the shed next to the ship – MacDonald looked it over carefully, dusted here and there, looked for non-existent scratches, opened up the boot, replaced the mascot – a Silver Bonzo doing full speed ahead – replaced the side mirror, checked the tyres and then carefully placed his bowler in the boot, put on his chauffeur's cap and gloves, and we drove off in style to 400 Park Avenue. My doorman was most impressed and said to me in awe the next day, 'Do you know, Madam, those cars cost $20,000?'

The return trip was Jack's and Suzzie's honeymoon on the maiden voyage of the *Caronia*. Suzzie recalls:

There were masses of chums on the ship, including Sir Alexander Maxwell, then the President of the British Tourist

Board. He gave a dinner party for us in a private room on our first night at sea. There were several Cunard big shots on board. Mr Baker was chief steward and everything was done to make us comfortable and happy. We had two first class staterooms which had been filled with flowers and there were cables from all over the world. MacDonald was perfect as valet for both Jack and me. Unlike Green, he seemed to take our marriage in his stride and reassured me as he brought in our breakfast tray on the first morning at sea 'You'll just have to get used to me, Madam'.

When we arrived at Southampton, Captain Sorell invited us on to the bridge as we came up Southampton Water on a grey winter's afternoon, made spectacular by the whistles and streaming hoses of the fire ships, all welcoming the newest lady of the Cunard Line. Then when we got to Aldford House there was champagne waiting for us from some of our fellow passengers and a card saying 'Happy to have been part of the maiden trip of the *Caronia* and the Buchanans'.

During their married life, Jack and Suzzie crossed the Atlantic ten times – almost always on one of the *Queens*. These were their happiest times together. Their privacy was respected and they had a chance to unwind – away from telephones and urgent messages about the immediate problems of Jack's theatre, film, radio, television and business interests. Their routine was well established. As soon as they reached their cabin, Suzzie would make arrangements on the telephone for their massage, turkish bath and swim times. Then Jack would say 'Baby, why don't you go and pick up some Bloods?' 'Bloods' were the murder mystery books which both Jack and Suzzie enjoyed reading. When Suzzie asked if he had anything special in mind, Jack would reply 'You know, the usual thing. "A shot rang out in Berkeley Square. There was a blood curdling scream . . ." One that I can get right into'. When Suzzie reached the ship's library, the librarian would greet her with a pile of books all ready and the remark 'I saw you were on the passenger list and I put some specials aside for Mr Buchanan'.

On most of the trips, Theo came too. This required some patience on Jack's part since the three of them travelled on occasions with forty-seven pieces of luggage – a constant nightmare of packing and checking. But Jack loved having Theo on board. She was able to enjoy shipboard life to the full. She was always included in their lunch time drink sessions sipping a coca-cola while Jack and Suzzie had their gin and tonics. They would solemnly exchange the toast of 'Rabbit's Ears' instead of 'Cheers' – another reminder of the family affection for the mythical 'Harvey'.

In the evening, the Buchanans would go up to their special

table in the Verandah Grill where the Chief Steward, Mr Thomas, was waiting to greet them. He would say, 'What can we do for you from our specials today? What about blinis and steak and kidney pudding?' which he knew were among their favourites.

After dinner on board, the Buchanans went to see a film almost every night. This was a good opportunity to catch up with many of the films which they missed when Jack was working. In the morning, they would put on heavy sweaters and make their early morning rounds on deck with the sea air in their faces, greeting the sailors who were swabbing down the decks. Then it would be time to go back to their cabin for an enormous breakfast in bed of sausages, eggs, bacon and kippers. They would read the ship's newspaper and then have another 'zizz' before getting up in time for lunch. Suzzie sums up their life on board: 'I really think that heaven is like a day on board the *Queen Elizabeth* in those marvellous plush days'.

Radio – 'Man About Town'

MAN ABOUT TOWN WAS the perfect title used for some of Jack's most successful radio programmes in the fifties. In this series, he brought to the radio his revue skills in performing many of his original sketches and musical numbers. He also showed an expertise and 'mike side manner' which was the product of many years' radio experience.

In the years after the War, Jack turned increasingly to a radio career to supplement his more limited theatrical opportunities. In its turn, the B.B.C. showed a growing awareness of Jack's ability in front of the microphone. His intimate style was ideally suited for a wide range of programmes both as a solo artist and as a performer.

In the seven years between 1949 and 1956, Jack was principal performer in 36 programmes. His range of activity was enormous and involved with subjects as various as *Musical Memories, A Queen Arrives* (on the *Queen Elizabeth*) and *Top of the Form*. There were extracts from his shows and films and Jack was a contributor to the tribute programmes on Ivor Novello, Gertrude Lawrence, André Charlot and Fred Astaire. Public interest in Jack was exploited for charity in his appeal on behalf of Boston House for Working Lads in Edinburgh in *The Week's Good Cause*. Similarly, he was constantly interviewed for *In Town Tonight, Personal Choice, Welcome to Britain, Preview, Show-case, London Magazine* and – perhaps most memorably – by Roy Plomley in *Desert Island Discs*.

In this programme, Jack gave an interesting insight into his appreciation of his fellow performers in choosing the eight records which he would take with him if stranded on a desert island. Significantly, two of his choices were for records by Bing Crosby, 'So Tall a Tree' and 'Swing Low Sweet Chariot'. Jack explained that he had literally hundreds of Bing's records in his own collection, adding 'I'm a tremendous fan of his. I think he's got the friendliest voice I know – and because of that, it's one of the very few voices that wouldn't sooner or later get irritating on a desert island'.

Jack's other choices were the Duke Ellington version of 'Limehouse Blues'; the Glasgow Orpheus Choir singing 'The Dashing White Sergeant'; Benny Goodman's orchestral arrangement of 'For Every Man There's a Woman'; Guy Lombardo's recording of 'Who'; Peter Lind Hayes singing 'Life Gits Tee-jus, Don't It?' and the Melachrino Strings playing 'The Donkey Serenade'.

Perhaps Jack's most notable appearance in post-war radio programmes were in the 'Big Shows' and radio series which – before the widespread ownership of television – commanded massive world-wide audiences.

In *Hi Gang* in 1949, Jack, Michael Wilding and Vic Oliver were the guests of Bebe Daniels and Ben Lyon. Ben introduced Jack as 'a star as well loved in America as he is right here in Britain'. Reflecting his recent return from America, and his interest in being up to the minute, Jack took advantage of the novelty spot in the show *If I had a chance* to perform a Bebop number with Stanley Black and the Orchestra, 'Hey-ba-ba-re-bop'.

In shows like *Star Bill* and *Variety Playhouse*, Jack worked as the compere in all-star variety. In *The Big Show* in 1951, he shared this responsibility with Tallulah Bankhead. This show was a joint production by the B.B.C. and the National Broadcasting Company of America to mark the N.B.C.'s 25th Anniversary. Other New York based artists appearing in the show included Beatrice Lillie, Fred Allen and George Burns.

In *The Forces Show* which was broadcast on the 20 September 1953, Jack worked with his good friend Bob Hope in a show which was heard in forty countries with an estimated listening audience of twenty million. Performing before a Service audience in a programme which was primarily designed to entertain the Anglo-American forces in the Korean War, Jack and Bob worked up a nice line of patter which they were able to use on a number of subsequent occasions. It reflected the warmth of their friendship and the ability to give and take so that, in their final duet, 'Put it there, pal', they were able to work in some relaxed ad libbing.

Jack's stature as a radio performer in the fifties was reflected in the two radio series he undertook in 1954 and 1955. In *Home and*

Away, there was an obvious attempt to take advantage of his current success in *As Long as They're Happy* in which he was then appearing at the Garrick Theatre. *Home and Away* had the same kind of family comedy theme. Jack was joined by members of The Gang. Elsie Randolph played the part of his wife and Dave Hutcheson had one guest appearance. Another of the regular members of the company in the four part series was David Jacobs.

This series was pleasant and agreeable entertainment. Its successor *Man about Town* was a far more ambitious enterprise. Broadcast in eight parts between June and August 1955, it gave Jack a perfect opportunity to live up to the show's title. The script written by Gale Pedrick evoked the true Buchanan style and microphone warmth. Roy Speer's production also struck a skillful blend between Jack's association with hit shows from the past together with some excellent new material written by his long standing admirer, Hubert Gregg. This consisted of the title song, together with a different song in each of the eight part series about London. This was a happy marriage of the talents, bringing together Jack's West End image with Hubert Gregg's outstanding ability as a writer of songs about London.

This versatile performer today recalls:

I first spoke to Jack at the Garrick Theatre. I went backstage and introduced myself because I had one particular song 'If I Could Pick, I'd Pick Piccadilly' which I had written thinking 'Jack Buchanan could do this marvellously with a suggestion of soft shoe and a quiet soft rhythm.' When I went to see him in his dressing room, he sat me down and gave me a drink and then he talked about my songs. He said how much he liked them – which I said was just as well, as I had something special for him. He suggested that I came round to his flat in Mount Street the next morning when he told me about his forthcoming work in the *Man about Town* radio series. This was an extraordinary coincidence as – this was no song writer's gambit – many years before, during the War, I had written a song called 'Man about Town'. I thought 'If he's using the title *Man about Town*, I wonder if he wouldn't like to use my song as his theme.' So I played it to him and he said 'Oh yes. That's exactly what I'm looking for.' It was extraordinary. Then he said 'Would you like to be in the programme?' I said 'Yes, of course.' So he suggested that I should write a few songs for the series and then we got the idea of my supposedly – and sometimes actually – composing a new London song for him in each of the eight programmes.

Although Hubert Gregg's admiration for J.B. as a performer was enhanced in this first opportunity of working together, he found it necessary to adapt to the problems of rehearsing with him.

He recalls:

Because of his many commitments, it took Jack a long time to learn my songs. We would have these wonderful rehearsals at the Garrick Theatre and all the marvellous performers who Jack had as his guests would wander in and out. Often we seemed to have everyone there but J.B. which worried Bill Shepherd who did the musical arrangement and whose singers would support Jack. If there was something difficult either musically or in the lyrics they would take over if required. As the series went on – always with these shows you have too little time for rehearsal – we had very little time to work with Jack. He would get his song on a Monday and we'd have to record it on the Thursday. Then, the pressures became so great that he would pick it up at the first band call when we were doing the show that night. He would read it off the music and he wasn't too happy working in this way. One day, he came in and we had a fairly difficult song. Bill Shepherd had practically written him out of it so that almost all the singing was done by his chorus and Jack only came in for about eight bars. We were all very worried about what Jack would say but, anyway, we gave this arrangement to him. He took one look at it and saw the amount he was going to be asked to sing and said 'Ah well, I see you rumbled me'.

In *Man about Town*, Jack had a regular company which included several old friends; Coral Browne, Fred Emney, Alan Melville, Vanessa Lee, Hubert Gregg, Pat Coombs and David Jacobs. In successive programmes they were joined by Leslie Henson, Spike Milligan, Eric Barker and Pearl Hackney, Bernard Miles, Cicely Courtneidge, Joan Sims, Charlie Chester, Elsie Randolph, Adele Dixon, Irene Handel, Terry-Thomas, Peter Butterworth, June Whitfield, Tony Fayne and David Evans and the President of the Cambridge Footlights Review, Brian Marber.

With this enormous wealth of talent, Jack was able to recreate many past successes. With Coral Browne he performed a comic version of the Romeo and Juliet scene and, with Elsie Randolph there was, inevitably, 'Fancy Our Meeting'. Perhaps the classic comedy performance of the entire series was the 'Pukka Sahib' sketch in which Jack was joined by Leslie Henson as two Indian Army Officers in the box of the theatre at which Hubert Gregg is desperately trying to recite 'The Green Eyed Goddess'.

For David Jacobs, this series was one of the first major opportunities which he had at the start of his broadcasting career. As one of the youngest members of the company, he acquired a special respect and affection for Jack:

He really was incredibly generous to me in the professional

sense. Even before we worked together in the radio series, he had recommended me to Jack Hylton for a television series from the Albany Club when he felt that the work wasn't suitable for himself. Now in *Man about Town* I had an opportunity of working as compere in Jack's own show.

I think that Jack was perhaps the most elegant man I had ever known. This was reflected in his attention to the smallest details. His wallet and his gold cigarette case were superb and his shoes had a mirror shine, the like of which I have never seen before or since. When I asked him about this, he told me that Green had 'boned' his shoes over many years and that particular pair were twenty-six years old.

Man about Town was the last major series of radio programmes which Jack undertook for the B.B.C. In many ways it was a fitting climax, bringing together many of the best-known West End performers in support and allowing Jack to show off many of the versatile talents which had first made him a great revue artist. Looking at the list of Jack's own personal contributions to the series is to review many of the highlights of his career.

In 'Lily of Laguna', Jack paid tribute to his first great inspiration 'The Dandy-Coloured Coon' Eugene Stratton from whom he had learnt so much in the years long ago before the First World War. In 'There isn't any Limit to My Love for You', 'Who', 'So Green', 'There's Always Tomorrow', 'This'll Make You Whistle' and –most appropriate of all – 'And Her Mother Came Too', Jack, in successive programmes, recaptured for new generations some of his greatest past successes.

§

Suzzie and life with 'Johnnie B'

LIVING TODAY IN A lovely house in Maryland, Suzzie Sage – now happily married to De Witt Sage, a charming American country gentleman – is in many ways a different person to the Suzzie Buchanan of this account. Today, she is keen on country pursuits and a crack shot. Then, she was a hothouse flower, a product of Nassau sunshine who found the transition to the world of the theatre and life with a hardy Scot an enormous challenge. Blessed with total recall, she gives a witty and charming account of 'Life with J.B.' in the journal she kept at the time and in her talks with the author.

It was through their travels together that Suzzie came to know Jack best. As we have seen, life aboard ship allowed time for the Buchanans to relax. The same was true – to a lesser extent – on their tours in Britain and their holidays on the Continent and in the United States.

For their holiday trips, the Buchanans alternated between staying with friends in the South of France and in visiting the family in the United States. Jack loved the Riviera from his earliest days of filming there and they would often stay with their chum Richard Greville. Suzzie's first visit there was on her own as Jack could not leave the tour of *King's Rhapsody*. When she came back twelve days later, it was just in time to see Jack appearing in a midnight matinée at the Palladium. She recalls: 'Jack was happy then, sitting up on a little terrace outside the theatre drinking champagne as the dawn came up and eating cold chicken sandwiches. "I'm happy it did you good, baby, but I won't let you go on your own again" he said. "Every time you go away for a few days, I'm frightened. Suppose something should happen and I should never see you again?" '

In Suzzie's notebook, she once made out a statistical and factual profile of Jack. It reads as follows:

Height – almost six feet. Weight – 11st 4lbs. His favourite food – sole, herrings, fillet steak, sweetbreads, eggs and bacon. His favourite flowers – lilacs, tulips, spring flowers and always the clove carnation for his buttonhole. His favourite colour was a superstituous preference for green. He never drank whisky and liked Gordon's Gin and Schweppes Tonic, Champagne and Pouilly Fuisse white wine. He hardly ever drank claret or port and preferred Kummel to brandy. His favourite cocktails were Angel's Delight (which was a rum cocktail he first discovered in Nassau), South Side (a gin cocktail with iced lemon and mint which came from the South Ocean Club at Nassau) and a Major Bailey which was like a Tom Collins.

Suzzie's list of Jack's wardrobe for one of his films shows that, in the mid-fifties, his three dressing gowns included one especially made for *King's Rhapsody*, his pin-stripe suits were grey and blue, he had two dinner jackets and a full range of morning dress, top hat and tails.

Aside from these vital statistics, Suzzie's notebook also lists the adjectives used to describe Jack's strengths and weaknesses. She wrote:

Impatient, gentle, courteous, kind, quixotic, sexy, graceful, quick, sentimental, loyal, enthusiastic, curious, nervy, depressed, irritable, helpful, trusting and stubborn.

In conversation with the author, she expanded on these last two attributes:

Jack's trusting qualities were constant despite the many occasions when people let him down. In the matter of money, for example, he was over-generous. After we were married, he had to think more about our future. Yet there were still many who expected him to maintain his old lavishness. I remember, one day, he came home for lunch and was especially quiet. When I asked him what was wrong, he told me an old friend had called at the office and asked for a loan of five hundred pounds. Jack had told him that he was unable to help because of his heavy television finance commitments. 'Do you know, Suzzie' he went on, 'he borrowed the twenty pounds I had in my wallet. We took a taxi together and when we got here he insisted on paying and he gave the driver five pounds telling him to keep the change. I didn't mind helping him out but I'd never have done it if I knew he was simply going to play the big shot with my money. I'd have much rather used the cash to buy you a pretty new titfer!'.

If you wanted to see Jack's stubbornness at its most obvious, you only had to be with him when he was driving the car. Never in nine years of marriage did I know him to successfully reverse a car – or at any rate, not without a frightening crashing of gears and a great deal of cursing under his breath. Mac-Donald, bless his heart, always pointed the car in the right direction but as Jack frequently drove himself with me beside him and MacDonald sitting in state in the back, we sometimes had problems. If we missed a turning, the performance of backing up the road took all Jack's perseverance and much of my self-control because one never suggested on these occasions that Mac might do it – or wasn't he bored driving, or weren't the gears exceedingly stiff? One sat, trying not to giggle, while the dialogue went as follows: 'I've missed the turning, have I, MacDonald?' 'Yes, Sir' 'Can't I turn right up ahead somewhere and come out on the same road?' 'No, Sir' 'Perhaps I can just turn around and swing into the other lane' 'No, Sir, I'm afraid there's too much traffic coming our way, you can't make it in one turn. Why not back up a bit?' 'Back it up, eh?' 'Yes, Sir'. This is where I usually lit a cigarette. By this time the traffic was whizzing by with irate hoots of the horn. This didn't do much to calm the master. 'Very well, I'll back up'. This was a tremendous decision. MacDonald and I gave each other apprehensive looks – we both relished and feared any excursion when Jack was at the wheel. I would puff deeply at my cigarette and look out of the window. The gear grinding noises start, the motor stalls and the air is rent with Scottish curses. MacDonald makes small and deprecating noises from the back seat – almost whimpering noises – thinking about his beloved car, which, it seemed to me, held together and ran through pure love and skill. After several minutes of this, the car moved grudgingly backwards despite its brutal treatment.

Of course, on the matter of age, Jack would never admit that he was too old to do anything, or even that he was not as young as he was. I don't believe that he ever admitted to himself that he was anything over thirty-five. He believed sincerely that he could do all that a youngster could do and just as well. He didn't train or practice his dancing and yet he could just pick it up again as though he'd only left off dancing the day before. If he noticed a little shortness of breath, after a good work out, he would quietly cut down his smoking.

His control was amazing and his will to be young, think young and to work as he always had never ceased to amaze me. He had the constitution of a bull elephant. His weak spot was his tummy and he suffered from nerves more than anyone I had ever known. This intense nervous feeling can be transmitted. When Jack's nerves were building up before an opening or first night, I found that I would be shaking with nerves after lunch at home which I had spent soothing, calming and distracting him. His vitality was amazing. In the years that we were married, he never missed a single performance. I have seen him go on with a temperature and 'flu and perform in plays in which he was seldom off the stage after eighteen hours of tummy sickness and practically no food. I was never successful in keeping him in bed. As curtain time drew near, he would say he felt better and it was simply no good threatening to call the doctor. No arguments worked. He'd feel better when he got the 'slap' on – the understudy was under-rehearsed, or ill, or someone else in the cast was off. Green could give him some milk and soda, he'd be fine. 'Concentration makes you feel better, you'll see darling, Don't worry.'

Off he would go and I would sit in agony. Minnie would come in and say that Mr B. was really in no shape to go to the theatre and I should have stopped him. 'How Minnie? That's what I'd like to know. How do you stop these mad actors?' I would ask.

The phone would ring. It would be Jack at the interval. 'I'm much better, darling. Don't worry. Come down and have my drink ready for me when I come off, that's a good girl'. I would arrive as usual just as 'The Queen' was being played in time to pour out his gin and tonic and hand it to him as he came in the dressing room door. I would say to Green 'How is he?' 'Fine, Madam, much better'. Green would smile at me with that sweet understanding look which said 'You don't know about the theatre, Madam' and Jack with his head held high would be springing with energy, rubbing his hands saying 'There's my baby with my lovely snort. Damned good house tonight and a lovely audience, weren't they, Green?' They would be feeling fine and I would be feeling exhausted. I never cease to marvel at the self-discipline of the theatre – they will themselves better and it's literally a case of mind over matter as with running noses, pounding heads and missing heartbeats, they play and play and play.

Television

DURING THE POST-WAR television boom, Jack was seen as a regular performer on both British and American networks. He had first appeared in scenes from 'When Knights were Bold' in the B.B.C.'s inaugural programme from Alexandra Palace in 1936. In the late forties and early fifties, he became a B.B.C. regular as a compere in variety shows and in feature programmes.

In *Know your Partner*, he and Suzzie were in separate sound booths guessing the answers which each might give to a range of questions. When Suzzie was asked 'Which song does your husband think he has sung most often?' she replied 'And Her Mother Came Too' only to find that Jack's reply was 'Fancy Our Meeting'.

In *Gay Rosalinda* Jack made one of his most ambitious British television appearances. He appeared opposite Tara Barry (who had been in the original production at the Palace Theatre) and Isobel Bigley (who had made her name in the Drury Lane production of *Oklahoma*) in a full scale operetta. Also in the cast were his chums Dave Hutcheson and Lord Peter Graves. The performance – which went out 'live' – was a near disaster. Jack was currently appearing in *Castle in the Air* and there was little time for rehearsal.

Peter Graves takes up the story:

> I can't imagine why Jack had agreed to take this part on. Some of us had been in the original production at the Palace Theatre but I don't think Jack had seen that or *Die Fledermaus* on which *Gay Rosalinda* was based. Anyway, his part as Von Eisenstein called on him to do a great deal in the way of singing and recitative of a kind which he had never really experienced before.

He rehearsed every day with his hat getting further and further over one eye. Tara Barry who was playing Rosalinda said to me 'Do you think I'm ever going to see his face?' I said 'No, dear, I can promise you you'll have to wait until the performance itself.' Apart from not seeing his face, the rest of us could hardly hear his voice during rehearsal because when we got in front of the cameras at Alexandra Palace, Eric Robinson and the Orchestra were on another floor and Jack could only just hear the music. It was all right for those of us who had appeared at the Palace and knew the orchestral lead-ins, but Jack didn't know them and had the greatest difficulty in connecting his lines to the music.

We were asked to come half an hour before the actual performance and, to my amazement (because the show went out live), I found Coral Browne, Elsie Randolph, Frances Day and Suzzie all attending as guests and sitting in the control room. Just before we started, Jack came on the set and Dave Hutcheson nudged me saying 'Will you look at the Scottish comedian?' He had a red wig on. I cannot imagine why. It had nothing to do with the show or the part. Anyway, Coral Browne made a few extraordinary remarks, but he kept it on and, very uncertainly, started the first act. By the middle act, he was in a terrible state of nerves, sweat was pouring off him but somehow we managed to get through. However, in the third act, they had to get the blackboards out with his lines on them because he had a great deal to do in the last part. By the end, he was done. He was exhausted. But somehow it worked and in the version everyone saw, he made a great success.

Jack did not rely on this ability to 'get away with it' during his American television appearances. In the early fiifties, he appeared in successive years in the Bob Hope, Ed Sullivan and Max Liebman shows. By definition, these were lavish productions involving weeks of rehearsals. Suzzie's journal describes how this often meant a major excursion to America:

Jack was to do the famous American colour T.V. programme, the Max Liebman Spectacular on 5 December in New York. We took Theo with us – planning to send her to a tutoring school in New York rather than being away from her for two months, lent our flat at Mount Street to Betty and Pete Selsdon who were between houses, and arranged to rent Bea Lillie's flat in New York for our stay. Jack had been many times to her flat high over the East River in New York, and thought it would be much more homelike for our stay and less expensive in the long run than taking a suite large enough for all three of us in a hotel. Bea was in the provinces, on tour prior to London, and I made all arrangements with her manager on the telephone, checking on the accommodation and even arranging to take over Bea's maid and her New York secretary.

The sequel was less happy. On arrival in New York, the Buchanans were met by a representative of Jack's New York agent, M.C.A. who was high-powered and efficient. When they reached Bea's flat, however, they found it was still occupied and their only consolation was three bowls of flowers addressed to them and a note saying 'Welcome to New York'.

Suzzie's journal continues the story:

Theo and Jack and I trailed back in the lift, and into a taxi, each of us holding a vase of flowers in our laps. We sat in dismal silence, each with our own thoughts. The taxi came to a grinding stop at a traffic light and simultaneously we screamed. Each of us had received a lap-full of cold water from the flowers. Jack started to laugh and Theo to giggle. I was close to tears, but as we started to mop up each others laps, trading back and forth the bowls of roses and tulips and carnations, we cried with laughter. And Jack looked at me and said between the guffaws of laughter 'God bless her, it's exactly like Bea, I know she meant it to be lovely for us, but she just forgot to arrange it – she hardly ever rents her flat, but said she would to me because it would be so much nicer to have a home – and then didn't remember. But I am sorry for you, Suzzie, with all your little lists and preparations. But never mind these nice people at the Lowell will look after us, and we'll be more comfortable in the long run.'

And so we settled down in the Lowell Hotel quite happily, if more expensively. And Bea sent flowers and apologies, and being Bea one forgave her and forgot the inconvenience and disappointment.

Jack was busy with his rehearsals, and tremendously happy. He was to co-star with Jimmy 'Schnozzle' Durante and little Jeannie Carson, who had come over from England to do a T.V. series, and was rapidly becoming a favourite with the Americans. Jack loved the enthusiasm and the professionalism of his fellow pros, and the equipment and T.V. studios were then far in advance of their counterparts in England.

The ninety-minute show sped along with a skillful mélange of revue sketches, solo spots and dance routines and speciality numbers. Jack did his favourite 'The Fox has Left His Lair', the tried and true number written for him by Duggie Furber and first performed in *Sunny*. It was a sketch that had all the elements of Jack's type of comedy, particularly that of lowered dignity, and earnest endeavour and I can't believe anyone will ever be able to touch him in his interpretation. Jack also worked a sketch with little Jeannie Carson and Jimmy and did a splendid spoof production number called 'Choreography'. The show went like a bomb and Jack made a tremendous personal success with the millions of viewers throughout America that night, which was echoed by the reviewers the next day.

While making television appearances in America, Jack was also working hard on his commercial interests in this field. His commitment to television went back long before he became involved as a performer. One night, early in 1925, as he was leaving the stage door of the Empire Theatre after his show he was surrounded by the usual supplicants as well as fans. Elsie Randolph has recalled how he said 'Gather round everybody – here comes another touch'. At this point, one of the less presentable characters waiting at the stage door called out 'Hello Chump'. Recognising his old school nickname, Jack turned to find it was his boyhood friend, John Logie Baird. He told Jack of his difficulties in arousing any interest in his new invention, the television.

A few weeks later on 1 May 1925, Jack gave a large lunch party for him at Romano's. Performers, the Press and potential backers were invited to meet Baird and to witness his television demonstration. The comedian Davy Burnaby has described the sense of amazement everyone felt when Baird arrived with tin boxes, string, bottles and other odds and ends. The *Morning Advertiser* said 'Mr Baird gave some interesting details but clumsy handling of his delicate apparatus when being conveyed to the Strand had unfortunately put it out of gear. Nevertheless, all those present were invited to take it in turns in looking into the camera where the rest of the audience were able to see the hazy outline of Mr Baird's face so that a wink and the opening and closing of the mouth was visible.'

The *Daily Graphic* commented 'Jack Buchanan introducing his friend Logie Baird was a surprise. He was never at a loss for words and he spoke sense. He said that Mr Baird had achieved his aim by the aid of all sorts of rough apparatus. Unfortunately he had exhausted his private means and could not go on. A few months now, with the necessary money and a perfected instrument would bring the invention to completion. The possibilities were enormous and it might be possible to achieve for seeing what broadcasting had done for hearing. When the system is perfected, we should be able to see the finish of the Derby, or any other topical event, in our own homes at the moment of occurrence.'

Within a decade, Jack's prophecy was to be fulfilled, and with his help Baird was successful in attracting the further capital which was needed for development work. When E.M.I. Marconi was chosen by the B.B.C. in preference to the Baird system in 1937, the inventor turned all his brilliant skills to the development of colour television. In this work, he received continued support from Jack. By the time Baird died in June 1946, Jack was heavily committed to a direct financial stake in their company, Television Limited.

Above, *Jack supported his old school friend, John Logie Baird (centre), from the earliest days of his first television inventions – Long Acre Laboratories, 1928.* Below, Man about Town *B.B.C. radio programmes with Coral Browne and Alan Melville.*

This company was one of the first in Britain to concern itself with both the manufacture and rental of television sets. The first thousand sets were manufactured by George Benning at Treforrest near Cardiff. Each set had, as its insignia, a picture of Jack together with his technical partner Edward Anderson.

George Benning recalls:

> Initially, there were three retail outlets for renting our sets at Harlow New Town. The problem in making a business of this kind pay is in the first three years or so when one is carrying the heaviest financial load in promotional costs and bad debts. One of our major problems was that J.B. simply did not understand cash flow forecasts and statements. So we seemed to live from one crisis to another.
>
> Another real problem was Jack's trusting nature. He would get very upset if you challenged the word of any of his business partners. As some of them – especially those after the American rights for our sets – were real 'fast buck' merchants, I'm afraid that we were taken for a ride.

But Jack was by no means a passenger in Television Limited. His skills were at their most evident in selling. Roy Plomley recalls how he and his associates negotiated with Jack for the American distribution rights of one of the first British television feature films. He was much impressed by Jack's mastery of detail when it came to assessing commercial prospects and he made a powerful case for working through his American contacts.

Although this deal did not come to fruition, Jack's major attack on the American market was a brilliant technical success. His collaborator in this venture, Edward Anderson, had been Baird's principal assistant. He was now in charge of research and television servicing and repair facilities in some small houses at Hammersmith which Jack had retained for the Company's use after he had sold the adjoining Riverside Studios.

Their joint venture was nothing less than the production and sale in America of the first mini-television set which could work indoors without an aerial. When this project got underway in 1947, they were many years ahead of their competitors. Suzzie's journal records their first practical demonstration in New York and the sad sequel.

> He brought this with Andy and his wife to New York hoping to break into the American market, which was then desperately needing sets as the domestic manufacturers couldn't keep up with the demand. Jack had tremendous faith in the enormous future of television and at that time when British exports for dollars were so important, he was excited at the prospect of finally cashing in on his long pioneering in T.V. and he was proud to have British television advances demonstrated and

sold in America. Again he was ahead of the game, because there was no portable set of equal quality on the market at that time for the price.

There was tremendous excitement when he docked with Andy. The precious prototype sets had been developed only through test instruments since the American scan of lines was different to the English. Jack and Andy brought the set directly to my apartment at 400 Park Avenue to try it out. The superintendent of the building happened to be in the foyer when they arrived and when he saw Jack with the set getting into the lift said 'Gosh, I'm sorry, Mr Buchanan, but that won't work in this building; we haven't got an aerial yet; all the tenants are complaining they can't get T.V. sets.' Jack said 'Well, I hope in a few months they will be able to; come up and see how this works in Mrs Bassett's flat.' The unbelieving man joined Jack and Andy and we all stood in my drawing room waiting for Andy to change the plug, and then the moment when all was ready and we switched on, all of us gazing riveted on the little set, made and designed in England, the first for the American market. The set warmed up, the signal came through and then a perfect test picture. The sound reproduction was excellent.

The set did work like a dream and at last justified Jack's faith and battle to keep on, after already having lost a great fortune in every aspect of television, since its earliest days. He came back to England with an order for many sets. And with the order in his hand, for dollar exports, he was unable to raise the finance to make the sets. He had put every penny he could spare and borrowed more to accomplish the prototype and keep his business going, and he couldn't raise another cent. The Board of Trade were full of praise for his efforts in breaking into the American market with British T.V. receivers, but he was stymied at every turn trying to raise the necessary finance. I think this was the greatest heart break of Jack's life. It came near to breaking his spirit of adventure and pioneering and it was the only thing in his life that I ever heard him discuss with bitterness and defeat. Always with disappointments and failures he could rise above despair – and even with people he loved when they let him down – as indeed they did – he never allowed bitterness in his heart or on his lips. But the failure to swing this American venture because of money (he who had given so much to every Tom, Dick and Harry, the softest touch in showbusiness) scarred his spirit and remained with him until the day he died.

ᴒU

United States For 'The Band Wagon'

JACK, SUZZIE AND THEO sailed on the *Queen Elizabeth* for New York on Wednesday 25 June 1952. The object of the trip was nothing less than a concerted attack which would bring Jack back to Hollywood as the major star he had been when he left there over twenty years earlier. Suzzie's journal takes up the story:

Jack very much wanted to film in Hollywood again. For a perfectionist like him modern filming was a good medium and meant that he could earn the same annual income without being tied down as he was with his enormous range of interests. He wanted more time with the family and felt that a limited season of plays and a film or two a year would leave us with time to spend in Nassau and the South of France.

We realised that Jack's ambition to make another film in Hollywood after so long an absence might take some considerable time to realise. Happily all Jack's old friends rallied round when we arrived in Beverly Hills. We had drinks on our first night there with Clifton Webb and we saw a great deal of our special chums, John and Bonnie Green. We did everything; the Farmers' Market with Clifton; a film preview in Pasadena with Bob Hope; lunch at Romanoffs and golf for Jack at Lakeside with Bing and Bob and Randolph Scott. Jack was like a child. He was so excited with all the marvellous hospitality but it wasn't all plain sailing.

Soon after our arrival, Clifton Webb and his mother Mabel gave a party for us. My heart sank when I found myself sitting next to Humphrey Bogart. He was always terrible to anyone he didn't like and I had the distinct impression that he felt Jack had acquired an American wife with too many airs and graces

208

and an English accent to boot. Sure enough, after a moment or two, Bogie fixed me with a beady look and said 'Your hair looks terrible. Why don't you do it this way?' As he said this, he reached over the table and pulled my hair down over my eyes. Jack looked stricken, wondering how I would take it and what he should do. But there was such a lovely gleam in Bogie's eye that I ran both my hands through my hair and pushed it up so that it was standing on end and said 'Oh, I think it would look even better this way'. Bogie let out a delighted whoop and said 'I hoped you were a good girl. We couldn't have old Jack with a stuffy one and you're all right. Waiter – bring two B and B's.' I'd never had a B and B with lobster salad and curry before but decided that this was no time to argue. After that, Bogie and I always got on and he beamed approval whenever he saw me.

Despite the 'star treatment', Jack had not forgotten some of his friends from the early days including his oldest friend of all, The Guv, André Charlot.

Life was by no means easy for The Guv, as he felt out of things and filled in with occasional bit parts in movies. Otherwise, he lived happily enough in his little house in North Hollywood with his devoted wife and daughter. When Jack went to see him, he thought it might arouse some of the old French impresario's interest in talking about the possibility of reviving material from the Charlot Revues for use on television. Jack had had discussions with a number of the companies, who expressed interest. When he met André Charlot, The Guv reverted immediately to full scale impresario when terms were mentioned and Jack had to give up the idea. He smiled when he told Suzzie, 'He wanted to produce, control and receive a massive sum for the sketches, darling. I can't explain to him that T.V. is a different medium and one in which he has no experience. I wish he would be more amenable because this way the whole deal will go out of the window and actually much of our stuff has dated very little and would be perfect for the material-eating monster that television is – but he'll never change, the dear old boy, and you must remember he's a Frenchman and careful with the Francs.'

Jack's other old Hollywood friend from the First World War was the former sweetheart of the American Expeditionary Force, Elsie Janis. Suzzie went with Jack to see her and recalls:

She had become practically a recluse living for years in a funny little house just off North Crescent in Beverly Hills away from the fashionable part. It was really like something out of *Sunset Boulevard*. She had a strange kind of chauffeur/bodyguard. Otherwise, I don't think she'd seen anyone for years, except perhaps an occasional visit from an old cameraman or dresser whom she'd worked with in the early Hollywood days. Apart from this, the only thing she seemed to do was to go out to the Veteran's Hospital and read to them several times a week. It was sad but touching that in this way she probably recaptured her memories of the marvellous work she had done for the American Forces in the First World War.

The house itself was terribly creepy. It was kept exactly as if it was a set for a nineteen twenties' movie. There was one of those awful satin dolls over the telephone (which I suppose would now be fashionable as art nouveau), there was a studio couch with tasselled pillows, and everything was terribly musty. There were hardly any lights and we sat in the shadows. Elsie Janis obviously felt happier away from the light although she was lean and spare and still very bright.

Recalling her total devotion to her mother, Jack said, 'I know you must miss her. I often think about the days when we were all together.' Elsie said 'Oh, mother's here. She's down in the bottom of the garden. I'm going to take you there after we've had some tea.' Jack gave me one of his raised eyebrow looks. Sure enough, after tea, we went down into the garden where we found an aviary. In it was one bird and this, Elsie announced, was mother. And 'She's delighted to see you'.

Between all these social rounds, Jack was actively pursuing his interest in making a film. His good friend, Bob Hope, arranged that his own agent, Louis Shurr, would help Jack, and early in August, word came that M.G.M. would like to see him. Jack told Suzzie that 'They want to have a good look to see if anno domini have caught up with me.' In fact, M.G.M. was considering a test for Jack in the part of Jeffrey Cordova, the flamboyant actor/manager role in M.G.M.'s forthcoming musical *The Band Wagon* in which Fred Astaire was already committed to appear.

The film was to be one of the last of the great M.G.M. musicals produced by Arthur Freed and directed by Vincent Minelli. The screen play had been written by Betty Comden and Adolph Green and the part of Jeffrey Cordova had originally been intended for Clifton Webb. It required someone who could play the role as a take-off of José Ferrer, Olivier and all the great actor/managers rolled into one. Clifton Webb had refused the part as he was unwilling to take lesser billing than Fred Astaire. Edward G. Robinson and Vincent Price were also under consideration but Clifton suggested that Jack would be perfect casting.

After his initial discussions with M.G.M., Jack came back to the Belair Hotel where he and Suzzie were staying. Her journal records:

He was shivering with delight and expectation and praying, 'Let the test be right'. We thought about the possibility of Jack working with his old friend Fred Astaire in a full scale musical of this kind. We thought 'What a set up!' and we went over the

210

small scene he was to do for the test over and over again.

He tested at M.G.M. one Wednesday morning and we left for New York by plane that evening. It was always Jack's policy never to hang around. If they wanted him, they could telephone him in New York. There were other things that he could do and he wasn't going to sit on his backside and wait for the phone to ring. However, a reaction to this bold front set in after we had been in the air about an hour and a half. He was sitting next to the window and we had another four hours before we came down in Chicago, when he turned to me and said in a very strained voice 'Baby, I've got to get out of here'. And he meant it. 'I can't breathe, I must have some air'. The plane was full and there was no room to roam around. We were flying into darkness with the night ahead of us. I rang for the stewardess, gave her a look and she gave me some sedatives. Jack took two and I loosened his collar, put the airstreams above directly on his face and gently rubbed his arms. Thank heaven the pills worked quickly and he went off to sleep until we got to Chicago. Then he woke up absolutely fit and full of energy and ate his way through an enormous breakfast at the airport while the plane refuelled. He had quite forgotten he had decided to leave the plane or turn it around a few hours before.

While we were in New York, the marvellous news came through that he'd got the part in *The Band Wagon*. They wanted him to start in September but, typically, Jack had promised Tom Arnold that he would take *King's Rhapsody* for a month in Glasgow. Although they never had a written contract, he and Tom always kept their agreements and so we sailed for home on the *Queen Elizabeth* on 20 August, even though we knew it was going to cost us far more to go home than Jack would possibly earn in Glasgow.

While Jack was there, we were working frantically on our move to Hollywood which would be for at least three months and then – we hoped – some time in Washington, New York and Nassau. We had sent the trunks on ahead by the *Queen Elizabeth*, including all the clothes which Jack needed for the enormous dress plot of *The Band Wagon* and, of course, the famous dressing gown, now so patched and worn, but essential for superstitious reasons when he began work in Hollywood.

The last few days were chaotic. 44 Mount Street was buzzing with people – Carl the barber was there to give him a last minute trim, Manny gave him his manicure and all the news from the Garrick Office, his manager Gilbert Brown was in and out with cheques to sign and reminders of things still undone; Reginald Eagle was constantly on the telephone about T.V. business, the tax situation and expenses of the film; chums would drop in for a drink; Green was hard at work on the last minute packing and unpacking and Mac was always there to answer the door and play his usual part of being the most helpful and resourceful person in the world and ready with the Rolls outside the door to take us to the airport.

We were making our first flight together across the Atlantic. We much preferred to travel by sea but we had no option as Jack had to report for work in Hollywood on 1 October. I had a new Michael black and white tweed suit which I thought was terribly smart with the tightest, straightest skirt ever seen. Of course I went mad trying to get into the sleeping berth on the plane. But Jack and I were both so alight with excitement and anticipation that we could hardly eat Minnie's special farewell lunch, let alone sleep on the plane. In the last few hours before we left, while the flat was still crowded with people, Jack would whip out of his study for a moment and come into my room and give me an enormous bear hug 'Can you believe it, baby. My God. I hope I can do a good job. When I finish with all these people, you and I will have a quiet drink just by ourselves.'

So we were off on the Great Adventure to Hollywood. To do just what Jack wanted to do most in the world – make a big musical comedy in the United States.

When Jack reported for duty at M.G.M., he faced an immediate and unforeseen challenge. In his talks before signing the contract, chief emphasis had been laid on the musical numbers which he would perform with Fred Astaire, Cyd Charisse, Nanette Fabray and Oscar Lavant. Now he found that his opening scene in the film would show him at work as a great dramatic actor playing a scene from *Oedipus Rex*.

Jack looked stricken when he came home from the studio after his initial costume fittings and trying out the mask and wig needed for the role. 'Damn our luck, baby', he said 'Why I should have to start with this scene I can't think. I can't do the bloody classics but its essential that this first scene should go well to establish the character. If I can get over being self-conscious and have a bash I might get away with it.'

'I saw Louis Calhern in the dressing room this afternoon and told him my troubles and he invited us up after dinner tonight to try the part out with me.'

Suzzie's journal once again takes up the story:

We went up to Louis' house and he and Jack bellowed into a tape recorder the terrifying lines which Oedipus utters after he has torn out his eyes. There were blood-curdling moans going out into the still Beverly Hills night. Fortunately, Louis was a wonderful booster for Jack's morale. 'That's it, Jack. Hit it hard. Give it full voice. Moan so they hear it in the gallery.' After a rather timid start, Jack was standing in front of the tape recorder making the volume needle hop about like mad. 'The only way I can do it, Louis', said Jack, 'is, if you'll excuse the expression, to ham it up'. 'But my dear fellow', said Louis 'That's the whole secret. We're all hams. That's the satisfying thing about doing the classics, or the Bard, play it up and play it out. Use your lungs. Get satisfaction and force. We're all hams – now let's try again.'

We took the tape home after that session and played it back hour after hour making new recordings to measure Jack's progress. He was splendid and he soon began to love it. 'My God, it's satisfying, darling, giving full voice and good earthy words to say.' When Jack shot the scene with his coach, Louis Calhern standing on the sidelines, he absolutely sailed through and came off and slapped Louis on the back and said, 'There's nothing to it, my dear Louis. Watch out now, I'm going to get into your branch of the racket before long. Stratford here I come – Sir Laurence look to your laurels'. And so with a blood-curdling laugh, he strode off in his Oedipus costume. He looked nine feet tall but then of course he was wearing wedge soled shoes to lift his six feet to nearer seven. It was a king size performance of Oedipus by Hollywood standards. Hammed it, he did, burlesqued it, maybe, but it came off and he loved it and it started the picture from his point of view with confidence and fun.

The Band Wagon is one of those M.G.M. musicals which its aficionados like to see again and again because of its many successful musical numbers and the scenes in which Jack played such a prominent part as the flamboyant actor/manager. Overall, the film conveys a sense of gaiety and charm in the face of the theatrical adversity which is the chief ingredient of the plot. Nevertheless, as so often in the entertainment world, the reality was much tougher.

Cyd Charisse remembers Jack with particular respect. 'He was,' she says, 'so extremely hard working' and 'able to take the inevitable production snags in his stride'. Her comments may well relate to one scene which was not used in the picture. This was intended as a dance routine for Jack and Cyd as the Devil and one of his minions. Suzzie recalls: 'She had to slap Jack and avoid hitting him with her heavy bracelet. Every time she slapped, the bracelet came off and they had to shoot the scene again. They tried it for hours and, by the end of the day, Jack was scarlet and sore. Cyd was practically in tears because there's nothing more difficult than trying to pull a punch – especially when it's repeated many times. What with their frustration over the bracelet and not wanting to hurt Jack and still get the damned thing right, by the end, she was very upset, but the mutual respect of the two actors was there for all to see.'

The other female lead in the picture, Nanette Fabray, also found at least one of her scenes with Jack physically arduous, and the whole picture – her first appearance in Hollywood – had something of a nightmare quality for her. She recalls:

The 'Triplets' number was typical of the really tough and demanding work which went into the film. In order to make Jack, Fred and I appear like small children, they bound our ankles up to our thighs and made casts of our legs in that position. They they fastened little shoes on to the front of our knees to give us some sense of balance. If you want to have an idea of how difficult that is, try holding your feet up behind your back and try walking around on your knees. The most difficult thing about doing 'Triplets' was when we jumped out of the three highchairs on to the floor we had to land on our knees without falling forward. We had to do many takes before we got that part right.

What made everything even more grisly was that I had laid open my knee in an accident during the 'Louisanna Hay Ride' sequence and poor, dear, darling Jack had had major dental surgery. Because of his treatment, we had to delay shooting the 'Triplets' sequence until eventually we ran almost out of time before he was due to go back to England. Eventually we had to shoot the sequence despite my bleeding leg and the fact that he had only just come back from another round of dental treatment. So when we started work, they had to give me a pain-killing injection in my leg and then we had to wait until Jack's Novacaine wore off as half his face was frozen. As a result, his lips weren't moving properly and we began the sequence by long shots, the three of us just jumping out of our chairs. We all worked very hard to get the number done but it was an absolutely tortuous nightmare. Between takes, they would have to stop and clear the blood away from my leg and off Jack's mouth. You can't imagine – this fun, gay number was just a living nightmare.

Despite these problems, Jack found his work in *The Band Wagon* immensely satisfying. He and Suzzie were fascinated by the way in which the studio grapevine worked when things were going well for a particular performer. During the first few weeks of shooting, the armed guard on the studio gate kept Suzzie out when she called for Jack or dropped him in the morning. Suddenly the word began to get around that this British actor, Jack Buchanan, was just sensational in the new film with Astaire, and Suzzie was ushered in and out by the guard who began to greet Jack by name. Three weeks later, 'Mr Buchanan' was 'Jack'. Before the film was completed it was the 'old chums' act – a slap across the shoulders – and 'Understand the rushes are great, Jack, just great'.

Jack found that, similarly, it took some time before he was accepted in the barber's shop and the make-up department of the studio. He subsequently discovered that following the influx of British actors in the immediate post-war years, they had acquired a reputation as being snobbish, selfish and mean which, in some cases, was well-deserved. One of the electricians told Jack that a certain famous British star was such a son of a bitch that he'd be lucky if he got through another film without having an arc light dropped on his head.

Jack, with his tact and warmth of spirit, soon won over all those involved in making the film with him. In the case of the extras, this warmth was heightened by professional respect. In one of the most complex scenes in the film, Jack was shown inside a penthouse set when selling the (as yet unwritten) play by using his vivid imagination on a large number of naïve potential backers. The scene involved a very complicated set-up of cameras covering several different angles looking through the various windows of the penthouse where Jack was doing his stuff. During the course of the action, he rolled all over the floor, hamming it up as he half strangled himself with cries of 'Fire and brimstone, hell and damnation' in his intended role as Faust. Suzzie was allowed to visit the set when this scene was shot.

I was there and I wondered how Jack would get on, conscious as he must have been of the cameras pointing at him from so many different angles and the need to give the impression that he was making up the whole thing as he went along. He had to wait all morning for the cameras to be set up. Then, when they came to shoot it, he did it in one take. All the extras clapped and cheered and they printed it just as it was the first time round. It was a tremendous *tour de force*. He got the right pace and never stopped and it is still one of my favourite scenes in the picture.

Many of those involved in the film have particular favourite scenes involving Jack. Many of these stemmed from the brilliant script by Betty Comden and Adolph Green. For the first time in many years, Jack was given a really 'meaty' film part, and he made the most of the role of the actor/manager whose conceit verges on egomania.

For Betty Comden, Jack's first entrance and the sequence which follows were 'a sheer joy'. He is first seen making his curtain exit in *Oedipus Rex*. In a moment of tragic intensity, his self-imposed blindness required that he be led off the stage. The moment he reaches the wings, he turns to his world-weary assistant, Hal, and – while the audience wonders what effect the moving tragedy has had on the great actor – says, 'Get someone to slip out for a ham and pastrami on rye. No mustard'.

As Betty Comden says 'Very few actors could have carried this off the way that Jack did and, indeed, his flow of non-stop chat which reveal his total self absorption'. The sequence she refers to begins as Jack, having ordered his sandwich, carries on with comments and instructions to all concerned:

Max, what happened to that amber spot? It was way off. I must have some more light on me. Don't let's keep it a secret that I'm in the show. Hullo, sweetheart (putting an arm round a passing statuesque blonde 'walk on' player), you look wonderful. Hal, call a full dialogue rehearsal – Friday, for the full company. Sloppy diction. The original was in Greek but this is in English – don't let us keep it a secret. Oh, and I want to catch the matinée tomorrow of *Man and the Mousetrap* (Hal: 'You can't do that, you've got to give a drama lecture at Princeton'). Oh well, we'll work something out.

Moments later when Fred Astaire has been introduced to Jack with the idea of working together in putting on a musical comedy, Fred queries whether this is really up Jack's street. Jack replies:

Musical, musical, I'm sick of these artificial barriers between the musical and the drama. In my mind, there is no difference between the magic rhythms of Bill Shakespeare's immortal verse and the magic rhythm of Bill Robinson's immortal feet. Hal, Hal, write that down! I'll use it at Princeton tomorrow. (Hal: 'You already did, last year') All right. I tell you – if it moves you, if it stimulates you, if it entertains you, it's theatre. When the right combination gets together and it spells theatre, well, I've got to be right in there up to my armpits. (Hal: 'That's higher than usual').

The beauty of these scenes came not only from Jack's superlative playing but also from the skill in Betty Comden's and Adolph Green's dialogue in creating a part that, in film terms, fitted him better than any other he had previously attempted.

The same was true of the composing skills of Arthur Schwartz and Howard Dietz. In the 'Triplets' and 'That's Entertainment' numbers, they provided material that showed off Jack's musical comedy versatility at its very best. But it was in 'I Guess I'll Have to Change my Plan' that they produced one of the greatest high style song and dance duets ever filmed.

The beauty of this number is its economy. Jack and Fred Astaire are seen, immaculate in top hat, white tie and tails, lit by twin spots in front of a glittering stage curtain. They stand motionless, side by side, with their hands resting on their canes as they begin to sing.

At the end of the chorus, Jack and Fred move into the most graceful soft shoe duet with taps from their canes in time with the staccato beat of the music. Their dance is brief, as is their song, but, as director Vincent Minelli said, 'It was just enough to show why and how these two had made themselves the two greatest white tie and tail performers we've ever seen'.

Nanette Fabray has revealed, however, that behind the apparently effortless technique in this number lay many hours of toil and sweat. She recalls:

Jack came in one day after he had been rehearsing with Fred and said, 'Oh, God, I hope I can survive this. Fred is such a perfectionist. I welcome that. I like it but I can't always do what he wants me to do. I can't do Fred Astaire. When you dance with Fred Astaire, you have to do Fred Astaire'. But, you know, when I saw the number I thought he was probably even better than Fred because he had his own style. And it was such a surprise to many in the American audiences who had grown up since the War to see this marvellous musical comedy man. He held your attention in that number and that's about the greatest compliment you can pay to anyone who has ever worked with Fred Astaire.

Jack certainly found working with Fred Astaire an immense challenge. But, on considered reflection (rather than during the trauma of rehearsal) he was thrilled by the experience and intrigued by the things which he found they had in common. As Suzzie recalls: 'Fred and Phyl invited us to dinner. They led a completely un-Hollywood life and we found them charming. Fred had no time for high jinks. He worked so hard – on Saturdays as well as weekdays – and that suited my boy just fine.'

Jack found that he and Fred shared the same nervousness and the same superstitions. Fred even had the same lucky dressing gown which he used for first nights and the start of pictures. They also shared the same lugubrious sense of humour when it came to considering their personal attributes. One day after they had completed an exhausting rehearsal, Jack and Fred sat gloomily looking at themselves in the wall mirror. Fred turned to Jack and said 'My God, I'm a knife. Nothing but a knife'. Jack replied 'You're lucky. I'm a horse. An absolute horse'.

When *The Band Wagon* was released in New York in July 1953, the director of the film Vincente Minelli sent the following cable:

JACK BUCHANAN GARRICK THEATRE LONDON ...
DEAR JACK ... YOU HAD AN ENORMOUS PER-
SONAL TRIUMPH
LAST NIGHT ... I AM VERY PROUD OF YOU ...
LOVE VINCENTE

In the opinion of several American critics, Jack's work was so outstanding that he had virtually stolen the show from the great Fred Astaire himself. Under the heading 'Buchanan humour gives *Band Wagon* bright glow', Edwin Schallert wrote: 'Jack Buchanan is the performer who gives *The Band Wagon* a big shot of adrenalin. He demonstrates what his long experience in the theatre has meant through impersonation of a man who boasts he can do anything in showbusiness, be it acting, directing, producing and even re-writing a script. Buchanan is a whizz in his travesty on such a theatrical Jack of all trades.'

Perhaps *Cue* magazine summed up all the praise which was heaped on Jack's performance when it wrote: 'The best thing in the film, perhaps, is the presence of fabulous Jack Buchanan, who has come over from Britain to play the singing, dancing, hammy, tragedian-genius. It's wonderful to have Buchanan with us – even for one picture – and perhaps he'll stay and make it a double.'

What *Cue* magazine and Jack's agent could not forsee was that *The Band Wagon* was one of the last great musical films made in Hollywood. Such films were soon to become prohibitive in cost, but, for the moment, Jack was back on top of the world. He had been discovered by a new generation who had only heard of his great musical comedy days before the War. When one British critic asked him how he still kept up his dancing, he gave a typical down to earth reply: 'Dancing, old boy? It's like riding a bicycle. Once you've learnt, you never forget'.

Right, 'The knife and the horse.' Below, Fred Astaire, Nanette Fabray, and J.B. experiencing real-life blood, sweat and tears in 'The Triplets' number in The Band Wagon.

ᵛV

Variety and Other Shows

JACK'S SUCCESS IN HOLLYWOOD had reminded British theatre moguls of the fifties that he was still capable of captivating an audience with his uniquely elegant top hat and tails routines. If prohibitive cost and changing fashion ruled out the big glamorous musicals of the twenties and thirties, it was in occasional variety appearances that London audiences now had their chance to see Jack at his inimitable best.

He had always been in demand as a solo performer for charity midnight matinées. At the Ivor Novello memorial performance on Sunday 7 October 1951, Jack came on to the stage of the London Coliseum in overcoat, white scarf and black homburg hat. The show – in aid of Redroofs, Ivor's house which was now an actor's home – consisted of the best of the Welsh composer's musical numbers. Jack was upset when he found that his turn was to follow a strenuous dance routine by Joan Heal and some of the bright young things then appearing in the Lyric Revue. He felt the contrast between their vitality and his own relaxed style might make his work seem dated.

But from the moment he came on, lit by a single spot, and sang 'My car will meet her . . . and her mother comes too' the audience was spellbound. Jack's performance brought back memories of both Ivor's and his own first great revue success in *A to Z*. As he moved into the lithe, not quite soft shoe, not quite tap dance routine there was not a sound from the audience. But with the final lines of the refrain, the applause rolled out from stalls to gallery. 'It went', Suzzie recalls, 'like a dream', and Jack who had assumed the mantle of Ivor's part in *King's Rhapsody* was hailed by the critics as star of the show.

220

The Coliseum performance was a fully rehearsed show, but Jack sometimes found himself ad libbing in charity shows where a previous run through was impossible. One such occasion was at the Stoll Theatre on 21 September 1952, when the Variety Club of Great Britain presented *Sunday with the Stars*. Bob Hope – who was appearing at the Palladium – organised the cast which included Pat Kirkwood, Jerry Desmonde, Donald Peers, Peter Sellers and 'additional surprise stars'.

As Bing Crosby was in Britain at the time, there was speculation as to whether he might be one of the guests. When the curtain went up, however, the first surprise of the evening was revealed as Jack strolled on to the stage. Prevented from wearing 'stage costume' by Sunday theatre regulations, Jack was in a lounge suit and bow tie as he began his work as compere for the evening. His reception was warm – the usual Buchanan welcome – made all the friendlier by the audience's knowledge that he had literally popped in from Hollywood between tests and the start of shooting of *The Band Wagon*.

Jack introduced the turns with his usual charm but there was a feeling of anticipation which made it hard for the earlier turns – great artists though they were – to distract the audience's mind from the obvious question – when would Bob Hope appear and would Bing Crosby be with him?

As the orchestra struck up 'Thanks for the Memory' Bob Hope made his expected appearance. He and Jack began to trade the wisecracks and insults which had worked well in their radio and television programmes. But it soon became clear that their ad libbing had an almost frenzied purpose in keeping the show going until Bing could be found. 'The Old Groaner' had agreed to appear but, typically, had been delayed on the golf course.

As the show went on until, by now, a late hour, the audience appreciated to the full Jack and Bob's ability to keep them entertained without a script or prior rehearsal long after their loosely planned routine was due to end. Finally, to the strains of 'Where the Blue of Night meets the Gold of the Day', Bing appeared. Casually dressed in blazer and flannels, he had not bothered with his toupée and offered his left side to Jack, Bob and the photographers with 'I've got more hair there'.

It was planned that Bing would simply appear to take a bow at the final curtain. The audience, by now, was in no mood to let the three Kings of comedy, song and dance leave without performing for them. There were hurried consultations; what number, if any, did all three and the orchestra know well enough to tackle 'cold'? Eventually, Jack announced that 'Carolina in the Morning' would now be rendered – perhaps literally – and 'everyone should feel free to leave!'

221

No one showed the slightest interest in doing so and – for the first and last time on any stage – Bing, Bob and Jack went into their song and dance routine. The singing was easy enough but the dance routine depended heavily on Jack with flashes of Bob's early 'buck and wing' training and Bing's total faking. At the end of the number, the two greatest all round American entertainers showed their appreciation to link man Jack with a kiss from each side which, happily, the photographers were there to catch.

Recalling this occasion at his home in California in 1976, Bing Crosby said:

> That night at the Stoll certainly was off the cuff. I never got to see either of the others until I arrived at the theatre. We didn't even have a few minutes together in the wings. All of a sudden I was on. There were a lot of things Bob and I had been doing in the army camps but it is always very difficult to go on cold. That was where Jack was so clever. Hope and I knew each other's work pretty well but Jack just fitted in with the wisecracks and the song and dance as though we had all been working together for years.
>
> I was in awe of Jack. He was such a distinguished looking fellow and he had such a variety of talents. It was like Laurence Olivier today. That was what he represented to me. He was very crisp and spruce. I just liked his style. He was my idea of a great English actor.

Bob Hope, too, has the happiest memories of working with Jack. This – as we have seen – was not confined to charity shows but to radio and television work in Britain and the United States. Still the supreme variety artist himself, early in 1977 Bob Hope summed up his impressions of Jack:

> He had a great and immense talent with a comedy and musical style all his own and he had a great sense of humour. Those spots with Jack and Crosby at the Stoll in 1952 were genuinely ad lib and there were a lot of unprogrammed activities going on, but working with two people like that, I felt pretty secure out on stage.

When Jack returned from Hollywood, he accepted several proposals for variety dates. In 1954, he appeared in two of the most prestigious bills ever presented at the London Palladium and kept his long standing promise to appear at the Café de Paris.

Noël Coward had traditionally staged *The Night of 100 Stars* which had succeeded the theatrical garden party as the profession's main fund-raising effort. This year, the show was called 'Midnight Cavalcade'. It was presented on the night of 18 March 1954 with virtually every West End star in the company. In the first half, Jack's turn was preceded by the appearance – among others – of Bobby and Sally Ann Howes, Jack Hawkins, Richard Burton, Gladys Cooper, Emlyn Williams, Paul Scofield, Margaret Lockwood and John Mills. Item 8 on the programme said simply 'Jack Buchanan and Laurence Olivier'.

When the curtain went up there was a roar of appreciation from the audience as Jack and Larry were found immaculate in top hat, white tie and tails moving smoothly into *The Band Wagon* Astaire/Buchanan hit number 'I guess I'll Have to Change my Plan'. Laurence Olivier had told Jack of his secret desire to perform as a song and dance man (which ambition was to lead him to play the part of Archie Rice in *The Entertainer* only a year or two later). Today he recalls how Jack showed endless patience in several weeks of painstaking rehearsals in which he broke down every step into the simplest component part. The end result was a pleasing performance which – if not quite up to the Jack and Fred film routine – carved out its own special place in theatrical history.

During the summer, Jack made his long awaited début at the Café de Paris. As ever, he was nervous before his opening night. He was following immediately after enormous personal successes there by Noël Coward, Bea Lillie, Marlene Dietrich and other cabaret specialists. He was also particularly conscious on this occasion of the many friends and well wishers who were in the first night audience which included Princess Margaret. He had been reluctant to use much of his old material and had commissioned several new songs, including the opening number 'There's No Café Like This Café' based on Irving Berlin's classic 'showbusiness' song. There was also a daring – by the standards of the mid-fifties – song about divorcees who could and could not enter the Royal Enclosure at Ascot.

These numbers went down well as did 'I Hate the Morning', a parody of the *Oklahoma* hit 'Oh, What a Beautiful Morning'. But there was less enthusiasm when Jack persuaded three couples to leave their ringside tables to participate in a draping contest with a bottle of champagne as the first prize. During this interlude and through most of his forty-two minute act, the unspoken question remained: 'When are we going to hear his great hits from the past?'

Right at the end of the evening, Jack obliged with 'Fancy Our Meeting', 'Goodnight Vienna', 'Who', 'Dancing Honeymoon' and, inevitably, 'And Her Mother Came Too'. The audience were, said one reviewer, 'exceptionally generous and when he brought back memories of the songs they had cheered before the war they were there to cheer him on his way again'.

Jack's variety work received the ultimate professional recognition when he was invited by Prince Littler and Val Parnell to

Left, *Bing and Bob show their appreciation of Jack's work – Midnight Matinée, Stoll Theatre in 1952. Below, 'I Guess I'll have to change my plan' – Jack rehearses Laurence Olivier for their 1954 Midnight Matinée.*

perform in the Royal Command Performance on 1 November 1954. Before the show, he and Suzzie were presented to the Queen, Prince Philip and Princess Margaret. Jack appeared in a scene which was a take-off of a First World War musical called *The Shopgirl Princess* in which the other principals were Diana Churchill, Gladys Cooper, Binnie Hale, Leslie Henson, Thora Hird, Frankie Howerd, Elsie Randolph, Peter Sellers, Joan Sims and Donald Wolfit.

Noël Coward who, with Bob Hope, was to provide the two big solo spots in the show has recalled how Jack was his usual mass of first night nerves. Jack told Suzzie that a Royal Command Performance audience was the toughest in the world adding: 'You can see them sitting there dressed up to the nines, saying "We've paid twenty guineas a head for our seats so amuse us if you can".' John Barber in the *Daily Express* wrote of an audience which 'remained cold throughout' but he and the rest of the London Press had no doubt about Jack's role in making a success of the evening. 'His presence,' said *The Times*, 'was most welcome'. John Barber added, 'For charm there was Jack Buchanan, aged sixty-three, impersonating a dapper World War One officer . . . and there was no actor on stage with half his sparkle.'

Jack's variety and cabaret appearances were fitted into a crowded programme of radio, television and film work. They were also restricted by his determination to play in his own theatre, the Garrick. In April 1953, the theatrical manager, Bill Linnit, rang Jack and asked him if he would go down to Southsea to look at the new Vernon Sylvaine comedy which was on its prior to London tour. Bill was losing money and felt the provincial reviews and the general feeling about the play were far from right and doubted whether he should bring it into London. Bill hoped that when Jack saw it, he might make suggestions for its improvement and, perhaps, consider playing in it himself.

Suzzie's journal takes up the story:

> Jack and I drove down with MacDonald and, on the way, he told me that his old chum Dave Hutcheson was playing in the show, as was Dickie Murdoch, who was unhappy about the play and likely to leave shortly. By the end of the first act, Jack was sufficiently intrigued with the play to begin mentally reconstructing. After the show, Bill Linnit said that unless Jack would come into the play, he would definitely take it off. Jack's plan was to take over the role of the father in the play (which was then played by Dave Hutcheson) and put Dave into the part which Dickie Murdoch was leaving – that of a crying crooner.'

Behind Suzzie's account lay a tremendous emotional tussle for Jack. The play was the first occasion on which Dave Hutcheson had the leading role and it was obvious that his wife Mary – who was a great friend of Suzzie's – bitterly resented Jack's proposed take-over of the lead. However, there is little doubt that the play would not have come on in London unless Jack had been willing to come into the company and, in the event, both he and Dave Hutcheson were to score great personal triumphs.

The play's success, was, however, by no means easily assured. Jack went out for a six-week tour prior to London. One of the problems was that Vernon Sylvaine had originally made his name as a serious playwright and *As Long as They're Happy*, as the play was called, was an uneven mixture. Jack as a stuffy stockbroker married to a retired actress (Dorothy Dickson) has to cope with the antics of three daughters; one is married to an *avant-garde* playwright, the second to a cowboy, and the third is infatuated with a crying crooner. These partnerships meant that there were jokes about existentialism and other abstruse matters.

On the opening night on 8 July 1953, the audience seemed unsure how to react. As the *Evening Standard* reporter said 'With a barrage of ironical laughs, the gallery announced its presence while I sat frozen, squirming alternately at the audience and the play.' Things were getting so bad that Jack's manager, Gilbert Brown, actually summoned two policemen, fearing a major demonstration.

As John Barber, writing in the *Daily Express*, said, 'The most astonishing thing that happened was not the appearance of the policemen. The surprise came later. Honest guffaws slowly built into prolonged roars of joy and, when Jack Buchanan burlesqued a sobbing crooner, singing 'Cry', applause stopped the show for nearly five minutes. I had never before heard threatened disaster throttled and turn into emphatic success.'

Jack's presence in the show literally, as the *Evening Standard* said, 'saved the evening . . . The audience cheered; Mr Buchanan bowed in gratitude and relief; and the gallery, mollified by this recognition of its power, allowed the play to proceed without further interruption.' But if Jack had saved the opening night, the show was still to face some difficulty. As Suzzie's journal recounts:

> That Coronation Year was one of those rare English summers when the hot weather kept the audiences away from the theatre. But Jack had tremendous faith in the play after all the blood, sweat and tears that had gone into working out the changes on the road. He took no salary for months after the London opening. Dotty Dickson and some of the youngsters also took cuts in their salaries and, by the end of August, the play was established as a firm hit. It settled down to a good run with full houses and enthusiastic audiences and Jack's belief

that the comedy had the right audience-appeal was rewarded when he was asked to appear in a film version of the play.

Part of the play's success was undoubtedly due to the fascination of West End audiences with Jack's impression of the crying crooner. He made a record of the Johnny Ray song 'Cry' which sold well. In a full page feature in the *Illustrated* magazine, David Clayton wrote:

Buchanan is demonstrating nicely what he thinks of crooners. Although the song is Johnny Ray's, he manages to convey, in 32 bars, all the antics, the grimaces, the winces, and every slippery glissando that any crooner has ever employed to make a bobby soxer squeal. It lasts three minutes and is one of the funniest things in the West End this season.

Buchanan, being an experienced artist, wise in the way of audiences, varies his microphone gymnastics from show to show. When the audience is mainly of an age which deplores the fact that the crying crooners earn more than the entire Cabinet put together, he lets himself go.

On other nights, to younger audiences, he stays immobile, in a hilarious half trance. The teenagers love it. It is true that they would rather be tearing buttons and bows from their idols but sometimes they squeal at the Garrick as fervently as they do at the Palladium.

Above, As long as they're happy, *Garrick Theatre 1953 – J.B., Virginia Hewett, David Hutcheson and Dorothy Dickson.* Below, As Long as they're Happy – *film version with Diana Dors.*

'Weep No More My Baby'

IN ONE OF JACK'S most charming songs, written for him by Johnny Green in the thirties, he sang:

Try to forget
Get a smile upon your face
Face the sun and let it find us
Weep no more my baby
You're baby's home again

The message might almost have been written as an epitaph for Jack's and Suzzie's last few years together. Perhaps, too, the lyrics written by Edward Heyman stayed clear in his mind. Jack rarely wrote letters to Suzzie, preferring to make their partings as infrequent as possible, and spending a fortune on telephone calls when he was away from her. But a little note he wrote to Suzzie after she came back from a trip to America sums up their relationship. He wrote 'Ah's singing cos mah baby's home'. Unlike the other 'babies' – the leading ladies and girl friends who had preceded her – Suzzie was *'mah baby*'.

Jack's simulated deep Southern drawl was always a sure indication of his inner contentment. His last years seemed to fulfil him as a man, as a husband and stepfather. Suzzie christened him 'Old Iron Claw' because of his tendency to gaze transfixed for long periods when they played Gin Rummy. 'He always lost' she recalls, 'and he owed me millions on paper whenever we played'. When Suzzie called him 'Old Iron Claw' he would say: 'Do you hear what she called me? Me. One of the great figures of the British theatre!'

Jack enjoyed this kind of de-bunking and even managed to make fun of his professional skills. Once when he stubbed his toe on an iron bedstead at Mount Street and aroused peals of mirth from Suzzie and Theo, he said while hopping, half dressed, on one foot: 'Look at the sympathy I get. Me, the great dancer. My prospects ended for life for all you care'.

Such jokes reflected Jack's ability to take setbacks in his stride. He needed these qualities as – in the Britain of the fifties – there were some managements who seemed totally oblivious to his skills. As Wilfrid Hyde White recalls:

'He was actually asked to audition for one play in which he was considering a 'takeover' part. It was unforgiveable that anyone should have asked this of such a great artist'.

When faced by such set-backs, Jack came increasingly to appreciate the value of his home and family. As Duggie Furber said 'Professionally his last years may not have equalled his brilliantly successful years before the war. But at a personal level, They brought him immense satisfaction.' Prendy agreed and, even today, recalls that these 'were the happiest days of Jack's life'.

For Suzzie, too, the last few years with Jack brought their own special reward. Much of this stemmed from her part in helping Jack with his film and stage work, in as she describes it, 'my theatrical education'.

Much of this arose naturally from Jack's ownership of the Garrick Theatre. For Suzzie, this became a second home and many of those who worked there were extensions of Jack's family; Maxine Maxwell on the switchboard, Miss Mann ('Manny'), Jack's old manicurist and now tea maker; Bill Ireson in the Box Office and Sam Gardner, the carpenter.

John Hallett came into partnership with Jack at the Garrick in the mid-fifties. He recalls: 'Jack said to me, "Just give the old place the once over, ol' boy and let me know if everything is shipshape". Well, I was very young at the time but it didn't need much experience to see that the office was a burglar's dream. I went to Jack and pointed out that the safe where all the takings were kept was in the box office in full view of the paying public. Jack's manager, Gilbert Browne, said that it was impossible to move it without knocking the wall down. I went over to the safe, fiddled with it for a moment, and the whole thing came away from the wall. It had no back on it and anybody could have just helped themselves'.

Gilbert Brown was in the office opposite to Jack and had been his manager since 1940. He has told how, on the stroke of 12.45, Jack would come out of his office and break into his Southern routine.

Massa Brown – is you there, Massa Brown?
I'se right here, Massa Buchanan
How's about joining me for a little snort, Massa Brown?

Gilbert Brown would readily agree and large gin and tonics would mark the end of the morning's work. Jack would usually go home for lunch with Suzzie and would often return for more work in the afternoon. It was said that taxis would often crawl slowly round the Garrick Theatre at lunchtime and again at 44 Mount Street afterwards, knowing that Jack would never walk in the West End if he could help it. On one occasion, he told the taxi driver that he had to have a quick lunch at home and would he like to come back for him. Such was the driver's regard for Jack that he offered to wait outside. Typically, Jack said 'Well, ol' boy, if you're sure you've nothing better to do'.

Teatime at the Garrick involved a set ritual. Jack would have his pot of tea and a boiled egg brought in whether or not he had a visitor at the time. Even if Suzzie appeared at this particular moment, she would find the Master with his long legs up on the desk, the grey trilby on his head and, in the words of Jack's song hit 'Everything Stopped for Tea'.

Jack came increasingly to rely on Suzzie's help with his work. On tour, she would pass the long evenings – in the three week stops in Birmingham or Leeds – answering Jack's mail. She recalls:

> Some of it was terribly sad. People would write sending a photo of their child who died last year. I could type and I would try to answer whenever I could – weeding out the many, many begging and crank letters. I also had to learn to read scripts. We would get many unsolicited efforts from aspiring playwrights. These were a real problem. Sometimes, they would send their only copy and the first thing I knew about it was when a letter arrived saying 'Where is the play I sent you four years ago?'
>
> Fortunately, I had majored in English at college and, if they were any good, I would type up a skeleton for Jack. He also kept me busy going to plays when he was on tour. Often, if he was away, he would ask me to check on the new productions at the Garrick. I found I couldn't take chums because it interfered with my concentration and I had to face Jack's professional inquisition at the weekend. 'What did you think of the lighting?' 'How did the first act curtain go and how did the new sets look?' I became more and more professional because I was reasonably observant and Jack didn't have time to see everything himself.'

Suzzie's help was soon extended to Jack's film work. Although Jack had been unable to capitalise on his success in *The Band Wagon* in America, in England he worked virtually non-stop on three films in British and Continental studios. *As Long as They're Happy* was the film version of Jack's stage success. It had an inauspicious beginning. Suzzie recalls:

> One of the first scenes which was shot was one in which Jack is playing the City chap who lives somewhere out in the hinterland dressed in bowler hat, striped trousers, briefcase and umbrella, running for his bus. It was a dolly shot and they hadn't swept the road. He twisted his ankle on something and although he got on the bus all right, he pulled both his Achilles tendons. As he had to do a dance later in the picture, I had to make him put his feet up whenever possible at home, and every night a masseur would give him treatment. He had to go out at six in the morning and do his dance all strapped up.

Two of Jack's co-stars in the film, Jeannie Carson and Diana Dors have recalled how impressed they were with his great courage in working in complete agony. Jeannie Carson also recalls how the younger members of the company reacted to Jack's insistence on maintaining his own high standard of elegance:

> At this time in the mid-fifties, those of us who had come into the theatre and the films recently followed the current trend for casual wear. Before and after work most of us were in sweaters and jeans. Jack, however, would always arrive and leave looking absolutely immaculate. Some of us used to make fun of him when we were chatting together at the studio, but, privately, I am sure that everyone very much admired the way in which he maintained his standards.

As Long as They're Happy was released by the Rank Organisation early in 1955. Meanwhile, Jack had begun work on a new film at Shepperton Studios. Here he demonstrated an increasingly relaxed approach to the Press in agreeing to an interview on the set with Margaret Constable, who wrote:

> Jack Buchanan, when I saw him this week, was smooth, impeccable about the tailoring but nevertheless offering unvoiced prayers that John and Roy Boulting would be finished with him in his film in time to enable him to be in New York next week.
>
> He is due there for a major spot on Ed Sullivan's *Toast of the Town*, one of those impressive coast to coast hook-ups with a comfortable allotment of dollars attached.
>
> Although Jack is in his sixties, he doesn't look a day over forty-six. When I watched him on the set, he was giggling like a schoolboy at Peter Finch's failure to stop burping during a scene in which he and Jack have consumed gallons of ginger ale. Despite the fact that ten takes were required while I was there, not one of the repeats could be blamed on Jack himself.

He showed a faultless timing, every repetition looking as spontaneous as though he had just thought up the whole thing.

Jack had been reluctant to work in his new film *Josephine and Men*. It was based on the Nigel Balchin 'Uncle Charles' books and Jack thought that the uncle whose niece (Glynis Johns) confides in him, was too old a part for him. Over lunch with Al Parker at the Mirabelle he was half persuaded. Suzzie finished the job by suggesting that the character was intended as an attractive, mature man – a member of White's rather than the Athenaeum. In the event, Suzzie's encouragement was justified. Jack appeared as a dashing clubman – a member of The Parasites Club – who confides in an understanding barman, while constantly peering anxiously over his shoulder for fear of pursuing ladies. Suzzie felt that this was one of Jack's happiest films and also one in which he gave a truer picture of himself than almost any other.

Before *Josephine and Men* had its première, Jack was already committed to a new film which would be made in Paris. This was *Major Thompson Lives in France* – a satire of the Englishman as seen through French eyes and based on the current best seller by Pierre Daninois. The film was to involve the Buchanans in almost a year of commuting between London and Paris in making a bilingual version.

Meanwhile, their life moved at an ever increasing pace. In April 1955, Jack sailed for New York on the *Queen Elizabeth* to appear in the *Ed Sullivan Show*. He brought his mother-in-law back to stay in the new flat which Suzzie had been cleaning and decorating in his absence at Lewes Crescent in Brighton. This was to become their new weekend home. It also encouraged Jack to accept a long standing invitation to appear for Melville Gillam at the nearby Connaught Theatre in Worthing for two weeks between his film and other commitments. Jack would not normally have considered playing the 'Worthing Rep' but he was tempted by Melville Gillam's brilliant direction of the Connaught Theatre and the opportunity to play in *Harvey* for a limited run of two weeks.

This became something of a cult performance. Many of Jack's old friends travelled especially to Worthing to see his interpretation of the part of Elwood P. Dowd. Liz Allen and Anna Neagle came over to see the show. So too – all the way from Yorkshire – did Prendy. He had seen Sid Field and Frank Fay create the part in London and New York. Today, he still recalls Jack's performance as 'the finest of them all. It was the only one which really made you believe that Elwood P. Dowd could see a rabbit which was invisible to the rest of the audience'.

After the family holiday in Monte Carlo in July, Jack started shooting on *Major Thompson Lives in France* at the end of the month. This was to prove an exceptionally strenuous assignment. He did not have a day off until the film was complete and the process of dubbing for the bilingual version was to mean that work on the picture went on until the middle of 1956 with constant visits to Paris. For his French version, Jack relied on the assistance of a French teacher, Madame Jolly, who became virtually a member of the Buchanan household.

Despite the irritation of constant trips to Paris – largely because Jack's co-star, Martine Carol, had more difficulty with her English than Jack had with his French – there were compensations to part-time living in France. There were meetings with old friends; Maurice Chevalier rallied round to greet his old film partner and arranged lavish parties for Jack and Suzzie to meet some of his friends. James and Gloria Stewart were in Paris for much of the same time on filming work. They soon established a regular foursome with Jack and Suzzie which included one all-night birthday party for Jimmy Stewart, literally under the bridges of Paris in a *Bateau Mouche*

As a result of her experience in being close to Jack in so many of his last film and theatre commitments, Suzzie gained a remarkable insight into the entertainment world. Much of this inevitably centred round Jack's work in the theatre, which was always his first and best love. She summarised her thoughts in her journal as follows:

The first time I visited Jack backstage I inadvertently whistled. Green and Jack looked at me in horror. 'Out, out you go' said Jack, opening the dressing room door into the corridor, 'Turn round three times and bow'. 'Why?' I complained, doing as I was told as his look and tone brooked no refusal. 'I thought everyone knew that it's bad luck to whistle in a dressing room, like putting shoes on a bed, or saying the last line of a play at rehearsal'. That was my first backstage lesson, and one of many I had to learn. Going backstage held its fascination for me and always will; it's the threshold to the land of make-believe.

Almost every night when Jack was playing I would go through the stage door to his dressing room just after he left it to go on for his last scene. I timed this very carefully, because to most actors any foreign element introduced backstage during a performance (and non-pro wives come under this category) is a distraction and can break the continuity of thought and concentration necessary for an actor to 'come across' night after night during a long run. I do know pros who can seemingly listen to the radio, watch T.V. and have a few drinks in their dressing rooms before the performance, and still play the piece well. But not many do and last. Certainly not the top people, who like Jack would never have a drink until after the final curtain, and who discouraged between-the-acts visitors.

My job, once in the dressing room, was to time fixing Jack's first drink of the evening with the final curtain. I would stand at the dressing room door, glass with gin and tonic and ice (which Green charmed from the stalls barmaid wherever we were) in hand as I heard the applause die away, and 'The Queen' played over the Tanoy system. Seconds later the sound of footsteps and in practised motions, a quick kiss, transference of glass, a cigarette lit, and long legs stretched out as he sank into his chair, a sip and a sigh of contentment. A few moments satisfaction of the job done for the day before the return to reality.

And then the visitors arrived. These backstage callers are a mixed blessing of theatre life. When an actor comes off after two hours or so in front of the public, he wants to relax and unwind. He has been working at full pitch, with tremendous concentration, and it takes at least a half hour to come down to a normal pace. Not all visitors are sensitive to this fact, since their working day has normally ended some hours before, and they have had a relaxing and enjoyable evening, and they don't think of acting as work.

Jack put backstage visitors roughly into three categories. First the management and the director, on business to do with the performance, secondly the fellow pros, actors and actresses who are 'resting' or between films, and thirdly the chums, non-theatrical friends, or friends of friends and fans from all over the world. The last group are the difficult ones. The friends of friends bring other friends who have never been backstage, and are quite naturally intrigued. They think the dressing rooms are too small, which indeed they are if you try to stuff the entire 'Giles' family into them, and serve them with a drink at the same time. And the non-pro visitors have a proclivity to try out the make-up on the tray, or putting on any false noses or wigs or comic props. This is frowned upon, obviously, and makes an awful mess. Green was jolly nippy at covering the make-up tray before the onslaught, and then he kept 'watch' at the door.

Jack never liked to know if there were any special friends or celebrities in the audience during the performance. He said that if he did he felt self-conscious and might try too hard to please. He preferred to play to an anonymous public, not individuals. But he was delighted to see them afterwards and to hear what they had to say, although he never asked them for an opinion. Any more than he ever read his press notices after an opening night. He said he would know soon enough by the box-office business and the audiences whether or not he had a success. I suppose that between the pre-London tours, and the run in London, I would see Jack's current play at least a dozen times in its entirety. And seeing snatches of it from time to time and listening to it over the loudspeaker in the dressing room, I would unconsciously know much of it by heart, and would snap to attention if someone muffed a line or embroidered on the original script. Sometimes I would hear new laughs creep in, with no change of dialogue and I would ask Jack about it. He would say 'I put in a bit of business, and it came off I think, anyway it got a good laugh'. Every night the audience differs, and so do the performances, I was to find out.

One night during the run of *Castle in the Air* we were having a quiet drink alone in the dressing room. It had been a particularly satisfying performance from Jack's point of view, a full house obviously enjoying themselves, laughing in all the right places, quiet when the dialogue indicated it, and that liaison between stage and audience had happened. Relaxed and thoughtful, Jack said: 'When I am old' . . . 'which you will never be' said I 'or when I retire' . . . 'which will never happen' I said again 'or maybe when we're on holiday in the sun and I have time to think' . . . 'that's better' I agreed.

'Well when that happens, Suzzie, I'm going to write a book about comedy. It is really the only thing in the world that I think I know about. You cannot make people laugh. If they feel it inside they will; the audience knows better than the actor, what amused them, and will behave accordingly. And thought comes across the footlights quicker than lines – if the thought is right. But if the actor doesn't think it through, particularly in farce, with tremendous sincerity and concentration, it just doesn't go over the footlights. Some of the funniest lines ever written can go for a 'Burton' if the chap who says them is thinking about what he'll have for supper.

People say I have a good sense of timing – and I think I have, but that's something you're born with and develop through listening. Tonight as I listened to the first act over the Tanoy I realised it was a very sticky audience. They seemed tired out, perhaps they'd overeaten, or been racing in the fresh air, and the stuffy atmosphere of the theatre made them sleepy. They seemed to sit there, unconsciously saying or thinking to themselves, "All right, we've paid for our seats, now entertain us". It's almost as if they dare us to make them laugh.'

'I know what you mean, darling, since I've been married to you I've become very sensitive to audiences, and it amazes me how they differ.'

'Well darling' said Jack 'that's just it. It is up to the actor on the stage to listen to the audience, and do his damnedest to get their attention. But so many of these youngsters on the stage nowadays don't listen to the audience. They realise the laughs aren't coming, but don't know why. They slow down and become discouraged and almost bloody minded, because they at least sense they aren't going over. I take my cue from the audience reaction before I go on, listening carefully to the first lines over the Tanoy or just off stage. When they aren't reacting as usual, I go on and throw the lines faster and harder. Speed up the tempo. The other actors automatically perk up and so does the audience. They snap out of their lethargy and sit up and take notice. And I keep throwing the lines faster until I feel their reaction, and the laughs and silences are coming in the right places as they should.'

He got up, stretched and sighed, 'It's the most fascinating business in the world, Suzzie, and that's why, when we're in it, we can't imagine anything else in the world so satisfying.' Characteristically, he rubbed his palms briskly together, head tilted on one side and said 'Fix us another little snort, baby, and I'll change. What's Minnie got for dinner, steak and kidney pud?'

XYZ

'The Happy Ending'

IN ONE OF JACK'S earliest silent films, *The Happy Ending*, the promotional blurb described how 'he died as a man might wish to die'. Life can often mirror art and so it was with the last year of Jack's life.

Towards the end of 1956, tests showed that he had cancer of the spine. For a long time, Suzzie and his doctor were able to conceal this from Jack. But even if – as is probable – he half suspected the truth, it was typical that Jack should meet this situation by continuing to work as hard as ever and in playing his full part in family life.

He went out on the road with a new comedy, *The French Mistress*, which he hoped to bring to the West End. The play was a light piece about the effect of a new and attractive French mistress on the life of a school in which Jack played the head-master. Melville Gillam had persuaded Jack to appear in the play and recalls how, even at the end, Jack maintained his 'larger than life' style.

> When the play was on in Manchester, I went to see Jack at the Central Hotel. He had the usual massive suite and I discovered that he had invited the Royal Ballet – who were also appearing in Manchester at that time – for drinks that evening. This was not just a question of entertaining Nureyev and Fonteyn, who were the principal dancers. He had literally invited all the company to be his guests for the evening.
>
> Soon afterwards, Jack took a break which we all said would allow him to rest before the West End opening. But in our hearts – and I suspect in his – we knew it would never happen.

Despite his growing ill health, Jack made a tremendous effort

238

to fulfil two major commitments in 1957. First, although by now in great pain, he took Suzzie to the Royal Garden Party, since he knew it would allow her to 'be presented' and, in turn, for Theo to be a débutante in the following year. Second, he appeared as the principal guest artist at the opening of Scottish I.T.V.

This – his last professional appearance – was singularly appropriate. Jack – the theatre's greatest backer of British television – was paying tribute not only to his Scottish boyhood friend, John Logie Baird, but to the homeland which had launched him – however uncertainly – in the entertainment world.

Jack and Suzzie were, by now, spending more and more time in Brighton, where their closest friends were Bill and Liz O'Bryen. Jack had known Bill from his earliest days as a great producer and theatrical agent. He was equally devoted to Liz O'Bryen who – as the actress Elizabeth Allen – had given up a brilliant stage and film career when her husband was taken ill. She discussed with Suzzie whether or not Jack should take part in the Scottish T.V. opening – given the obvious strain on his failing health – and ended the conversation by saying, correctly, 'There's no way on God's earth that you will stop him from doing it. He's made up his mind and he'll go on even if they have to carry him.'

In the event, Jack's determination once more showed the 'mind over matter' capacity at which Suzzie had always marvelled. He appeared, inevitably and fittingly, in top hat, white tie and tails to perform some of his best-known numbers. He showed all his old skill to the extent that the reviewers wrote with relish of the prospects of his further appearances in another play or film.

So well was the secret of Jack's illness kept that, only a few weeks before he died, there were serious offers for him to take over in Noël Coward's new play *Nude with Violin* and the touring version of *My Fair Lady*.

It was this ability to stay at the top of his profession to the last that was part of the happy ending. So too was his unchanged appearance. Apart from a neck brace which he covered with a scarf, Jack looked in MacDonald's words 'the same as ever and you wouldn't have known he was ill'. It was as if nature relented to the extent that he still had about him the look and the air of a man at the height of his power.

To read Suzzie's journal of their last days together is heart-rending. The treatment of cancer twenty years ago was unable to prevent acute suffering and Jack and Suzzie lived through many days and nights of pain without sleep. 'It was', as Coral Browne said, 'terrible that such a lovely man had to suffer so much.' The mental agony for Suzzie was no less. All that was left to sustain them was their love.

That this was Jack's greatest comfort there is no doubt and it was this which, above all else, ensured the happy ending. When, finally, at the beginning of October, he was taken secretly – since he and Suzzie did not want the pressures of massive publicity – to the Middlesex Hospital, he showed flashes of his old humour. The ambulance men were putting him on his stretcher leaving Mount Street when Jack called out to Green, 'Whatever are you thinking of – sending me out without my hat'. The pearl grey trilby was produced and J.B. went out with it resting on his chest.

Only a few days later, Green had a heart attack. He had been to see 'The Guv' daily and Suzzie made an excuse when he did not appear. He died a week or so before Jack, having already lost the focal point of his life. Manny at the Garrick said 'Oh, he's gone ahead to prepare Mr B's dressing room up there'.

Jack died peacefully on 21 October 1957. Mercifully, he was spared pain in his last few days.

After his death the Press asked Suzzie the secret of their undoubted happiness together. There was a small silence before she replied:

Oh, how I wish I'd met Jack's mother. You know, she knew the secret of how to instill respect for women in a man. Somehow Jack always made you feel feminine and wise. It was a natural thing with him. He didn't even know he was doing it. I think this was a lot to do with his success on the stage. His respect for women leapt across the footlights and spread among the audience.

I was Jack's best friend as well as his wife. We were a team. Perhaps subconsciously we both knew there was so little time. Perhaps that's why we crammed a lifetime of happiness into nine, short, wonderful years of marriage.

There were two memorial services for Jack, one in public and one in private. The private occasion was unique. Suzzie wrote to Cunard White Star officials reminding them of Jack's love of the sea and his last wish that his ashes should be scattered from the deck of one of the *Queens*. Cunard had previously refused to allow this kind of ceremony but, remembering Jack had made more than fifty crossings with them, agreed that this could take place in the strictest secrecy. Thus, one grey morning on board the *Queen Mary*, Captain Law commended Jack's ashes to the deep in Southampton Water.

On the same day, the official memorial service took place at the chief Scottish church in London, St Columba's in Pont Street, Westminster. Among the ushers were Tom Arnold, Robert Nesbitt, Fred Emney and Alan Melville. Bill Kendall read the lesson and Vanessa Lee sang from the organ loft 'And Then a Violin Began to Play' from *King's Rhapsody*. Dr Scott, a former moderator of the church of Scotland, who conducted the service, spoke of Jack's 'ready wit and merry laughter, the high integrity of his art, the warmth and faithfulness of his friendship and the joy of happiness he brought to many'.

Suzzie and Theo were supported by Richard Greville and, in the congregation were many of the greatest names in the theatre. They included Laurence Olivier, Henry Kendall, Frank Lawton and Evelyn Laye, Cicely Courtneidge, Adele Dixon, Robertson Hare, Elizabeth Allan, Elisabeth Welch, Elsie Randolph, Anna Neagle, Zena Dare, Clive Brook, Geraldo, Leslie Henson, Naunton Wayne and Peter Graves.

Outside, there were other mourners in the streets around St Columba's. There were the Gallery Girls – the faithful fans over so many years, members of the public and, it was said, scores of old actors weeping unashamedly.

Suzzie received many hundreds of letters of condolence. From Jack's professional colleagues, the tributes came warm and genuine. Douglas Fairbanks sent a five page telegram. Anton Dolin wrote of the happiest year and a half of his life when he forsook classical ballet to work with Jack in *Stand Up and Sing*, adding 'His loss to his friends is irreparable, for such loyalty and friendship is rare'. Laurence Olivier described 'the admiration I felt for him as a person and as an artist', while his wife, Vivian Leigh, said, 'London will never feel the same without him'. Jack Strachey who had composed songs for Jack long before his success with 'These Foolish Things' said 'He, more than anyone else living, revived the nostalgic memories of our youth'.

The Press, too, reflected an almost unique appreciation of the affection Jack had aroused with critics as well as the public. This was all the more striking as Fleet Street had long described Jack as 'The male Greta Garbo' because of his aversion to personal publicity. Yet, for the *Daily Telegraph*, he was 'the most popular musical comedy artist in Britain'. Cecil Wilson said that the greatest tribute to Jack's work was his ability to stay at the top for forty years. Recalling his return to Hollywood for *The Band Wagon* with Fred Astaire, he added 'The film was a triumph for the two boys of the old top hat brigade, but Jack Buchanan smiled when it was hailed as his come-back. He had never really gone away'. Perhaps *The Times* put Jack's place in the theatre world into its apt perspective when it described him as the last of the 'Knuts' adding, 'He belonged to the gay tradition of dude comedians who will be remembered most affectionately for the seemingly lazy but accomplished grace with which he sang, danced, flirted, and joked his way through musical shows between the Wars'.

Press comment in America was equally fulsome. For the *New*

York Times, 'Few British musical show comedians have been more popular here'. The *New York Herald Tribune* recalled how, with *The Band Wagon*, Jack had 'made himself known to an entirely new generation in designing a new career to suit them'. Richard Watts, Jr in the *New York Post* who – with the other 'Butchers of Broadway' had sometimes been severely critical of Jack's later choice of material in America – nevertheless summed up his views simply: '. . . In a time when all sorts of performers are loosely called "great", the late Jack Buchanan was one who really deserved the title'.

Perhaps the most elegant and personal Press tribute to Jack came from his fellow Scot, Logan Gourlay, in the *Daily Express*. He wrote: 'Jack Buchanan died as he lived. Quietly. With dignity. Without fuss. It is not irreverent to say that he died with his hat on – the pearl grey trilby which he wore with such panache – even indoors on occasions.'

By his bedside when he died was a copy of his national and favourite poet – Robert Burns. And from Burns, I take the epitaph that fits like the hat that never left him:

'I've play'd mysel a bonie spring
An' danc'd my fill'

There was one aspect of the reporting of Jack's death which had a certain cruel irony. Almost every report suggested that he died one of the richest men in the theatre. As Cecil Wilson wrote, 'Just how rich, his Scot's caution would never allow him to reveal. But he was something more than the Beau Brummell of the West End stage, something more than a national idol, who reflected every man's vain dream of himself. He was the shrewdest business brain that ever came out of the musical comedy chorus.'

This view was shared on the other side of the Atlantic. Only a few weeks before Jack's death, Robert Coleman, writing in the New York *Daily Mirror* had described a discussion of the Broadway Historical Society at which it was generally agreed that the world's richest actor was Jack Buchanan, adding 'He owns theatres and is greeted like a Lord when he passes down Threadneedle Street. Ironically, the clever Jack, unlike Laurence Olivier, Ralph Richardson and John Gielgud, hasn't been knighted. He just owns tons of pounds.'

It came as a distinct shock when Jack's Will was published showing that he had left £24,489. As he had agreed to buy a new Mayfair penthouse only weeks before his death, the net value of the estate was reduced to £1,489.

It was then that the Press recalled Jack's reputation in the theatre as 'God's almoner'. The *Daily Mail* commented: 'People were surprised to learn what was left of Jack Buchanan's fortune. They knew he earned lavishly, spent lavishly and lost lavishly in business ventures. But until now the real reason for the disappearing thousands was Buchanan's secret – he also gave lavishly. And he never wanted anyone to know. A few years ago, he lent a theatre manager ten thousand pounds. Buchanan never saw the money again. But that did not worry the Good Samaritan of Shaftesbury Avenue. His old friend, Jack Prendegast, an executor of the will, said, "He wanted to die rich in friends". And in friends he was a millionaire'.

In assessing Jack Buchanan's place in the social as well as theatrical history of the twentieth century, perhaps the most remarkable feature was his durability. For those over forty, he will always represent the epitome of West End elegance, the days when musical comedy was part of a national confidence in which, like Jack's own on stage self-confidence, one showed one's best face to the world at large whatever one's private worries.

For many under forty, Jack Buchanan is part of a theatrical legend which still exerts its spell today. But, inevitably, it was those who had the good fortune to see Jack at the height of his career who can best sum up the affection so many felt for him. Sir Harold Hobson – the doyen of London dramatic critics – in a special appreciation for this book writes:

I believe that in Kipling's 'Song of the Banjo' there is a verse which, slightly paraphrased, says:
'I am Memory and Pleasure, I am Town,
I am all that ever went with evening dress'.
That was what the great Jack Buchanan, with his tall, slim, elegant figure, nonchalantly dancing the foxtrot as no one else could with such ease and grace, meant to me in the days in the twenties when I saw him in *Sunny*, *That's a Good Girl* and in Charles Cochran's incomparable revues.

To those of us who were up at Oxford at that time it meant tail coats, white ties and waistcoats, and gleaming top hats; Leicester Square, and the lights blazing from the London Palladium in a Piccadilly Circus that was still a credit to a world of pleasure beyond my reach. There was a magic to life at Oxford, too, but always beyond Magdalen Bridge there was the glitter of London, and the irresistable lure of the world of chorus girls and tap dancing and romance in which Jack Buchanan lived and had his suave and civilised being.

Now it is evident that I, who have seen Beckett, and Olivier, and Ashcroft and Feuillère, and Richardson, would not in my articles refer to the 'great Buchanan' as often as I do, if he were no more than another accomplished dancer like Fred Astaire. He was in fact that most potent of magical things, a myth. We all thrill to the moment when the tortoise beats the hare. The greatness of Buchanan, his memorability, lay in the opposite of that. *His* supreme moment was when the hare lost to the tortoise.

He was always the handsomest man on the stage; always the most graceful; always the most accomplished; always the one best qualified to play the conquering hero. But he never did play the conquering hero. With all his brilliance, he chose to be the one who was invariably defeated, and put off with the second best. If there were twenty men on the stage in tails, and one in a dinner jacket, that one was Jack Buchanan. When he took part in an operatic quartet, it was always Jack Buchanan's music sheet that fell to pieces. With all his talents, he affected to be rather slow-witted. In *Sunny* he uttered an epigram I have never forgotten. He stood in the middle of the stage, and pondered with immense concentration the problem 'Whether it is better to keep one's mouth shut and be thought a fool, or to open it and remove all doubt'. But, handsome and glittering, he carried through his defeats and disappointments with a modest refusal to be discouraged, even with a certain quiet satisfaction. He was the exemplification of the great truth that to win is not the important thing, but to wander through defeat with happy nonchalance.

But the final words on Jack must come from two of those whose work gave them special opportunities to pay tribute to him. Both have spent their lives in the theatre. One is an international star and the other totally unknown to the public at large.

For Wilfrid Hyde White, Jack's death was more than the loss of a professional colleague. He felt then – as he does today – that Jack's contribution to the theatre was unique. On the night of 21 October 1957, he was appearing in a play at Coventry. He recalls his remarks at the final curtain:

> I merely said, there was some very grave news. Jack Buchanan had died that morning – an event which would affect directly or indirectly every single member of the English-speaking theatrical profession and every single listener or member of an English-speaking audience. I said some actors have style, some have grace, some have elegance but Mr Buchanan had these admirable qualities to a unique extent. I didn't know him well but you didn't have to know him well to have affection, respect and admiration for him. He wrote his name in large letters in the theatrical dictionary.
>
> Look under the 'B' for Buchanan or for beauty; look under 'G' for glamour; 'R' for romance; 'M' for magic; you will find him in all of these. Also, as a manager, if other producers and impresarios had run their affairs as he did, there would be no reason for shop stewards, or Equity, or for the electricians or stagehands to be protected. Then I finished by saying it will be

a long, long, time before he is replaced and the end of time before he is forgotten.

Betty Daly retired recently from the Garrick Theatre where she and her sister, Marie, had worked for over thirty years. Even earlier, they knew Jack when they had worked in the chorus of shows when he was first beginning. At the Garrick, Marie was in charge of the cloakroom and Betty took the tickets on the door.

From the day that Jack died until their retirement, they put fresh flowers in a little vase under the picture of him by Baron which still hangs in the foyer. One night, a year or two ago, when the author stood looking at this picture, Betty Daly asked, 'Do you know about Jack Buchanan?' When she was assured that this was the purpose of the present book, she said simply, 'Bless him, there'll never be another one like him.'

The picture by Baron which still hangs in the foyer of the Garrick Theatre.

Career of Jack Buchanan

(Born in Helensburgh 2 April 1890. Died in London 21 October 1957)

The chronological list which follows covers the highlights of Jack Buchanan's work on stage, screen and television. Details of theatrical productions are almost all confined to the part played, the name of the show and the principal theatre concerned (since much additional information is given in the text of the book). Except as noted, the more detailed chronological film listing is based on the British release date and other information is provided in the following sequence: title, producing and distribution companies (in brackets), producer, director, co-stars (normally leading ladies) followed by supporting actors (listed alphabetically), song titles and any miscellaneous information.

1911	First professional appearances in Scotland in variety at Pickard's Panoptican, Glasgow and at the Edinburgh Empire followed by a small part in *The Elder at the Plate* at the Grand Theatre, Glasgow.
1912 September	First London appearance as M. Deschamps in *The Grass Widows* at the Apollo.
1913 April	Understudy for Vernon Watson and Lionel Mackinder in the revue *All the Winners* at the Empire.
1913 Christmas	Appeared as specialist dancer in *Little Miss Muffet* at the Theatre Royal, Birmingham.
1914 March	Fourth billing in *A Mixed Grill* at the Empire, Leicester Square.
1914 (End)	Touring as understudy to Jack Hulbert in *The Cinema Star*.
1915–1917	Touring as Dudley Mitten in *Tonight's the Night*.
1917 May	Took over from Jack Hulbert as Phyllis Monkman's leading man in the Charlot revue *Bubbly* at the Comedy.
1917 July	Pearly in *Round the Map* at the Alhambra.
1917 October	*Auld Lang Syne* (British and Commonwealth – Unicorn). Director Sidney Morgan. With Violet Graham, Henry Baynton, George Bellamy, Sydney Fairbrother and Roy Travers.
1918 June	Returned to Charlot revue in *Tails Up* at the Comedy.
1918/1919	Appeared with Phyllis Monkman in show for the B.E.F. at Wimereux and in Volterra's revue at the Casino de Paris.
1919 March	*Her Heritage* (Ward's Films). Director Bannister Merwin. With Phyllis Monkman, E. Holman Clark, Winifred Dennis and Edward O'Neill.
1920 January	Hon. Bill Malcolm in *Wild Geese* at the Comedy.
1920 June	In revue *Bran Pie* at the Prince of Wales.
1920 September	Max Roper in *Her Dancing Man* at the Garrick.
1921 April	Faust in *Faust on Toast* at the Gaiety.
1921 August	Peter Bassett in *The Trump Card* on the Strand.
1921 October	Returned to Charlot revue as partner to Gertrude Lawrence in *A to Z* at the Prince of Wales.

1922 December   Entered management when appearing as Alfred Butler in *Battling Butler* at the New Oxford.

1924 January   Appeared with Gertrude Lawrence and Beatrice Lillie in *André Charlot's Revue of 1924* at Times Square Theatre, New York.

1924 May   Anthony Prince in *Toni* (also produced) at the Shaftesbury.

1924 October   *The Audacious Mr Squire* (British and Commonwealth). Producer Edward Godal. Director Edwin Greenwood. With Valia, Forbes Dawson, Sydney Paxton, Fred Rains, Dorinea Shirley, Russell Thorndike and Malcolm Tod.

1925 January   *The Happy Ending* (Gaumont). Director George A. Cooper. With Fay Compton, Joan Barry, Pat Doyle, Jack Hobbs, Benita Hume, Gladys Jennings, Eric Lewis, Doris Manswell, A. G. Poulton, Donald Searle and Drusilla Wills.

1925 March   Lord Algernon Kenilworth in *Boodle* at the Empire.

1925 July   In *Charlot's Revue* at the Prince of Wales.

1925 October   *Settled out of Court* (Gaumont). Director George A. Cooper. With Fay Compton, Jeanne de Casalis, Malcolm Keen, Kinsey Piele, and Leon Quartermaine.

1925 November   *A Typical Budget* (Gainsborough) Director Adrian Brunel. Producer Michael Balcon. A solo performance in one of the Gainsborough Burlesque shorts.

1925 November   *Bulldog Drummond's Third Round* (Astra-National) Director Sidney Morgan. With Juliette Compton, Betty Faire, Frank Goldsmith, Allan Jeaves, Austin Leigh, Phil Scott and Edward Sorley.

1925 November   Returned to Broadway with Gertrude Lawrence and Beatrice Lillie in *Charlot's Revue, 1926* at the Selwyn.

1926 October   Jim Demming in *Sunny* at the London Hippodrome.

1927 November   *Confetti* (First National – Pathé). Producer Harry Ham. Director Graham Cutts. With Annette Benson, Sydney Fairbrother, Robin Irvine, Audree Sayre and Georges Teroff.

1928 June   *Toni* (BIP – Wardour). Director Arthur Maude. With Dorothy Boyd, W. Lawson Butt, Frank Goldsmith, Forrester Harvey, Hayford Hobbs, Moore Marriott and Henry Vibart.

1928 June   Bill Barrow in *That's a Good Girl* at the London Hippodrome.

1929 September   Appeared in variety at the London Palladium.

1929 November   *Paris* (First National Pictures). Producer Bobby North. Director Clarence Badger. With Irene Bordoni, Margaret Fielding, Louise Closser Hale, ZaSu Pitts, Jason Robards. Songs: 'Among My Souvenirs', 'Crystal Girl', 'I'm a Little Negative Looking for a Positive', 'I Wonder what is Really on his Mind', 'Miss Wonderful', 'My Lover' and 'Somebody Mighty Like You'. (Note: The release date shown is that of the American première.)

1929 December   Appeared with Jessie Matthews in C. B. Cochran's revue *Wake Up and Dream* at the Selwyn, New York.

1930 May   *The Glee Quartet* (Warner Brothers) (Note: This sequence was based on the Quartet from *Sunny* and was originally shot for the Warner Brothers all star revue, *The Show of Shows*. It was released separately as a comedy short.)

1930 August   *Monté Carlo* (Paramount). Director Ernst Lubitsch. With Jeanette MacDonald, Claud Allister, Lionel Belmore, Erik Bey, Tyler Brooke, Albert Conti, Helen Garden, Donald

Novis, David Percy, ZaSu Pitts and John Roche. Songs: 'Always in All Ways', 'Beyond the Blue Horizon', 'Day of Days', 'Give Me a Moment Please', 'I'm a Simple-Hearted Man', 'She'll Love Me and Like It', and 'Trimmin' the Women'. (Note: The release date shown is that of the American première.)

1931   *The Invisible Enemy* (Note: This short film was an appeal made by Jack Buchanan on behalf of the West End Hospital for Nervous Diseases.)

1931 March   Rockingham Smith in *Stand Up and Sing* (part-author) at the London Hippodrome.

1931 December   *Man of Mayfair* (Paramount British). Producer Walter Morosco. Director Louis Mercanton. With Joan Barry, Lilian Braithwaite, Charles Quartermaine, Cyril Raymond, Sebastian Smith, Nora Swinburne, Ellaline Terris, Warwick Ward and J. Fisher White. Song: 'Alone with My Dreams'.

1932 March   *Goodnight, Vienna* (British and Dominion – W. & F.) Producer/Director Herbert Wilcox. With Anna Neagle, Muriel Aked, Joyce Bland, Herbert Carrick, Peggy Cartwright, O. B. Clarence, Clive Currie, Clifford Heatherley, William Kendall, Gina Malo and Gibb McLaughlin. Songs: 'Goodnight Vienna', 'Just Heaven', 'Living in Clover' and 'Marching Song'. (Note: In the United States this film was released under the title *Magic Night*.)

1932 December   Michael Bramleigh in *Pardon my English* at the Garrick, Philadelphia.

1933 January   *Yes, Mr Brown* (British and Dominion — W. & F.) Producer Herbert Wilcox. Directors Herbert Wilcox and Jack Buchanan. With Elsie Randolph, Margot Grahame, Clifford Heatherley, Vera Pearce and Hartley Power. Songs: 'Leave a Little Love for Me', 'Yes, Mr Brown'.

1933 September   *That's a Good Girl* (British and Dominion – U.A.). Producer Herbert Wilcox. Director Jack Buchanan. With Elsie Randolph, Kate Cutler, Antony Holles, Dorothy Hyson, William Kendall, Garry Marsh, Vera Pearce and Frank Stanmore. Songs: 'Fancy Our Meeting', 'Now That I've Found You', 'Oh! La! La!' and 'So Green'.

1934 February   Dick Whittington in *Mr Whittington* at the London Hippodrome.

1935 January   *Brewster's Millions* (British and Dominion – U.A.) Producer Herbert Wilcox. Director Thornton Freeland. With Lili Damita, Allan Aynesworth, Fred Emney, Sydney Fairbrother, Dennis Hoey, Antony Holles, Ian McLean, Nancy O'Neil, Sebastian Shaw, Amy Veness and Henry Wenman. Songs: 'I Think I Can', 'One Good Tune Deserves Another', 'Pull Down the Blind'.

1935 May   René, in *The Flying Trapeze* at the Alhambra.

1935 November   *Come Out of the Pantry* (British and Dominion – U.A.) Producer Herbert Wilcox. Director Jack Raymond. With Fay Wray, Olive Blakeney, James Carew, Kate Cutler, W. T. Ellwanger, Fred Emney, Marie O'Neill, Ronald Squire, Ethel Stewart and Ben Welden. Songs: 'Everything Stops for Tea', 'From One Minute to Another'.

1936 January   *Limelight* (Wilcox – GFD). Director Herbert Wilcox. Note: Jack Buchanan made a guest apearance with Anna Neagle in this film which was released in the United States with the title *Backstage*.

1936 February *When Knights Were Bold* (Capital – GFD). Producer Max Schach. Director Jack Raymond. With Fay Wray, Kate Cutler, Aubrey Fitzgerald, Robert Horton, Martita Hunt, Moore Marriott, Garry Marsh, Aubrey Mather and Robert Nainby. Songs: 'I'm Still Dreaming', 'Let's Put Some People to Work'.

1936 September Bill Hopping in *This'll Make You Whistle* at the Palace.

1937 November *This'll Make You Whistle* (Wilcox – GFD). Producer/Director Herbert Wilcox. With Elsie Randolph, Marjorie Brooks, Jean Gillie, Antony Holles, David Hutcheson, Miki Hood, Maidie Hope and William Kendall. Songs: 'I'm in a Dancing Mood', 'There isn't any Limit to My Love for You', 'This'll Make You Whistle', 'Without Rhythm'.

1937 September *Smash and Grab* (Jack Buchanan – GFD). Director Tim Whelan. With Elsie Randolph, David Burns, Lawrence Grossmith, Lawrence Hanray, Antony Holles, Edward Lexy, Arthur Margetson, Sara Seegar, Edmund Willard and Zoe Wynn. (Note: Released in the United States in January 1941 under the title *Larceny Street*.)

1937 November *The Sky's The Limit* (Jack Buchanan – GFD) Directors Lee Garmes and Jack Buchanan. With Mara Loseff, Sara Allgood, David Burns, C. M. Hallard, Morris Harvey, Antony Holles, David Hutcheson, William Kendall, Barry Lupino, H. F. Maltby, Wally Patch and Athene Seyler. Songs: 'The Montreal', 'Swing Madame'.

1937 December Peter Anthony in *Between the Devil* at the Majestic, New York.

1938 January *Sweet Devil* (Jack Buchanan – GFD) Director René Guissart. (Note: This film was produced by the J.B. Film Company as a starring vehicle for Bobby Howes and Jean Gillie.)

1938 July *Break the News* (Jack Buchanan – GFD). Director René Clair. With Maurice Chevalier, June Knight, Felix Aylmer, George Hayes, Marta Labarr, Garry Marsh, Gibb McLaughlin, Guy Middleton, Gertrude Musgrove, Wally Patch, Athole Stewart, C. Denier Warren and Robb Wilton. Song: 'It All Belongs to You'.

1939 April With Gilbert Miller presented *The Women* at the Lyric.

1939 June *The Gang's All Here* (ABPC) Producers Walter Mycroft and Jack Buchanan. Director Thornton Freeland. With Googie Withers, Edward Everett Horton, David Burns, Charles Carson, Otto Kruger, Edward Lexy, Leslie Perrins, Walter Rilla, Jack la Rue, Ronald Shiner, Syd Walker and Robb Wilton. (Note: In the United States released as *The Amazing Mr Forrest*.)

1939 December *The Middle Watch* (ABPC). Producer Walter C. Mycroft. Director Thomas Bentley. With Greta Gynt, Romney Brent, Fred Emney, Leslie Fuller, Jean Gillie, Louise Hampton, Martita Hunt, David Hutcheson, Reginald Purdell, Bruce Seton, Ronald Shiner and Kay Walsh.

1940 March Returned to revue in *Top Hat and Tails* at the Imperial, Brighton and on tour.

1940 April *Bulldog Sees it Through* (ABPC). Producer Walter C. Mycroft. Director Harold Huth. With Greta Gynt, Googie

	Withers, Arthur Hambling, David Hutcheson, Aubrey Mallalieu, Nadine March, Robert Newton, Sebastian Shaw, Ronald Shiner, Polly Ward and Wylie Watson.
1940 December	Buttons in *Cinderella* at the Empire, Sheffield and on tour.
1941 March	William Blake in *The Body Was Well Nourished* on tour to Newcastle, Liverpool, Streatham Hill, Manchester, Oxford, Norwich, Bournemouth, Nottingham, Bradford, Sheffield, Leeds, Southport, Brighton, Reading, Torquay, Exeter, Cardiff, Cambridge, Tunbridge Wells, Dudley, Leicester, Cheltenham, Bristol, Carlisle, Dewsbury, Huddersfield and York.
1941 December	Buttons in *Cinderella* at the Theatre Royal, Birmingham.
1942 September	Produced *Waltz Without End* at the Cambridge.
1942 December	Buttons in *Cinderella* at the Theatre Royal, Birmingham.
1943 April	*Happidrome* (Aldwych – MGM) (Note: Jack Buchanan was co-producer with Tom Arnold and Harold Boxall of this film version of the B.B.C. Radio Series starring Harry Korris, Robbie Vincent and Cecil Frederick.)
1943 July	Willmott Brown in *It's Time to Dance* at the Winter Garden.
1944 March	Presented *A Murder for a Valentine* at the Lyric.
1944 June	Lord Dilling in *The Last of Mrs Cheyney* at the Savoy.
1944	*Some Like it Rough.* (Note: Jack Buchanan's voice was used in this Wartime Short.)
1945 October	In revue *Fine Feathers* at the Prince of Wales.
1946 November	Produced *Treble Trouble* at the Garrick.
1947 November	Geoffrey Lymes in *Canaries Sometimes Sing* at the Garrick.
1948 April	Elwood P. Dowd in *Harvey* at the 48th Street Theatre, New York.
1948 June	Produced *The Lady Asks for Help* at the Garrick.
1948 December ⎫ 1949 January ⎭	Daniel Bachelet in *Don't Listen Ladies* at the Booth, New York and the St James in London.
1949 December	The Earl of Locharne in *Castle in the Air* at the Adelphi.
1951	*A Boy and a Bike* (Note: Jack Buchanan was the Producer of this Short.)
1951 April	Nikki in *King's Rhapsody* at the Palace.
1952 May	*Giselle* (Craft – Ex). (Note: Jack Buchanan narrated the script for this short ballet film which starred Alicia Markova and Anton Dolin.)
1952 September	Appeared with Bing Crosby and Bob Hope at the Stoll Theatre Charity Matinée.
1953 January	Appeared in *The Bob Hope T.V. Show*, New York.
1953 July	John Bentley in *As Long as They're Happy* at the Garrick.
1953 July	*The Band Wagon* (M.G.M.) Producer Arthur Freed. Director Vincent Minelli. With Fred Astaire, Cyd Charisse, Nanette Fabray, Oscar Levant, James Mitchell. Songs: 'By Myself', 'I Guess I'll Have to Change my Plan', 'That's Entertainment' and 'Triplets'.
1954 March	Appeared in *Midnight Cavalcade* at the London Palladium.
1954 November	Appeared in *Royal Command Variety Performance* at the London Palladium.
1954 December	Appeared in *The Max Liebman T.V. Show* in New York.
1955 March	*As Long as They're Happy* (Group – GFD). Producer Raymond Stross. Director J. Lee-Thompson. With Jean Carson, Jeanette Scott, Brenda de Banzie, Dora Bryan, Diana Dors, Nigel Greene, Gilbert Harding, Charles Hawtrey,

	David Hurst, Hugh MacDermott, Athene Seyler, Joan Sims, Susan Stephen and Jerry Wayne. Song: 'Cry'.
1955 April	Appeared in *The Ed Sullivan T.V. Show* in New York.
1955 June	Produced *The Lost Generation* at the Garrick.
1955 December	*Josephine and Men* (Charter – BL). Producer John Boulting. Director Roy Boulting. With Glynis Johns, Peter Finch, Lisa Gastoni, William Hartnell, John le Mesurier, Victor Maddern, Hugh Moxey, Lawrence Naismith, Donald Sinden, Ronald Squire, Heather Thatcher and Thorley Walters.
1956 May	Appeared with Tommy Steele in Val Parnell's Saturday T.V. Spectacular at the Wood Green Empire.
1956 August	Touring in *The French Mistress*.
1956 August	Appeared in the first transmission of Independent Scottish Television at the Theatre Royal, Glasgow in *This is Scotland*.
1957 May	*The French They are a Funny Race* (Gaumont-Continental Distributing). Written and Directed by Preston Sturges. With Martine Carol, Catherine Boyle, Genevieve Brunet, Andre Luguet, Noel-Noel and Totti Truman Taylor. (Note: The release date shown is that of the American première. Multilingual versions of the film were released in Britain and France after Jack Buchanan's death under the title of *The Diaries of Major Thompson*.)

Discography

Two stories illustrate Jack Buchanan's ability as a recording artist at all times and in all places. First, Richard Murdoch describes how, in 1933, Jack recorded his first film record success, the title song from *Goodnight Vienna*:

Jack made it one morning on the stage of the Liverpool Empire. He invited the whole company to come and watch. I think he may have had a bit of a party the night before. Anyway after he sang the opening words 'Goodnight Vienna' way up there, he dropped a whole octave in the next line 'You city of a million melodies'. It was outrageous but he could get away with it. I wondered how it would come out because the Liverpool Empire was a vast barn of a place. He not only filled it for six weeks when we played there but his voice got right up to the back of the gallery. It was the same with the recording. He had that wonderful timbre in his voice and he put it over by sheer professionalism.

Second, Coral Browne tells how Jack's records are heard even behind the Iron Curtain:

Several years after Jack's death, I was playing with the Old Vic in Moscow when I received a message asking if I would go and see Guy Burgess. I was intrigued to meet this notorious runaway spy. When I got to his flat we had a rather miserable lunch because he couldn't eat anything (apparently he had trouble with his teeth and found it difficult to get treatment in Moscow). After lunch he revealed that the real purpose of the invitation was to ask me to take his measurements so that he could order some clothes in Saville Row. To cap this he told me that I couldn't leave for another two hours until he got a telephone message as he was under observation by Russian security agents and this was the only basis on which my visit had been allowed. To fill in the time, he suggested that we might have some music. He told me that he had only brought two things with him when he fled Britain and they were both gramophone records. When he put on the first record, I discovered it was one of Jack Buchanan's selections. There I was, two days before Christmas, it was snowing and one couldn't have felt more miserable to be away from home. What made it all the more poignant was sitting there in the most unlikely place in the world listening to Jack's voice forever perpetuating a light-hearted and carefree land of make believe.

In the detailed listing which follows, I am indebted to Brian Rust and Rex Burnett and General Gramophone Publications Limited for their permission to draw freely from *London Musical Shows on Record 1897–1976*. Unless otherwise indicated, each entry is in the following sequence: Accompaniment, venue and date of recording, Manufacturer's catalogue number, title, co-artists and composer's names (in brackets), record number or test details and, if not indicated earlier, details of shows or films represented. The record companies concerned are Columbia (Col) both U.K. and U.S.A., His Master's Voice (HMV), Brunswick (Br) and Metro Goldwyn Mayer U.S.A. (MGM)

Acc. by the Comedy Theatre Orchestra, cond. by Philip Braham. (All three titles are from *Tails Up*). London, c. 18 June 1918.
76182–1 Any Little Thing (w/Phyllis Monkman)   Col L–1254

| 76183–1 Gnee-ah! | Col L–1253 |
| 76184–2 The Special Cop (w/Phyllis Monkman) | Col L–1254 |

Orch. acc. cond. by George W. Byng. Hayes, Middlesex, 23 November 1921.

| Bb–703–3 | Keep Moving (w/Bessie Jones–Peter Dawson-Edward Halland behind Helen Trix) (Helen Trix) | HMV B–1301 |
| Bb–704–2 | Dapper Dan (w/Trix Sisters) (von Tilzer) And Her Mother Came Too (Ivor Novello) | HMV B–1302 HMV test (un-numbered) |

NOTE: The above three titles are all from *A to Z*.

Hayes, Middlesex, 17 January 1922.

| Bb–914–1 | And Her Mother Came Too (Ivor Novello) | HMV B–1319 |
| Bb–915–2 | My Alco Holiday (Kenneth Duffield) | – |

NOTE: Both the above titles are from *A to Z*.

Acc. by the Shaftesbury Theatre Orchestra, cond. by Thomas Tunbridge. London, 28 May 1924.

A–906	Blotto	Col 3451
A–907	Take A Step	–
A–908	Don't Love You (w/Elsie Randolph)	Col 3453
A–909	Do It For Me (w/June)	Col 3452
A–910	For My Friend (w/June)	–

NOTE: The above five titles are all from *Toni*.

Orch. acc. cond. by George W. Byng. Hayes, Middlesex, 9 April 1925.

| Bb–6021–1 Garden of Lies (w/June) (*Boodle*) | HMV B–2005 |
| Bb–6022–2 This Year, Next Year (w/June) (*Boodle*) | – |

Piano acc. by R. H. Bowers. New York, 17 November 1925.

| 141271–2 | A Cup of Coffee, a Sandwich and You (w/Gertrude Lawrence) (*Charlot's Revue of 1926* – Meyer – Rose – Dublin) | Col 512–D |

New York, 20 November 1925.

| 141295–2–3 | Gigolette (*Charlot's Revue of 1926* – Franz Lehar) | Col 514–D |

Orch. acc. cond. by ? Percival Mackey. London, 15 October 1926.

| WAX–2023–2 | Let's Say Goodnight till the Morning (w/Elsie Randolph) (*Sunny*) | Col 9147 |
| WAX–2024–1–2 | Who ? (w/Binnie Hale) (*Sunny*) | Rejected |

London, 19 October 1926.

WA–4292–1	When We Get Our Divorce (w/Binnie Hale) (*Sunny*)	Col 4141
WA–4293–2	I've Looked For Trouble (*Sunny*)	–
WAX–2024–3	Who ? (w/Binnie Hale) (*Sunny*)	Col 9147

Acc. by Debroy Somers' Band, cond. by Leonard Hornsey. London, 19 June 1928.

| WA–7519–1 | Sweet So-and-So | Col 4952 |
| WAX–3802–2 | Fancy Our Meeting (w/Elsie Randolph) | Col 9462 |

London, 26 June 1928.

| WA–7547–1 | Parting Time (w/Vera Pearce/Raymond Newell) | Col 4952 |
| WAX–3836–2 | The One I'm Looking For (w/Elsie Randolph) | Col 9462 |

NOTE: All the last four titles above are from *That's a Good Girl*.

Acc. by the London Hippodrome Orchestra, cond. by Harry Perritt. London, 14 April 1931.

WA–11451	Stand Up and Sing	Col DB–484
WA–11452	I Would If I Could	Col DB–486
WA–11453	Night Time	Col DB–484
WA–11454	It's Not You (w/Elsie Randolph)	Col DB–485
WA–11455	There's Always Tomorrow (w/Elsie Randolph)–	
WA–11456	Take It Or Leave It	Col DB–486

    NOTE: The above six titles are all from *Stand Up and Sing*.

Orch. acc. cond. by Ray Noble. London, 29 October 1931.

OB–1771–1	You Forgot Your Gloves	HMV B–4005
OB–1772–3	Alone with My Dreams (Film *Man Of Mayfair*)	–

Kingsway Hall, London, 18 January 1932.

OBR–100–1–2	Living in Clover	HMV B–4083
OBR–101–3	Goodnight, Vienna	–

    NOTE: Both the above titles are from the film *Goodnight, Vienna*.

London, 8 March 1933.

OB–6327–1	Yes, Mr Brown	HMV B–4398
OB–6328–1	Leave A Little Love For Me	–

    NOTE: Both the above titles are from the film *Yes, Mr Brown*.

London, 4 October 1933.

OB–5367–2	Fancy Our Meeting (w/Elsie Randolph)	HMV B–8026
OB–5368–2	Now That I've Found You (w/Elsie Randolph)	–

    NOTE: Both the above titles are from the film *That's a Good Girl*.

London, 5 October 1933.

2B–5369–2	Jack Buchanan Medley – Part 1 (Intro. Dancing Honeymoon (*Battling Butler*)/ And Her Mother Came Too (*A To Z*) Fancy Our Meeting (*That's A Good Girl*)/Who ? (*Sunny*)	HMV C–2630
2B–5370–2	Jack Buchanan Medley – Part 2 (Intro. Two Little Bluebirds (*Sunny*)/Goodnight, Vienna (from the film)/It's Not You /There's Always Tomorrow (both from *Stand Up and Sing*)	–
OB–5371–2	So Green (Film *That's a Good Girl*)	HMV B–8027
OB–5372–2	Oh ! La ! La ! (Film *That's a Good Girl*)	–

Comedy sketch with supporting cast. London, 6 October 1933.

OB–5373–6	Adapted From The French – Part 1	HMV B–8072
OB–5374–2	Adapted From the French –Part 2	–

Orch. acc. cond. by Ray Noble. London, 19 December 1933.

OB–5524–2	Oceans of Time (w/Elsie Randolph)	HMV B–8109
OB–5525–2	Who Do You Think You Are? (w/Elsie Randolph)	–
OB–5526–2	Weep No More, My Baby	HMV B–8110

    NOTE: The above three titles are all from *Mr Whittington*.

Acc. by Carroll Gibbons and Johnny Green on two pianos, with their Boy Friends (members of the Savoy Hotel Orpheans). London, 20 December 1933.

CAX–7027–1 Mr Whittington – Selection, Part 1 (Intro.   Col DX–566
Bow Bells Music/Oceans Of Time)
(w/Elsie Randolph)

CAX–7028–2 Mr Whittington – Selection, Part 2 (Intro.   –
What A Pleasant Surprise/I'm Simply
Wild About Horses/Weep No More, My Baby/
Who Do You Think You Are?/Oceans of
Time) (w/Elsie Randolph)

Orch. acc. by Ray Noble. London, 13 March 1934.

OB–5942–1 Not Bad (Film *Big Business*)   HMV B–8153

OB–5943–1 Like Monday Follows Sunday (w/Elsie   –
Randolph) (Film *Big Business*)

Acc. by Geraldo and his Orchestra, with chorus. London, 18 December 1934.

CA–14809–2 I Think I Can (Film   Col DB–1483; FB–1130
Brewster's Millions)

CA–14810–1 One Good Tune Deserves   –   –
Another (Film *Brewster's
Millions*)

London, 19 December 1934.

CAX–7373–1 *Brewster's Millions* – Selection, Part I   Col DX–662
(Intro. One Good Tune Deserves Another/
I Think I Can/Pull Down The Blind)

CAX–7374–2 *Brewster's Millions* – Selection, Part 2   –
(Intro. The Orange Seller/Caranza)

Acc. by Harry Perritt and his Orchestra. London, 31 May 1935.

CAX–7550–1 *The Flying Trapeze* – Selection,   Col DX–696 (part side)
Part 1 (Intro. Marie Louise/
Nellie)

CAX–7551–1 *The Flying Trapeze* – Selection,   –
Part 2 (Intro. Life In A
Circus/There Won't Be Any
Spring/The Flying Trapeze)

Orch. acc. London, 17 January 1936.

GB–7610–1 Everything Stops for Tea (Film *Come Out Of*   Br 02125
The Pantry)

GB–7611–1 From One Minute to Another (Film *Come Out*   –
Of The Pantry)

GB–7622–1 I'm Still Dreaming (Film *When Knights Were*   Br 02153
Bold)

GB–7623–1 Let's Put Some People to Work (Film *When*   –
Knights Were Bold)

London, 30 November 1936.

TB–2668–2 I'm in a Dancing Mood (w/Elsie Randolph)   Br 02348

TB–2669–2 This'll Make You Whistle (w/Elsie Randolph)   –

TB–2670–2 Without Rhythm   Br 02347

TB–2671–2 There isn't any Limit to My Love   –

NOTE: All the above four titles are from the film *This'll Make You Whistle*.

Acc. by the Winter Garden Theatre Orchestra, cond. by George Windeatt. London, 24 August 1943.
CA–19311–1   I'm Looking For A Melody   Col DB–2127
CA–19312–1   Everything Happens To Me   –
  NOTE: Both the above titles are from *It's Time to Dance*.

Acc. by the MGM Studio Orchestra, cond. by Adolph Deutsch. Hollywood, 1952.

Triplets (w/Fred Astaire-Nanette Fabray) (Film *Band Wagon*)	MGM 685, C–752	
I Guess I'll Have to Change my Plan (w/Fred Astaire) (Film *Band Wagon*)	MGM 686 –	
That's Entertainment (w/Fred Astaire-Nanette Fabray-India Adams) (Film *Band Wagon*)	MGM 687 –	

London, June 1955.
OX-EF3   Cry/The Hokey-Pokey-Polka
  3 and 4   (w/Diana Dors)/   HMV DLP C1
          I Don't Know Whether to Laugh or Cry

NOTE: The above titles are from the film *As Long As They're Happy* which were included in this record under the title 'The Story of J. Arthur Rank Organisation'.

ADDENDUM: Apart from the last entry, all the above titles were first released as 78 rpm records. Following Jack Buchanan's death. Many of them have been transferred and re-mastered on the EP (45 rpm) and LP (33⅓ rpm) records shown below.

45 rpm Extended Play Records
E.M.I. Records Limited
SEG7767   Memories of Jack Buchanan:
          Side 1 (There's Always Tomorrow/Who).
          Side 2 (I Think I Can/Sweet So and So).
7EG8307   Memories of Jack Buchanan:
          Side 1 (And Her Mother Came Too/Fancy Our Meeting/
              Who/Like Monday Follows Sunday).
          Side 2 (Two Little Blackbirds/Goodnight Vienna/It's Not You/
              There's Always Tomorrow/Weep No More My Baby).

33⅓ rpm Long Playing Records
Decca Ace of Clubs
ACL1140   London Screen Scene. The Thirties: Jack Buchanan with Elsie
          Randolph (Everything Stops for Tea/I'm in a Dancing Mood/Let's
          Put Some People to Work/From One Minute to Another/Without
          Rhythm/This'll Make You Whistle/There isn't any Limit to My
          Love).
  NOTE: These titles were on Side One of this record which was released in
1963. Side Two had Jessie Matthews' titles.

E.M.I. Music for Pleasure
MFP1160   The Debonair Jack Buchanan:
          Side 1 (Stand Up and Sing/Who/Yes, Mr Brown/I Think I
              Can/The One I'm Looking For/You Forgot your Gloves).
          Side 2 (Goodnight Vienna/There's Always Tomorrow/Fancy Our
              Meeting/Sweet So and So/Who Do You Think You
              Are?/And Her Mother Came Too).
  NOTE: Released in 1967.

Stanyan Records. Hollywood

SR10035 *Sunny* (Selection of original cast recordings including Jack Buchanan singing I've Looked For Trouble/Let's Say Goodnight Till It's Morning/When We Get Our Divorce/Who).

NOTE: These titles were on Side Two of this record which was released in the United States in 1975 under licence from E.M.I. Side One has original cast recording from *No No Nanette*.

E.M.I. World Records

SH 283 Jack Buchanan:

Side 1 (Two Little Bluebirds/It's Not You/There's Always Tomorrow/Dancing Honeymoon/And Her Mother Came Too/Who/Take A Step/Alone With My Dreams/You Forgot Your Gloves/Leave A Little For Me/Yes, Mr Brown/Now That I've Found You/Living in Clover).

Side 2 (Goodnight Vienna/Fancy Our Meeting/Weep No More My Baby/One Good Tune Deserves Another/I Think I Can/So Green/Oo' La' La'/Adapted from the French).

Bibliography

Agate, James. *Contemporary Theatre 1944–1945* (George Harrap, London, 1946)

Amherst, Jeffrey. *Wandering Abroad* (Secker and Warburg, London, 1976)

Appelbaum, Stanley. *The Hollywood Musical: A Picture Quiz Book* (Dover, New York, 1974)

Astaire, Fred. *Steps in Time* (William Heinemann, London, 1960)

Baral, Robert. *Revue – The Great Broadway Period* (Fleet, New York and London, 1962)

Barker, Felix. *The House That Stoll Built* (Frederick Muller, London, 1957)

Baxter, John. *The Hollywood Exiles* (Macdonald and Jane's, London, 1976)

Bodeen, De Witt and Ringold, Gene. *Chevalier* (Citadel, New Jersey, 1973)

Bowden, Liz-Anne, ed. *The Oxford Companion to Film* (Oxford University Press, London, New York and Toronto, 1976)

Busby, Roy. *British Music Hall: An Illustrated Who's Who from 1850 to the Present Day*, (Paul Elek, London, 1976)

Byng, Douglas. *As You Were* (Duckworth, London, 1970)

Carstairs, John Paddy. *'Bunch'* (Hurst and Blackett, London, 1948)

Cochran, Charles B. *A Showman Looks On* (Guild Books, London, 1941)

Cochran, Charles B. *Cock-A-Doodle-Do* (J. M. Dent, London, 1941)

Compton, Fay. *Rosemary* (Alston Rivers, London, 1926)

Coward, Noël. *Present Indicative* (William Heinemann, London, 1937)

Curtis, Anthony, ed. *The Rise and Fall of the Matinée Idol* (Weidenfeld and Nicolson, London, 1974)

Dean, Basil. *The Theatre at War* (George Harrap, London, 1956)

Dietz, Howard. *Dancing in the Dark* (Quadrangle, New York, 1974)

Ellis, Vivian. *I'm on a See Saw* (Michael Joseph, London, 1953)

England, John. *Across My Path* (Pennant, Weybridge, 1975)

Fairbrother, Sydney. *Through an Old Stage Door* (Frederick Muller, London, 1939)

Fairlie, Gerald. *The Fred Emney Story* (Hutchinson, London, 1960)

Fox, Roy. *Hollywood, Mayfair and All That Jazz* (Frewin, London, 1975)

Friedland, Michael. *Fred Astaire* (W. H. Allen, 1976)

Gifford, Denis. *British Film Catalogue 1895–1970* (David and Charles, London, 1973)

Goldblatt, Burt and Green, Stanley. *Starring Fred Astaire* (W. H. Allen, London and New York, 1974)

Green, Stanley. *Ring Bells! Sing Songs!: Broadway Musicals of the 1930s* (Arlington House, New York, 1973)

Green, Stanley. *The World of Musical Comedy* (A. S. Barnes, New York and Thomas Yoseloff, London, 1968)

Green, Stanley and Goldblatt, Burt. *Starring Fred Astaire* (W. H. Allen, London and New York, 1974)

Grossmith, George. *'G.G.'* (Hutchinson, London, 1933)

Harman, Bob. *Hollywood Panorama* (Dutton, New York, 1971)

Herbert, I. ed. *Who's Who in the Theatre*, sixteenth edition (Pitman, London and Cole, Detroit, 1977)

Holloway, Stanley. *Wiv a Little Bit of Luck* (Frewin, London, 1967)

Hulbert, Jack. *The Little Woman's Always Right* (W. H. Allen, London, 1975)

Hyde, Francis E. *Cunard and the North Atlantic 1840–1973* (Macmillan, London, 1975)

Janis, Elsie. *So Far, So Good!* (John Long, London, 1935)

June. *The Glass Ladder* (William Heinemann, London, 1960)

Kendall, Henry. *I Remember Romano's* (Macdonald, London, 1960)

Kimball, Robert and Simon, Alfred. *The Gershwins* (Atheneum, New York, 1973)

Kinkle, Roger D. ed. *Complete Encyclopedia of Popular Music and Jazz 1900–1950*, vols. 1–4 (Arlington House, New York, 1974)

Kobal, John. *Gotta Sing Gotta Dance: A Pictorial History of Film Musicals* (Hamlyn, London and New York, 1970)

Kreuger, Miles, ed. *The Movie Musical* (Dover Publications, New York, 1975)

Lawrence, Gertrude. *A Star Danced* (W. H. Allen, London, 1945)

Leonard, William T. and Parish, James Robert. *Hollywood Players; The Thirties* (Arlington House, New York, 1976)

Low, Rachel. *History of the British Film 1914–1918* (George Allen and Unwin, London, 1971)

Low, Rachel. *History of the British Film 1918–1929* (George Allen and Unwin, London, 1973)

Lupino, Stanley. *From the Stocks to the Stars* (Hutchinson, London, 1934)

Macqueen-Pope, W. *Ivor* (W. H. Allen, London, 1951)

Macqueen-Pope, W. *The Footlights Flickered* (Herbert Jenkins, London, 1959)

Mander, Raymond and Mitchenson, Joe. *Musical Comedy* (Peter Davies, London, 1969)

Mander, Raymond and Mitchenson, Joe. *Revue* (Peter Davies, London, 1969)

Matthews, Jessie. *Over My Shoulder* (W. H. Allen, London, 1974)

Melville, Alan. *Merely Melville* (Hodder and Stoughton, London, 1970)

Milton, Billy. *Milton's Paradise Mislaid* (Jupiter, London, 1976)

Minelli, Vincent. *I Remember it Well* (Angus and Robertson, London, 1975)

Mitchenson, Joe and Mander, Raymond. *Musical Comedy* (Peter Davies, London, 1969)

Mitchenson, Joe and Mander, Raymond. *Revue* (Peter Davies, London, 1969)

Montgomery, John. *Comedy Films 1894–1954* (Allen and Unwin, 1968)

Munden, Kenneth W. ed. *American Film Institute Catalogue 1921–1930* (R. R. Bowker & Co., New York and London, 1971)

Neagle, Anna. *There's Always Tomorrow* (W. H. Allen, London, 1975)

Nerman. *Darlings of the Gods* (Alston Rivers, London, 1929)

New York Times Directory of the Film (Arno Press/Random House, New York, 1973)

New York Times Directory of the Theatre (Quadrangle, New York, 1973)

Nichols, Beverley. *The Sweet and Twenties* (Weidenfeld and Nicolson, London, 1958)

Noble, Peter. *Ivor Novello* (Falcon Press, London, 1951)

Palmer, Helen M. and Williams, E. T. eds. *Dictionary of National Biography, 1951–1960* (Oxford University Press, 1960)

Parish, James Robert and Leonard, William T. *Hollywood Players: The Thirties* (Arlington House, New York, 1976)

Parker, J. ed. *Who's Who in the Theatre*, tenth edition (Pitman, London and Cole, Detroit, 1947)

Perry, George. *Movies from the Mansion* (Elm Tree, London, 1976)

Picturegoer's Who's Who and Encyclopaedia (Odham's Press, London, 1933)

Ragan, David, ed. *Who's Who in Hollywood 1900–1976* (Arlington House, New York, 1976)

Ringold, Gene and Bodeen, De Witt. *Chevalier* (Citadel, New Jersey, 1973)

Rodway, Phyllis Ismay Inshaw and Slingsby, Lois Harford. *Philip Rodway: A Tale of Two Theatres* (Cornish Brothers, Birmingham, 1934)

Schwartz, Charles. *Gershwin: His Life and Music* (Bobbs-Merrill, Indianapolis and New York, 1973)

Simon, Alfred and Kimball, Robert. *The Gershwins* (Atheneum, New York, 1973)

Slingsby, Lois Harford and Rodway, Phyllis Ismay Inshaw. *Philip Rodway: A Tale of Two Theatres* (Cornish Brothers, Birmingham, 1934)

Wall, Max. *The Fool on the Hill* (Quartet, London, 1975)

Weinberg, Harman G. *The Lubitsch Touch* (Dutton, New York, 1968)

Weissberger, L. Arnold. *Famous Faces* (Harry N. Abrams, New York, 1972)

Wilcox, Herbert. *Twenty Five Thousand Sunsets* (Bodley Head, London, 1967)

Williams, E. T. and Palmer, Helen M. eds. *Dictionary of National Biography, 1951–1960* (Oxford University Press, Oxford, 1971)

Wilson, Sandy. *Ivor* (Michael Joseph, London, 1975)

Winchester, Clarence, ed. *World Film Encyclopaedia* (Amalgamated Press, London, 1933)

Index

268

270

271